DON'T F*CKING PANIC

THE SH*T THEY DON'T TELL YOU
IN THERAPY ABOUT ANXIETY DISORDER,
PANIC ATTACKS, & DEPRESSION

KELSEY DARRAGH

THOUGHT
CATALOG
Books

THOUGHTCATALOG.COM
NEW YORK · LOS ANGELES

THOUGHT
CATALOG
Books

THOUGHT CATALOG BOOKS is a publishing imprint of Thought Catalog, a digital magazine for thoughtful storytelling. Thought Catalog is owned by The Thought & Expression Company, an independent media group based in Brooklyn, NY, which also owns and operates Shop Catalog, a curated shopping experience featuring our best-selling books and one-of-a-kind products, and Collective World, a global creative community network. Founded in 2010, we are committed to helping people become better communicators and listeners to engender a more exciting, attentive, and imaginative world. As a publisher and media platform, we help creatives all over the world realize their artistic vision and share it in print and digital form with audiences across the globe.

ThoughtCatalog.com
Thoughtful Storytelling

ShopCatalog.com
Boutique Books + Curated Products

Collective.world
Creative Community Network

Published by Thought Catalog Books. This book was produced by Chris Lavergne and Noelle Beams. Art direction, design, and illustration by KJ Parish. Special thanks to Bianca Sparacino for creative editorial direction and Isidoros Karamitopoulos for circulation management.

Visit us on the web at thoughtcatalog.com and shopcatalog.com.

Made and printed in the United States of America.

ISBN 978-1-949759-27-3

TABLE *of* CONTENTS

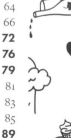

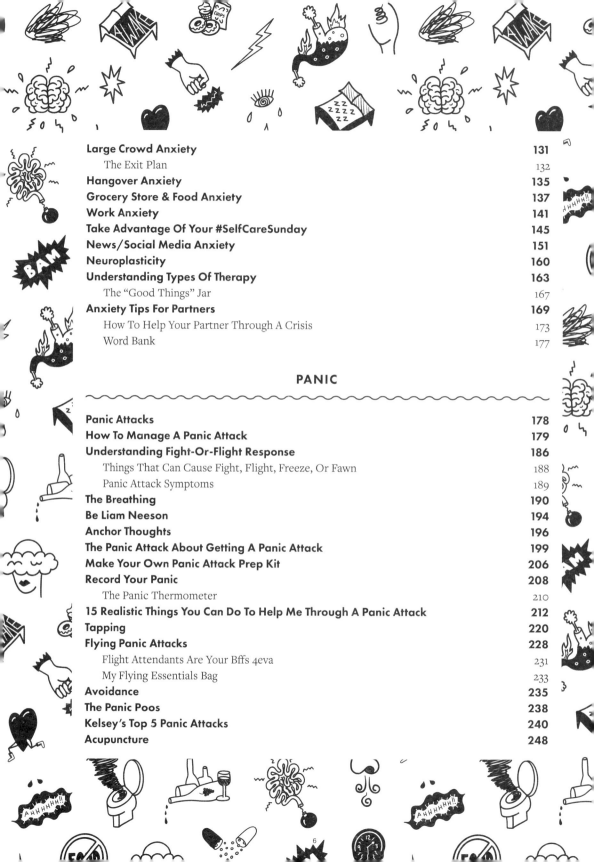

PANIC

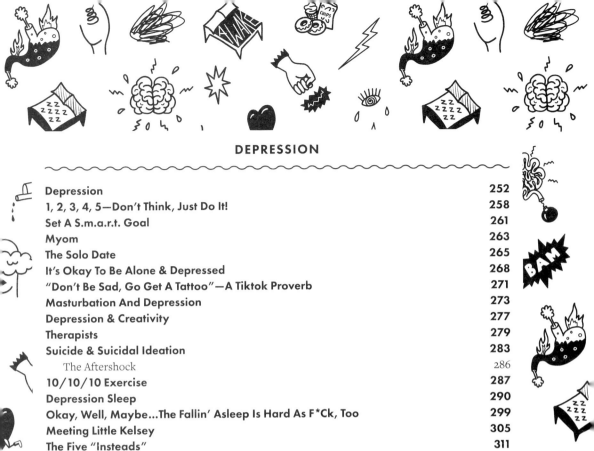

DEPRESSION

SO WTF IS THIS BOOK EXACTLY?!?

This is an honest-as-shit book of tips, tricks, and exercises for a generation afflicted by real-ass anxiety, depression, and panic that's hindering us from seizing our entire lives by the balls. This was not written by a doctor—in fact, our author dropped out of three colleges (THREE!!)—but by a real person who has spent her whole life desperately and successfully managing her mental health daily.

There are three sections to this book: Anxiety, Panic, and Depression...BUT! This isn't JUST a book about those things! No, no, no, this is a *many feelings book*! In DON'T F*CKING PANIC!, we're going to give you a myriad of tools to process all those feelings in a fun, ~*sometimes fucked up*~, and genuine way. Sometimes you *may* feel sad, anxious, or even panicked when reading this, and we'll explain why that's okay! In fact, it's ENCOURAGED! After all, *feelings are just* FEELINGS... *not* FACTS! We hope to quell those ruminating feelings and perhaps reverse them. Or, hell, maybe sitting in your feelings and having a good-ass cry over takeout! The journey will be as multifaceted as a human can be! DON'T F*CKING PANIC is an interactive workbook that's meant to be carried with you, reader friend. Something to be written in, laughed with, cried on, torn up, and shared with a stranger who, maybe, one day, might need a page more than you do.

This book is young, fresh, and f*cking brash as f*ck. Remember, Kelsey's not a doctor. She's here to keep it real, and sometimes that means being dark or funny or both, because when you're deep in mental-health management, it's like being in some fucked-up club you didn't ask for membership to, but since we're all standing in the same line, you're allowed to joke about it. The beauty of this book is that each page is a different working exercise, sometimes coupled with an anecdote or personal story of Kelsey's matching the page's theme. For example, the page that works on airplane anxiety also has a paragraph about Kelsey's suggestions for the best seat to sit in for anxious fliers, how to score free drinks, and the best way to keep the reader's hands busy if a seat-back movie just ain't cutting it.

Or, maybe you're having a panic attack RIGHT EFFING NOW and need relief. Kelsey gives you step-by-step advice that not only covers breathing exercises but also how to manage the anxiety shits that come with the rush of a panic attack (you read that right).

In our "Depression" section, Kelsey gets honest: If you're going to be depressed in bed for 12 hours a day, let's talk about how to make the most of those 12 hours in bed (she definitely recommends finding time to masturbate, because, as research shows, orgasming can help improve sleep as well as self-image, and reduce stress!).

There will also be conflicting ideas and methodology to read and practice along the way, because no one's mental health is exactly the same. Although we, as a society, like to classify people into groups and disorders, everyone's brain is completely different. What might work for one person might be totally useless to another! Kelsey encourages you to try them all; maybe what you thought was a stupid and silly technique upon first glance might be the thing that gets you through your next panic attack! Or, hey, something to put in your Rolodex the next time a friend of yours is having a hard time. NICE WORK, ANXIETY HELPER! YOU GO, GLEN COCO! Look at it this way: If there was one thing that worked for everyone, we wouldn't have *hundreds of thousands* of self-help books to choose from at bookstores and "suggested readings" all over Amazon.

This book is here to help people recognize their anxiety/panic/depression—accept it, and learn to manage it. Even if that management comes in the form of tracing Ryan Gosling's face in the name of mindfulness. So, are you ready to dive in? It's more of a "wading" into the water from the shallow end. We have blow-up floaties, a hot lifeguard, and extra oxygen tanks on deck here.

!!!!! BEFORE YOU BEGIN !!!!!

The exercises in this book are meant to be repeated as often as needed and are not limited to the space provided to write! If you need lots of room to process your feelings, my advice is to get a clean notebook to use alongside this book. Go nuts and write unapologetically...use all the paper you need! There are also some exercises you can download and print at home (see the Resource Index).

TRIGGER WARNING:

THIS BOOK WAS WRITTEN BY A (VERY) SENSITIVE COMEDIAN WHO OFTEN USES HUMOR TO COPE WITH HER MENTAL-HEALTH STRUGGLES. SINCE THIS WORKBOOK DOES CARRY SOME LIGHTHEARTED CON-VOS AS WELL AS THE DEEP DARK SHIT (HI, SUICIDAL IDEOLOGY! THANKS FOR CHECKING IN, YOU DIRTY RAT BASTARD!!! ARGH, COME OVER HERE, GIMME A HUG, YOU FUCK!), IT SHOULD GO WITHOUT SAYING THAT EACH PAGE COULD CONTAIN A TRIGGER WARNING WHILE TALKIN' 'BOUT THESE TOP-EES ("TOPICS." SORRY, I'M NERVOUS).

ABOUT ME, YOUR ANXIOUS, DEPRESSED, AND PANICKED PAL

I'm Fucked Up. I Have Problems. I am Not Normal. My Brain is Broken...Is Yours, Too? These were some of the titles I came up with when trying to name this workbook (omitted title: *I'M INCURABLE AND I'VE TRIED EVERYTHING ALREADY AND MOST DAYS I FEEL LIKE I'M LIVING IN THE TRUMAN SHOW AND MY WHOLE LIFE IS AN ACID TRIP AND IS YOUR HEART BEATING AS FAST AS MINE??? THE SKY COULD BEND AT ANY MOMENT LIKE THAT SCENE IN INCEPTION STARRING LEONARDO DICAPRIO.*) Notice how NEGATIVE all those titles sound???

FEAR NOT! This is simply my high-functioning, yet debilitating, anxiety talking. Just a peek behind my brain curtains! Welcome to the show!

I've lived with generalized anxiety, panic disorder, and major depressive disorder my whole life. I was diagnosed when I was 17, but could tell from a very early age that my brain didn't seem to function like everyone else around me. At the tender age of six, during a soccer match, while all my friends were focused on the game, I'd be walking up and down the bench, asking everyone how they thought our lungs were able to breathe on their own, and why did our veins pump blood, and how did I know my heart wasn't just going to stop beating at any moment?

After being rinsed and left out to dry by the healthcare system over 15+ years, I've spent the majority of my adult life advocating for mental-health issues in young people. I've made videos on YouTube that have amassed more than 250 million views to date. During the time of creating and writing this workbook, I went through some of the most challenging times of my adult life. I left my job of four years as a producer for the viral international entertainment conglomerate, BuzzFeed. I went through the most trying time of my three-year relationship with my partner. I stopped drinking alcohol (I NEVER could have predicted this one). I had fiery chronic pain flare-ups that left me wondering if I wanted to live in my body any longer. I visited over six countries, flying over 50 flights for work. (Have I mentioned that I have a paralyzing fear of flying?) OH YEAH, AND THE WORLD WENT THROUGH A GLOBAL PANDEMIC!!! NBD (no big deal). Needless to say, if there was anyone that could've used a workbook like this—**IT WAS ME**. I suffered, and in return, I would write out my feelings, turning that suffering into meaning. I learned that I am indeed stronger than I gave myself credit for. Using the pages in the book as my own form of therapy (although I have three human therapists, too), I found myself getting weirdly fervent after a particularly stressful time, as I knew it was material for this book. I truly believe that the universe gave me these mental hardships and disorders to use them for good to help others, like YOU!

For a long time, I would wake up every morning internally screaming, "WHY ME?? WHY THE FUCK AM I THE PERSON WHO HAS THIS SHIT??" Now, I see each panic attack, depressive episode, and anxious situation as material to connect with you all. I remind myself that I am not the only one who feels this way and I repeat to myself, over and over, "There are others just like me. This too shall pass... and will probably be a chapter in the workbook."

As a comedian, producer, and Internet person in Los Angeles, I've chosen a life in the public eye and in a constant state of freelancing, with no guarantee where my next pay-check comes from. My career involves being a public figure on the Internet, where I am regularly judged by millions of people, host live TV events, and work on million-dollar shoots where I have no excuse to drop out, lest I risk said millions of dollars, not to mention people's time and money—LOLOL, NO PRESSURE, RIGHT? WHY WOULD I DO THIS TO MYSELF??? Welp, for the simple fact that it's my passion. And while there have been days when my mental health has told me to quit—that there's no way I can have a sustainable career in this industry with all these "issues" flaring up at any moment—thinking about moving back in with my parents, getting a traditional 9-5, and giving up on my dreams gives me more anxiety than that does.

I'm grateful to feel things—even the shitty feelings. Can you believe it!?...You probably don't, and I don't blame you, because, 10 years ago, I would've told anyone that suggested I'd be grateful for my depression one day to fuck right off. I spent so many years trying to *escape* the uncomfortable feelings that it kept me from ever popping back in on those scary/sad feelings to see if I felt any different about them years later. That's right, YEARS. I was in DENIAL of my feelings, which, I found out, TO NO ONE'S SURPRISE, isn't the way to feel better. The feelings don't just disappear. If they do for you? GOOD FOR YOU! THIS ISN'T YOUR WORKBOOK. Perhaps we have feelings that we've buried so far down, we don't realize that they're even still there under all those dusty brain thoughts! It wasn't until I was finally on the edge of life—FURIOUS at what I had become (shivering, sad, suicidal, in and out of inpatient and outpatient programs, sick of speaking to doctors who saw me as a subject and not a person) and mad enough at myself (although I couldn't figure out why I was the target of my own anger)—that I realized I could no longer run from the big, bad, scary things in my head. The shit in my head made me believe I was the ONLY PERSON IN THE WORLD who thought these things. I thought I was "crazy." I found myself asking, "What does 'crazy' even mean?" I self-identify as "crazy" quite often. I feel like I'm "allowed" though, right? But though I found comfort in taking back the word, I was terrified of being labeled "crazy" by other people. I had repetitive thoughts of completely losing my mind and being locked away in a mental hospital, forgetting who I was and just living as a blob of skin until, finally, someone would put me out of my misery. And no amount of professional help (although incredibly vital) would be the thing that "fixed" me. In the end, I knew that it was up to ME to put in a lot of the hard work, including getting myself up to GO to those doctor appointments! If I kept running from myself, I'd dissociate forever and end up living exactly like that blob of skin I was so afraid of becoming. So, my dear reader, that is what this workbook is all about: facing those fears, taking a chance on yourself, and taking off all that shame, setting it down for a little bit. I'm so excited for you. Because, I've been you. I AM you. And always will be.

I've learned how to *manage* living, not run from what I fear.

We know there is not a single pill, or a spell, or a professional who can take it all away. *It's up to us to decide how we manage these feelings.*

Remember: You are not alone. You may feel frustrated, broken, and damaged, but *you are not those thoughts and feelings.* Creating this workbook has deeply changed how I view and approach who I am in this world. How I exist. How I turned all those scary and unfamiliar thoughts into friends. I changed how I viewed my anxiety, panic, and depression, turning my life around in a way that I never thought was possible. I hope these exercises and passages help you change the way you feel about yourself and all the shit you hate in your brain. I hope you learn that you can love that shit, too.

XOXO, GOSSIP GIRL
(*Just kidding, I'm Kelsey.*)

HOW TO USE THIS WORKBOOK TO ITS FULLEST FRIGGIN' POTENTIAL

(A.K.A. DON'T LET THIS BE ANOTHER CUTE-ASS BOOK THAT COLLECTS DUST ON YOUR SHELF)

1. **I am not a doctor.** In fact, I dropped out of three liberal arts colleges and smoked weed pretty much my entire high school experience. But what I lack in degrees, I make up for in psychiatry appointments, a stint in an inpatient mental-health rehab facility and an outpatient treatment center, so-many-therapy-appointments-I-couldn't-even-count, studying every book about mood disorders I could get my hands on, and a general "I've been fucking THROUGH IT" attitude. I know the American mental healthcare system in and out, and I know how frustrating, scary, and isolating it can feel. But as much as I've been through in my mental-health journey, I'm still not a doctor!! I simply offer tools to, hopefully, help rid you of feelings of frustration, fear, and isolation. I can't diagnose you or tell you that you need treatment, but I can tell you that *you are absolutely not alone.* According to the World Health Organization, one out of every four people will experience a mental-health issue in their lives, and 450 million people are *currently* living with mental illness. But I have a feeling these numbers will rise as we break stigmas and more people feel comfortable talking about their mental health out loud.

2. **Write all over this motherfucker!!!** This book is filled with exercises, games, graphs, charts, and stories to help you understand and learn more about managing your anxiety, panic, and depression. You can use this book at any moment. Having a panic attack RIGHT NOW? Turn to the chapter "HOW TO MANAGE A PANIC ATTACK RIGHT NOW!!" Know someone going through depression? Gain some insight on how to approach the subject, and rip out a page for them. Some passages might even conflict with methods

described on previous pages or chapters. Why? Because not all anxiety, panic, and depression manifests in the same way! Your brain does not fire synapses like mine; therefore, our mental health does not fire off the same patterns! It's like when a friend suggests a technique to "calm you down" or "cheer you up" when you're going through it, and it doesn't work, and you might want to scream at them, "THAT'S NOT GOING TO WORK RIGHT NOW, JAN." Or, "I'VE TRIED THAT BEFORE, BECKY!" Then, turn the page and try something else! What works for you may not work for me, and vice versa.

3. **GET A PEN THAT FEELS GOOD IN YOUR HANDS!** Make it a special mental-health pen with superpowers. When you pick it up, get in the feel-good zone. I've tried to include as many types of techniques and exercises as possible, from breathing and mindfulness to CBT (cognitive behavioral therapy) and DBT (dialectical behavioral therapy), to shit I've completely made up on my own that I've used personally in times of need. I've found that just one sentence from a self-help book, or a meme from Tumblr, or something smart a friend said in passing, would strike a chord with me and come in handy the next time I was struggling.

4. **Stop when you need to.** For me, sometimes *talking* about my panic disorder can trigger some physical symptoms inside of me. I don't want that for you! If you find yourself getting anxious reading this, stop for a moment and check in with your body. This book should make you feel uncomfortable at times while we dig a little deeper and get vulnerable, but I never want you to feel triggered. Only you know your limits, bb.

5. **All that is to say, learning more about WHY my brain and heart and soul do the things they do *does help* take the fear out of the worst panic, anxiety, and depression**. And that's empowering as hell. That's what a big part of this book is all about: giving you the power to take charge of your mental health in moments that seem impossible to get through. Some of it can sound like "work" or "homework," but, I promise, learning the language and vocabulary of these disorders will help you be able to identify and express your needs when you need to understand what is going on in yo head! And, on that note, vocabulary—some people who manage/suffer/deal with/ live with these connections in our brains and bodies might call them conditions, disorders, mental-health challenges, or simply "mental health." For the sake of writing and being sensitive to everyone's preferred use of terms, I'll use them ALL in various ways throughout this workbook. Please, don't be offended. I am sensitive, too.

6. **Use this in conjunction with therapy, if you can.** I'd be careless to mention this tip without acknowledging the privilege that comes with having accessibility and funds to go to therapy.

I know, I hear you; therapy is fucking expensive. If you're able to afford health insurance, or have it through your job, try to look in-network first. Although most therapists (as opposed to psychiatrists and psychologists) do not accept ANY insurance, you can always check out your insurance's mental-health benefits and try to get reimbursed, especially if you are going more than once a month. (Hi! It's me!) Additionally, most therapists work on a "sliding scale," which means they are willing to "slide" their fees down from the usual cost if you aren't able to afford their regular rate. However, if you don't have insurance, it may feel impractical to even consider this expense. There are low-cost therapy apps (resources at the back of the book!), psychoanalytic training centers that may offer free sessions with an MD in a specific type of therapy training, and free support groups that you can attend. The internet is yo friend!

> **BTW: What kind of doc am I looking for?**
> Let's break down the bare bones of the basic three: psychiatrist, psychologist, and therapist.
>
> **Psychiatrist**—Can diagnose mental illness and prescribe meds.
>
> **Psychologist**—Can diagnose mental illness but they cannot prescribe meds. Psychologists go to school longer than a therapist and often work with psychiatrists to monitor medication and changes.
>
> **Therapist**—Provides support and guidance while helping patients make effective decisions within their overall structure of support.

7. **We are going to get vulnerable up in this bitch, okay?** I'm asking you to go on an adventure with me into the deepest parts of yourself. We're not just diving in without a parachute, though; I'm too anxious for that shit. We're going to build a TOOL BELT filled with different types of safety tools that will allow us to take the leap. But as much as I can help you get ready, only YOU can promise to take a searching moral inventory of yourself, so—*be honest*. Sure, fibbing can be a type of self-protection, but let's agree right now to rid ourselves of any habitual cover-ups about our mental health. Sounds cool? Cool.

8. **This book is broken up into three sections: Anxiety, Panic, and Depression.** I did this not only out of selfishness, because these are the main mental-health struggles I deal with on a daily basis, but because science shows that these three "disorders" overlap. In each section, you'll find

stories, exercises, journaling prompts, and coexisting subtopics. Don't like to read? Great! Tons of writing exercises! Don't like journaling? AWESOME! There are tons of stories you're going to love, and I'm not just saying that because I WROTE THEM (okay, I am). See? A BOOK FOR ALL! My hope is that you can at least learn something new that eases your struggles, check on your own mental health with a different perspective, and maybe even... HAVE FUN?!

9. Anytime you see this ☼ W. O. W. ☼ symbol you are receiving some important "words of wisdom" or advice. Take it to heart!

eat
shit,
brain.

anxiety

OMGOMGOMGOMG

gurgle

f✹ck f✹ck f✹ck

help

PANIC

!!!

just a little inner scream. NBD.

OMG

ANXIETY

*The oldest and longest relationship
I can't break up with!*

omgomgomg

f*ck this
f*cking sh*t!

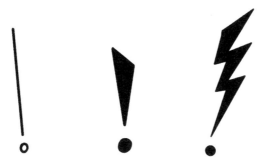

ANXIETY VS. ANXIETY DISORDER VS. PANIC ATTACKS

LET'S GO OVER SOMETHING!! VERY!!! Important! (!!!) What's the difference between <u>high anxiety</u> and <u>panic attacks</u>? Mainstream media often conflate the two, but they are VERY DIFFERENT.

A panic attack is your body's physical, sudden and intense, response to NORMAL thoughts and sensations. If you're being chased by a bear, then, my dude, you absolutely should be panicking in that life-threatening situation. But if you find yourself PANICKING "out of the blue," or even in high-anxiety situations, it will manifest *physically*: feeling a sense of impending doom, increased heart rate, sweating, dizziness, feeling pins and needles in your appendages, disorientation, loss of words, etc. More on panic attacks in section two. These suck ass.

Anxiety can suck ass in a different way. It *hits different,* as the kids say. As for anxiety, we can look at it two ways:

1. **Everyone has ANXIETY.** From the beginning of time, the first people on Earth all carried anxiety. Without it, they would've been complacent, and a complacent human is very easy to...well, kill! Our cavemen, cavewomen, and

cavepeople ancestors would've died QUICKLY trying to make friends with a saber-toothed tiger. They had *survival anxiety*, and we as evolved humans now have *social anxiety*. It is *psychological*: affecting and arising in the mind. **It happens naturally and manifests emotionally**. It's associated with excessive worry and stress. If you have a big meeting coming up, or maybe a first date (hubba, hubba—go, you!), it's safe to say that you might feel a little nervous and anxious. These types of situations can usually be referred to as "healthy anxiety." Then, there's number...

2. **HIGH ANXIETY**, which is what this section is mostly about. What we want to watch out for are areas of your life that are being INTERRUPTED by anxiety. Times of prolonged ruminating, intrusive thoughts, or performing rituals. If you find yourself avoiding parts of life or certain situations, and you realize this behavior is affecting your quality of life (trust me, I've been there and still struggle with this one), then we are entering into *anxiety disorder-ville*. Population: A LOT OF PEOPLE! WELCOME TO TOWN!! Stay as long as you'd like, or don't—it can be a beautiful but scary place. Watch out for unexpected and sharp turns that might throw off your entire day!!!

There are many types of anxiety disorders: generalized anxiety disorder [GAD], OCD [obsessive-compulsive disorder], PTSD [post-traumatic stress disorder], social phobia, and, drum roll please...PANIC DISORDER!!! That's right! **Panic disorder is a type of anxiety disorder.** Not to say that, if you have high anxiety, you will ever have a panic attack (lucky you!), but there's a chance you might have an anxiety disorder if you have more than one panic attack. So, in this book, when I refer to "anxiety," I'm talking about the debilitating, "beyond stressed out" kind = High Anxiety and Anxiety Disorders.

Another way to look at it is that **STRESS** is worrying about things that are tangibly affecting your life right now, while **ANXIETY** is worrying about things that *could* possibly go wrong, and your brain can't register the difference between the two. AND THAT'S NOT YOUR FAULT! Your brain is simply trying to protect you—and that's nothing you need to apologize for. Ever. SAY IT AGAIN FOR THE PEOPLE IN THE BACK! YOU NEVER HAVE TO APOLOGIZE FOR HAVING HIGH ANXIETY. Your brain is reacting to your environment in a way that has helped get you to where you are today and to stay alive. And, while everyone in the world experiences anxiety, those of us with more significant and severe anxiety should not carry any more of a burden. Anxious thinking happens when we think too much into the future or too far into the past. We have no control over what has happened and little control over what's coming. Finding a way to live in the present moment—the right here and right now—is the thing that's going to kick your anxiety's ass. KAH POW, in the keister, bitch.

All in all, I want to help you DO something with your pain. Do not let it go to waste. Do not let it become you. You're going to figure out something here—I can't wait for you to discover it.

There are all kinds of anxiety that exist in the world and in everybody's brain. So, let's check it out. Open up the hood and see what's inside. Try to be the *mechanic* here, not the car that is your anxiety-filled brain. Let's look at it together from an outsider's perspective:

DESCRIBE YOUR ANXIETY

What's it smell like? Feel like? Taste like?????

_____

_____

_____

_____

_____

_____

_____

_____

_____

_____

_____

_____

_____

_____

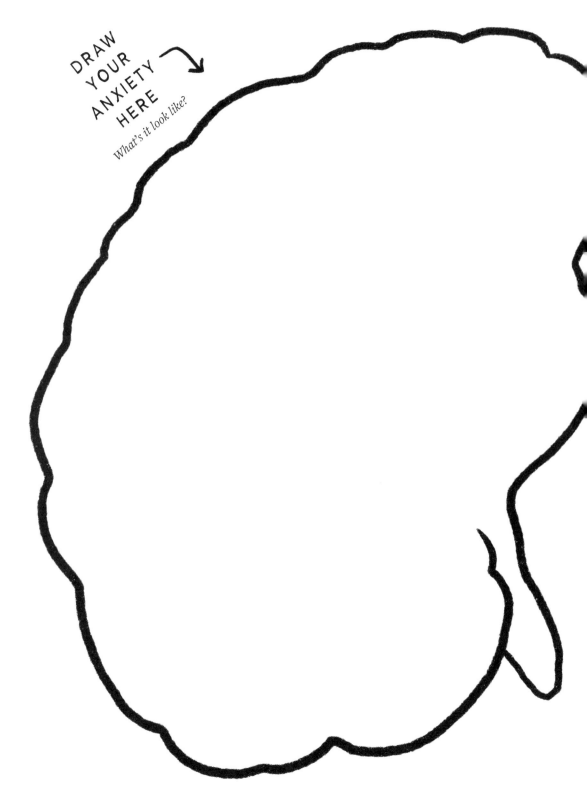

DRAW
YOUR
ANXIETY
HERE

What's it look like?

WRITE YOUR ANXIETY STORY

When did anxiety become a problem in your life? How old were you? Was it a specific scenario you remember, or a general time in your life, when it became intrusive? What was going on in your life then?

_____

_____

_____

_____

_____

_____

_____

_____

_____

_____

_____

_____

_____

_____

_____

_____

_____

Has your outward behavior or emotional state changed since anxiety became a negative pattern in your life? Tell me more:

_____

_____

_____

_____

_____

_____

_____

_____

_____

_____

What have been some of your worst moments with high anxiety that you can recall?

_____

_____

_____

_____

_____

_____

How do you cope now?

_____

_____

_____

_____

_____

_____

In a perfect world, how would you like to see your anxiety change after reading this workbook?

_____

_____

_____

_____

_____

_____

Do you feel ready to change your life? If not, what do you feel is stopping you?

_____

_____

_____

_____

_____

_____

Anything else?

_____

_____

_____

_____

The end. (J/K, we're just getting started...)

INTRUSIVE THOUGHTS

THE GAS FOR THE VEHICLE OF ANXIETY

My biggest fear in life is going "crazy." That one day, I'll simply lose all my marbles, all my brain wires will totally fry, and I'll run into traffic naked while screaming garbled nonsense about Neverland and never come back into my body or mind. I fear that everyone I love will give up on me and leave me to be brain-gooped in a mental hospital forever. I fear that my thoughts are too powerful for my brain to correct itself, and that these thoughts that take over are evil ones. And I'm terrified, each day, that this "insane alter ego" is bubbling under the surface, just waiting to JUMP out at me. Out of nowhere. For no logical reason. You may be surprised to find out that this is a fear many high-anxiety sufferers have.

'Tis an INTRUSIVE THOUGHT.

Perhaps a more relatable and lower-stakes example of an intrusive thought arising is that moment when you've left for work, minding your own damn business, and your brain taps on your forehead and says, "HEY! DID U REMEMBER TO TURN OFF UR STRAIGHTENING IRON??"

And you think, "Yeah. I did."

And then, your brain is all like, "YEAH, BUT ARE U SURE? LOL. BC IF UR NOT SURE, UR HOUSE MIGHT BURN DOWN."

You: "Brain, I did. Trust me." ***END DIALOGUE***

If the dialogue were to end here, we'd consider that a normal and healthy exchange of thought between your brain and body. However, an INTRUSIVE THOUGHT, paired with an ANXIETY DISORDER, is when the thought becomes distressing, disturbing, and interruptive.

In this scenario, the dialogue above would continue, so you're like, "Yes, brain, I did...at least, I think I did..."

And then your brain is all "AH-HAH! DOUBT! QUESTIONING!! YES!!! I THRIIIIIIVE ON THISSSS SHITTTTT! YOU DIDN'T TURN IT OFF, DID YOU?! LET IT BURN, BABY!! LET IT BURNNNNN!!! YOU'RE APARTMENT IS PROBABLY GONE ALREADY! IN A PILE OF ASH AND DUST! ALL YOUR LIFE MEMORIES AND YOUR HARRY POTTER COLLECTABLES ARE FRIGGIN' GONE FOREVER!!! YOU'LL BE OUT ON THE STREETS! WITH NO HELP! AND YOU SUNBURN EASY SO THAT'S REALLY GONNA SUCK FOR YOUUUUU!"

................fuckin' hell, brain.

In the brain of someone who lives with high anxiety, that INTRUSIVE THOUGHT would keep RUMINATING (*more on managing this cycle in the "Rumination" chapter!*), which means to think deeply about something until that thought interferes with your day. You'd start to see the image of your straightening iron pop into your head all day. How annoying. Or, maybe you mentally trace your steps from your morning over and over. UGH! Or, maybe the INTRUSIVE THOUGHT is so extreme you can't focus in your meeting until your roommate has sent you a picture of your straightening iron with the OFF button in full-view portrait mode.

So you're probably thinking (hopefully, not *overthinking*), "GREAT. HOW DO I STOP THESE INTRUSIVE THOUGHTS? Because I'm le' TIRED! This isn't rational!"

AND THERE'S THE RUB, MY ANXIOUS BEANS—High anxiety ISN'T rational! It's hard to pinpoint exactly WHY those worries, thoughts, and fears come up—*they are just there*. And we feel them. Usually, negatively.

There are varying levels of intrusive thoughts. Some might feel more extreme, like, when I'm cutting up apples in the morning for my smoothie, and this thought comes up to say hi:

〉 *"What if I just stabbed myself with this knife?"*

OR

〉 *"What if I stabbed my cats?"*

"WHOA! HOLY SHIT! WHAT! THE FUCK!?!" Is what you might be thinking and TRUST ME, it's what I think, too, when these thoughts pop up! Guess what? THIS IS TOTALLY NORMAL. EVERYONE—YES, EVERYONE—has passing intrusive thoughts. The thoughts are often unwanted and disturbing to the thinker, too! Varying levels of intrusive thoughts can be "creepy," incestuous, violent, and scary! I fear these thoughts are part of that "alter ego" sitting in the shadows. But here's the good news: You're having these wildly fucked-up thoughts because you are afraid of *being* that thought. Not because you *are* what you're thinking. It makes sense! Why would I want to be a cat-murderer?! I DON'T! It violates my belief of who I am. It is a thought, not an impulse.

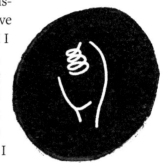

So, we're going to learn how to reverse-engineer those INTRUSIVE THOUGHTS so that the next time you wake up in the middle of the night thinking, "SHIT! I FORGOT TO TURN OFF MY STRAIGHTENER!" you can use these tools and exercises to rid the toxic INTRUSIVE THOUGHTS from your beautiful brain and get back to that vital slumber. Let's get into it.

Once upon a yoga class, a teacher said something to me that I'll never forget: "For the next hour, as we practice, leave all those intrusive thoughts behind— you can pick them back up in an hour when we are finished. *They will always be there.*" I couldn't help but think, shit, she's right! My mostly negative and intrusive thoughts will *always* be there to access. I control the brain gates! AND I SAY "NO" TO INTRUSIVE THOUGHTS DURING DOWNWARD LOTUS PINE WHATEVER POSE!

What are a couple negative and intrusive thoughts you could leave here, on this page, for now, as you move onto the next exercise? You can always come back to them, if you need them (*hint: you won't!*).

_____

_____

LET'S BREAK DOWN THAT INTRUSIVE THOUGHT

Separate reality from your feelings. **After all, FEELINGS ARE JUST FEELINGS—NOT FACTS.** *YOU ARE NOT YOUR THOUGHTS!* (Remember this phrase, cause ya girl is going to say it often in these pages!) Let's look at the facts, baby! INTRUSIVE THOUGHTS can easily spiral out of reality.

Let's see how a super-smart science person breaks this down:

> *"In a series of experiments, Harvard neuroscientist Joshua Greene described what he calls a 'dual-process brain.'* [1,2]. *He uses the analogy of a digital camera, which has an automatic mode and a manual mode. The automatic mode in our brains is driven by emotions. It is fast and efficient. The manual mode requires reasoning to do its work. It is slower, just like changing manual settings on your camera is slower. Problems come, Greene argues, when we use the automatic mode in situations that call for manual-mode thinking."*

To break that down for the people who dropped out of three colleges (me), people with high anxiety sometimes need to switch from *automatic mode*, which automatically creates negative and annoying thoughts, to a more *self-reflective manual mode*. It's extra work, but we have to break the cycle by getting outside of our own heads. The next exercise is going to teach us how to get our of our own way.

Often, we make our decisions based on *feelings* or *emotions* (*feelings = outward, emotions = inward*), and then we use our rational brain to create facts that justify our feelings and/or emotions. *But here's the thing:* They might not always be factual thoughts. Our brain is "reaching" for justification of that initial emotional thought response. Tricky fucker!

For example:

EMOTIONAL THOUGHT RESPONSE: I'm hurt and embarrassed my boss didn't acknowledge my recent project's success in the last company meeting.

THE REACH FOR "FACTS:" My work must not have been important. She avoided eye contact with me during the meeting, so maybe she's mad at me for something!? Remember that time four years ago when she didn't

---

1 Newell, Terry. *Feelings Are Not Facts: A Dangerous Confusion.* 5 Dec. 2016, www.huffpost.com/entry/feeling-are-not-facts-a_b_8726718.
2 "Dual Process Theory (Moral Psychology)." *Wikipedia*, Wikimedia Foundation, 2 Sept. 2020, en.wikipedia.org/wiki/Dual_process_theory_(moral_psychology).

respond back to your pitch email about allowing dogs in the office? She probably thinks you're some stupid, dog-obsessed freak. I should quit. Etc., etc.

All of these "facts" are your brain's way of supplementing your emotional response, therefore validating it!! And while it's natural for someone with an anxiety disorder to think this way, it's time to change the narrative! We want to REVERSE the process in yo brain waves. We want to look at FACTS first and THEN make an emotional response to those facts.

If you're still having a hard time understanding that YOU ARE NOT YOUR THOUGHTS, as I will often scream at you throughout this workbook, try thinking of it this way:

- **You are the awareness behind your thoughts—**not the thoughts themselves.
- **Did you exist before the thought occurred?** Yes.
- **Do you continue to exist after the thought leaves?** Yep!

Therefore, **you can't be your thoughts.** You are something greater! If you were your thoughts, you would disappear when the thought does.

I know this stuff can sound sciencey as fuck and may seem goofy to think about, but I can assure you that *separating facts from feelings is the first step in lowering your unnecessary and disruptive anxiety!* It's gonna take a li'l work to get it down—after all, your brain has gotten you this far surviving on emotional responses—But now that you've picked up this workbook I can tell you're tired of that shit. It's not serving you anymore. Time to try something different.

You must forgive yourself for doing whatever it took to survive.

Let's put it to werk, sis.

This fuckboi on Bumble ghosted me after we'd had amazing conversations, exchanged GIFS, and I even sent him a pussy picture (OF MY CAT, LARRY, YOU PERVS!...still, very intimate, okay?). So! My brain, being a Leo sun/double Gemini moon & rising, immediately will run to an emotional, self-destructive response.

(**Remember:** In moments of anxiety, it's easy and automatic to reach for *emotion* instead of doing the extra work to realize what might be TRUE and what might be your habitual brain doin' its self-destructive thinking.)

> **KELSEY'S EMOTIONAL THOUGHT RESPONSE:** I'm feeling lonely and unattractive and unworthy of love. Is my pussy ugly???

> **THE REACH FOR "FACTS:"** He decided I was an ugly-pussy owning, untalented loudmouth whom he could NEVER introduce to his family or see as a "girlfriend". He probably saw my internet videos and now thinks I'm a big ol' dumb slut who just wants attention and "likes" and...I could keep going, but I'll stop.

When I find myself thinking this way, I know it's time to *do the work*. I have to actively notice why all of a sudden I feel hella self-conscious and sad and realize it's just a *thinking pattern*. I try to rid the thinking of my emotional internal monologue's bias and look at the facts first and allow those FACTS to influence my emotional response. Let's get logical.

> **FACT:** He didn't respond to a Bumble message.

THAT'S ALL!!!! THAT'S IT!!! SO SMALL!! It's actually impressive how I was able to make such a small thing SO MUCH ABOUT ME, EH? There's a MILLION reasons (that have nothing to do with me, btw) that could be very logical as to why someone didn't respond to a dating app message. Maybe he met someone? Maybe he died? IDK. Us, Anxiety Queens, can practice removing ourselves from a negative internal narrative to focus on the outward, true facts of the matter.

Now it's time for you to try...**OUR FIRST EXERCISE!! HOW EXCITING!!**

You can come to these pages any time you find your anxiety causing an overwhelming emotional response. With these exercises, you'll start to deconstruct your own habitual thinking response.

INTRUSIVE THOUGHTS EXERCISE

I am worried/mad/sad/hurt that:

_____

_____

_____

_____

_____

_____

_____

_____

_____

_____

Now, try to notice what you are feeling and the facts that you've come up with to supplement that emotional response:

FEELINGS?   **VS.**   **FACTS?**

What's the worst that can happen?

_____

_____

_____

_____

How likely is it that this will happen?

_____

_____

_____

_____

REFRAMING

HOW TO TURN AN INTRUSIVE THOUGHT INTO A USEFUL ONE

It takes practice and can feel mantra-ish at times, but the good news is you CAN change your brain. (It's called neuroplasticity! There's a whole chapter about this later!) Like with learning any new skill, it takes time and practice, so try to be kind to yourself as you literally change the wiring in your brain! Let's take the intrusive thought you wrote down in the exercise above and combat it with its opposite, positive thought. How? Take yourself out of it. Don't get too self-centered in your thinking; we tend to put all the blame on something WE are doing instead of considering the world around us, the environment, other people, etc., as involved in our current situation. If you're having trouble reframing your own thoughts, try thinking of your thoughts as belonging to someone else you're helping to solve a problem.

Whenever you have an intrusive thought, _remember, it's your second thought that counts._

NOW YOU TRY!

Fill in the table below. I added some of my own examples to get you started. Remember, if you need more room to write, grab a notebook. Check out the Resource Index to print this at home.

Negative Intrusive	Evidence this thought is true?	Alternate Possibility? (unrelated to you)	Opposite Positive Thought
My presentation at work sucked ass and I messed up.	My boss had a resting bitch face the entire time.	They are looking for something else, or boss had a bad morning.	I'm brave to share my thoughts and ideas. I do good work and I learn from my mistakes.
He won't call me back because he hates me and I'm ugly/worth-less/stupid, etc.	He hasn't texted me back or liked any of my tweets.	He's busy, or he's not dating right now.	I can't control how anyone else feels. I am smart, kind, and beautiful, and anyone would be lucky to be with me and like my hilarious tweets!

Write down everything you're afraid of going wrong.

_____

_____

_____

_____

_____

_____

_____

_____

_____

_____

_____

Now, ditch the negative part of the sentence and write down the best-case scenario. **What does that look like?**

_____

_____

_____

_____

_____

_____

_____

_____

_____

_____

Example:

What I'm afraid of: I fail this meeting, look like an idiot, people talking about me behind my back, and I get fired.

vs.

Ditching the negative: I nail this pitch, my coworkers respect me more, I believe in myself more than ever, I make the deal happen. BAM!

Which thought requires less energy from yourself?

_____

_____

_____

_____

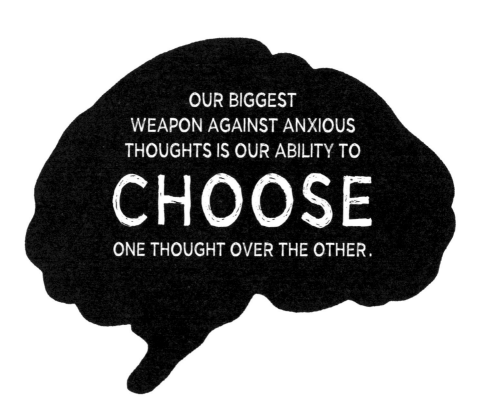

OUR BIGGEST
WEAPON AGAINST ANXIOUS
THOUGHTS IS OUR ABILITY TO

CHOOSE

ONE THOUGHT OVER THE OTHER.

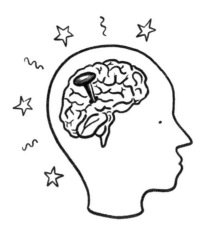

RUMINATION

You like to think a lot! Good for you! SHE'S A THINKER! Thinking = curious = growing = learning = optimizing self, right? Yes!

.....

....

....

Well, let me think about that for a second. This is true, unless you are someone with an anxiety disorder and tend to get stuck on the whole "thinking" thing. Unhealthy and disruptive thinking associated with anxiety is called RUMINATION. People that "ruminate," or mentally replay events, conversations, or thoughts that have happened in the past, or things that might happen in the future, border a fun line between striving for higher cognition and also thinking themselves into an intensive worry spiral. From our previous example, ruminating over whether I turned my hair straightener off before I left the house for work can easily spiral into deep thinking, worry, and self-criticism, and FAST. I cycle through thinking and thinking, which quickly turns into beating myself up ("Did my dumbass turn off the hair straightener before leaving?") and slips off the slippery slope into, "I'm such a fucking thoughtless idiot. How could I have done that? I don't pay enough attention. If the house burns down, it's my fault." The internal monologue (inner self-talk/the "voice in your head") of a person with anxiety disorder can be heavily tied to your feeling of self-worth and overall sense of self. Some research[3] has shown that negative self-talk can lead to exacerbating feelings of depression. If left unchecked, this could be quite damaging.

People who ruminate (hi, us) also tend to be people of creation and creativity, but have a hard time putting those thoughts into physical action. It can tend to feel like you are a professional procrastinator, instead of realizing that you're *simply overthinking more than the average person*. It's important to note that you are still very capable of completing tasks while having the never-ending notification that is your rumination. A helpful trick in managing rumination is GIVING YOUR INNER VOICE A NAME. They're the problem, not you! When you CATCH YOUR CRITIC acting up, you can blame it on them! For instance, my inner voice is named RILEY. Riley is wily and chaotic, and reminds me a lot of a Tasmanian devil. She's kinda a hot mess! So, when I find myself overthinking, I know it's just Riley acting up, being a thotty li'l buzzing fly in my head, focusing on the negatives. I have to talk to her gently and tell her to go take a nap.

Another way that Riley ruminates is with completely useless thoughts. FOR EXAMPLE: I'll just be chillin' in my garden, watering the grass, and then, for SOME REASON UNKNOWN TO CONSCIOUS KELSEY, my brain will start to have a convo with Chrissy Teigen in my head, practicing over and over all the things I'd like to say to her if we were to ever meet. I won't even notice my brain is DOING THIS until I find myself TALKING OUT LOUD TO MYSELF, "Wow, Chrissy, I also LOVE *Four Weddings* on TLC and always think those girls who rate a '7' are totally copping out of just going out and SAYING they didn't like the wedding. 7 is a soft rating. 7 is a bitch rating. It's like, have an opinion, ya know? Did you LOVE OR HATE THE BUFFET??"

...and then I will say that about 10-12 times, over and over, sometimes out loud, then back in my head, in varying tones, practicing the conversation before I realize that my brain has convinced me to have a REHEARSAL with myself about a FAKE conversation I'm having with a CELEBRITY that will 100,000% NEVER HAPPEN. This loud ass ruminating quick voice is called "inner speech." Inner speech moves 10x faster in our heads than the time it would take to use our mouths to say it. Inner speech is a bit different from "thinking" in that it feels more like a conversation than a random thought process. I like to think my brain is producing this completely useless conversation with Chrissy Teigen as a way of entertaining itself, but it can start to feel a bit exhausting. The best way to break this chain of thought is with mindfulness, which we will learn more about in the coming chapters.

---

3 Elizabeth Scott, MS. "How to Reduce Negative Self-Talk for a Better Life." *Verywell Mind*, 25 Feb. 2020, www.verywellmind.com/negative-self-talk-and-how-it-affects-us-4161304.

I experience rumination mostly with creative work. Each week, I host a podcast (go listen! Confidently Insecure: the podcast where we're absolutely sure we don't know everything! Shout out to my Confidantes!), and self-produce the whole damn thing, which I'm pretty proud of! But every week, after we release the episode on Monday morning, I have about 30 minutes of feeling content and accomplished in my brain...and then it's time to start thinking about the next episode! And, sure, I could block-shoot them, but then they won't feel relevant to the week's news. So, for the next six days, 23 hours, and 30 minutes, my brain is cycling in thought of what next week's episode will be. Who will I ask to guest? What will the listeners think? Are there any fun giveaways we can do? What about all the social media posts? Are we gaining listeners? Can we read an ad this week to pay for this whole operation? Will this week's topic last 45 minutes, or run into an hour and a half territory...? I could go on, but I'll stop with the inside baseball jargon.

These thoughts aren't classified as "intrusive," since there are no negative emotions attached, but BOY ARE THEY CONSTANT! Making it more...annoying...than anything. Before I fall asleep, I'm thinking of topic ideas, picturing the episode, randomly imagining Chrissy Teigen as a guest; it's like a fly I can't ever swat away. I won't feel that relief until that podcast audio file goes live on the airwaves.

BUT WHY?! Those smart sciencey people say it can be narrowed down to three basic reasons as to why we ruminate:

1. **The brain wants to repair.** My brain is ruminating, trying to gain insight into a problem to <u>fix</u> it. (I will be VERY PREPARED if I ever run into the problem of not having anything to talk about with Chrissy Teigen!!)

2. **There is unresolved emotional or physical trauma getting recognition.**

3. **STRESS!!!**

There are a couple of tricks to try, once you've noticed you're ruminating, to calm that rapid cycle before it takes you down an endless trip into a black hole brain blender of high anxiety.

1. **Distract yourself**. Yep. That simple. GO DO SOMETHING ELSE! Write, draw, tap your foot—really, anything to tell your brain, "Ah-ha! I've seen what you're doing...NOW LOOK OVER HERE AT THIS INSTEAD!"

2. **Take ACTION!** In the case of ruminating about my podcast, I could physically take action, whether that be writing an outline to get my thoughts and

worries out, calling a friend to brainstorm, or just DOING THE DANG PODCAST!

3. **Meditate!** Don't worry, this book is not going to be filled with "meditation" as an answer for everything. But in this specific case of thought repetition, meditation can actually help break the cycle! More in the "Meditation & Mindfulness" chapter ahead.

Another tip is to watch how often you are SHOULD-ING yourself in a negative or self-critiquing way. Telling yourself that you SHOULD or SHOULD NOT be or think a certain way can become discrediting or too demanding on the psyche. You are you—a special miracle—even if mental illness/bullies/society tries to tell us we are not "enough"! Try having a rumination "conversation" in your head without using the word "should" or "shouldn't."

Some examples of self-critiquing rumination are:

- **Recounting** that email you sent to your boss over and over again in your head, imagining your boss thinking you're incompetent based on how you space your paragraphs.
- **Thinking** about the last text you sent to that crush, wondering if you're even good enough for them, and how they're going to judge you based on which emoji you use.
- **Obsessing** about how you should be doing more of *insert thing you don't think you're doing enough of*.

It's helpful to write out the scenarios you ruminate on, not to try to *fix them*, but simply to *notice* that you are doing it.

What do you notice that you ruminate about?

_____

_____

_____

_____

_____

Do you find yourself should or shouldn't-ing yourself in this scenario?

_____

_____

_____

_____

Is it possible that you are being too self-critical about this situation? If yes, how so?

_____

_____

_____

_____

_____

Do you feel self-compassion in this scenario could be more useful? How?

_____

_____

_____

_____

Can you give your rumination a name and personality? What do they look like? How do they present themselves to you when they are actin' up?

_____

_____

_____

_____

I've always been a nervous person. I blame it on a mixture of my exploding personality and scattered hormones (I was a very late bloomer). My parents might tell you it's because I'm "the most dramatic person they've ever met," but I like to think that I'm just very *expressive*. Friends at work say I have a "face for thumbnails," A.K.A. I'm so hammy with my facial expressions that they make for eye-catching video thumbnails.

But back to me being nervous! There are good nerves and bad nerves.

Good nerves come to me right before a big shoot, like when I'm about to improvise a bunch of jokes on the set of my TV show, *Dating: No Filter*, or right before a big meeting, where I'm about to present an idea to my team ("Okay, so what if we try to toilet train my cats for a month?").

Bad nerves happen when the inner dialogue in my head starts to negatively affect my situation, like when I think, "Everyone on set is going to think my jokes about penises looking like freeze-dried eggplants are too politically incorrect," or "I'm not patient enough to toilet train my cats."

I've spent the better half of my 20's trying to retrain that little voice in my head to not be so dang tough on me! It's not easy! For some nervous people, that harsh, bitchy attitude we have toward ourselves is a big motivator to work harder, to do better. However, sometimes it gets carried away. **We fear success because we think reaching a point of contentment will stop us from working as hard.** We fear that if we're not successful *enough*, that means we're not working hard enough.

A big realization I've had as I become more self-aware is that I'm my own biggest critic. *No one is ever as hard on me as I am on myself*, which makes me think...**why am I so hard on myself?** Sure, my harsh inner voice is what makes me a perfectionist, but even though my high energy can be alluring, it can also be exhausting. And, despite the fact that I've had *plenty* of hard-ass coaches, teachers, and mentors in my life, I've always had the mentality that if I don't root for my own damn self, who will? But how can we find the balance of cheering ourselves on vs. punishing ourselves? We should listen to what our Lord & Savior, Beyoncé Giselle Knowles-Carter, preaches:

Me myself and I

That's all I got in the end

That's what I found out

And it ain't no need to cry

I took a vow that from now on

I'm gonna be my own best friend

Yas, Kween. Yas. **We all need to treat ourselves the way we treat our best friend when they're in need of some loving.** If I need to skip yoga because I'm too crampy, I'm not going to beat myself up about it. If I need a large pineapple pizza with a side of pad Thai with extra pineapples, I'm going to have it. If I'm feeling anxious, I'm going to talk to myself the same way I would comfort a friend.

So, let's all take a quick second right now to say something nice about ourselves. GO!*

_____

_____

_____

_____

_____

_____

_____

*I told myself, "Girl, I'm proud of you for putting yourself first…and good job hanging up all those clothes that you normally throw on that one special 'chair just for clothes to be thrown on' chair while getting dressed in the morning."

ANXIETY & PERFECTIONISM

THE PERFECT PIZZA

We all know them: the perfect people in our lives and in our social feeds. They just have it all: the career, the looks, the relationship, the Instagram aesthetic, the perfect jokes on Twitter, the latest and greatest gadgets—oh, and did we mention PERFECT FUCKING TEETH AND SKIN? WHO ARE THESE ROBOTIC FUCKS, and who are their dentists/dermatologists?!

Ahhhh, *perfectionism*, the art of being perfect. Or, at least *trying* to be. Because it really is an "art." It's an activity that requires hours of work, sweat, and tears just to maintain. Sure, while trying to be perfect can help drive motivation and shape us to be the "go-getters" we are, it can also totally fucking ruin our ability to function, because we are constantly reaching for an end goal that DOESN'T EXIST. It's a front! A facade! But our society (*especially* social media) doesn't want us to believe that is true. It wants us to think that "perfect" is something everyone seems to have...except for you.

A lot of my anxiety comes from the fear that my mental illness gets in the way of me reaching my full potential. I often find myself getting stuck on projects I'm passionate about, doubting my talents, and blaming my ADHD when I'm unable to finish a project. **It was becoming obvious that I had A FEAR OF FAILURE.**

CUE: DREAMLIKE HARP MUSIC THAT FLASHES US BACK IN TIME

When I was 15, I interviewed for my first real adult job at a pizzeria (shout out to the scars on my arms from the pizza oven). I'd never done a job interview before, and even though it was a summer job with the lowest stakes possible, I was—YOU GUESSED CORRECTLY—extremely anxious about it. I love pizza...but...what if I'm not good in pizzaesque environments? What if I'm bad at pizza-ing? I asked one of my high school buddies who had been working since she was 10 (definitely illegal, right?) for some tips on how to nail the interview. She told me that every interviewer will always ask the same classic question intended to trip you up, to reveal a negative quality about yourself: "What's your worst trait?" She told me to *always* turn this negative into a positive. Give a trick answer to their trick question. "Tell them you're a perfectionist," she said. 'Say something like, 'while most people would consider this a good trait to have, I just won't be able to send a pizza out until I know it's PERFECT. Some call it a gift. But it's my curse...' and they'll be all like, 'Wow this teenager is THOROUGH!' And they'll have no choice but to hire you!" Great, I thought! I've got the secret sauce (pun intended) to nail this interview.

And guess what? They DID ask me that question, and I DID respond that I'm a perfectionist. And then, guess what even freaking more? Turns out I wasn't lying. *I was a perfectionist* and didn't even know it until there was dough in my hands. Pizza brought out the anxiety of performance perfectionism. I really couldn't let a pizza leave my sight without making sure it was picturesque. The pressure of knowing something I'D created with MY OWN HANDS was then going into the hands of someone else and even further...INTO THE BODY OF SOMEONE ELSE, had my perfectionist bells a-ring-a-ding-dinging until, quickly, the "ring" turned into a blaring alarm! I was bordering on OBSESSION about where each pepperoni was placed...making sure the boxes were perfectly folded before housing a pizza, and slicing...oh god...slicing the pizza needed to be SMOOTH AND EQUAL. If not? TRASH THE WHOLE PIZZA. (Yes, I'm ashamed to admit, I tossed many pizzas in my day. A major waste.)

Imagine how my boss looked on, knowing I took 18 minutes to prepare each pizza, as opposed to the standard 4-6 minutes. My fears came true: I was an incredibly slow pizza-maker. When summer came to an end, I found myself so stressed that I knew I couldn't keep the job into the school year. My boss was definitely going to fire me, so I put myself out of my own misery instead. As I resigned the position, the owner of the pizza shop told me, "People don't want it perfect, they just want it fast and good enough." I was so afraid of making mistakes, of disappointed customers, fear of failing the creation of a freakin' pizza. I realized my perfectionist anxiety decreased efficiency. If I had the chance to do it all again, I wish I would've encouraged myself to make more mistakes, to learn that not everything needeth be perfecteth. But, of course, my high anxiety couldn't allow this to be a learned lesson, could it?

I berated myself, "How dumb are you to have let BREAD AND CHEESE cause you so much angst and stress that you had to quit your teenage summer job!?"

The point of PIZZA is not to be *perfect*. It's to be *delicious and fast*! Even the ugliest pizza is still delicious, ooey gooey PIZZA! **Not everything needs to be perfect to still be absolutely WONDERFUL!** *Consistency* is cool! *Progress* is dope! You must ultimately learn that being "perfect" isn't what matters, and in fact, it can be the thing that gets in your way of becoming the best version of yourself. And, no matter what version of yourself you're living in right now, you are GOOD ENOUGH. Say it with me out loud right now:

I AM GOOD ENOUGH.

AGAIN!

I AM GOOD ENOUGH!!

I was able to learn throughout the years how to separate my anxiety around perfectionism, from wanting to please other people (boo) to finding a way to please myself (yay!). Pleasing instead of self-abusing was based around letting go of "black or white" thinking. Meaning, I quit thinking if something wasn't "perfect," then it was a failure. All or nothing. I stopped focusing on flaws. I learned to feel satisfaction in PROGRESS instead of a final product! I tried to avoid BURNOUT. I set boundaries on working hours and fought the impulses that would BLOOP up into my brain by:

1. **Noticing them.**

2. **Saying, "thank you, brain, for this thought."**

3. **Reminding myself it's impossible to please everyone and it's not my job to!**

4. **KEEPIN' IT MOVIN'.**

By now, dear reader, you might be thinking that intrusive anxiety around perfectionism sounds eerily familiar to another disorder and symptom of anxiety...and that's how I found out about OCD.

OCD & ANXIETY

When writing this workbook, I learned something that I hadn't previously known about OCD.

This disorder is split into two types of diagnosis:

1. **Obsessive Compulsive Disorder** (OCD), which is a type of anxiety disorder; and

2. **Obsessive Compulsive Personality Disorder** (OCPD).

Most people (including me, up until an hour ago!) don't know the second exists, or the difference between the two! And, how should we know?! We don't study psychology! COLLEGE DROPOUT HERE, REMEMBER?! Instead, we've been trained by society to applaud highly organized and detail-oriented people!

The DSM-5[4] separates the two by labeling 1) OCD as an anxiety disorder, while 2) OCDP is considered a personality disorder.

THE BIGGEST DIFFERENCE TO NOTE BETWEEN THE TWO IS SIMPLE:

OCD comes from distress, and OCDP comes with pleasure.

Folks with OCD *know* their behaviors are not exactly reasonable ("Did I turn off that hair straightener before I left? Or not, like a fuckin' idiot? I *know* I did, but I better drive back home and check."); therefore, completing the behavior or thought helps them RELIEVE the stressful feelings.

People with OCPD find rituals, perfectionism, and rigidity pleasurable; it's very intertwined with the person's personality. There is no anxiety experienced with OCDP.

There are tons of resources online that go more in depth with OCD and OCPD, but because of my mild connection to OCD, I will be referring to its relationship with *anxiety* in this workbook. The kind of OCD that lives in the back of your head, its tiny voice constantly reminding you of those intrusive thoughts (btw, reader, have you tried the "Intrusive Thoughts" exercise in the beginning of this workbook? If you have, PRACTICE IT AGAIN!), OCD related to anxiety disorders overall is a coping mechanism. **It's about self-soothing.** OOOOooooOOo WOooooosaaaaaaa AhhhhhHH! Self-soothing is instilled in us from childhood. For example, baby-us

---

4 The DSM-5 is basically the Holy Bible of mental illnesses and diagnosis if the Bible was able to be edited and updated. And just like the book of the Lawd, the DSM 5 is widely debated and argued by professionals. Some live by it—some think it's a pile of trash.

had to learn how to fall back asleep without the coddling of our parents by self-soothing: maybe it's sucking a thumb, crying a bit, readjusting sleep positions, etc.

It's being able to recognize and *contain control.* Which can be tricky because, with OCD as a symptom of anxiety, control can be seen as a useful manifestation by your brain when, in fact, it can be disruptive. There is a level of management where the symptom of OCD doesn't feel like a BAD thing! It's okay if "needing to maintain control" is a constant thought you have—after all, society needs people like that! Disastrous thinking can be helpful for catastrophe planning or disaster management (which is another thing I didn't know existed until writing this workbook!). For example, if you have OCD tendencies, I bet your house would be the first place all your friends would run to during a zombie apocalypse, 'cause they know your shit is stacked and ready! IT'S OKAY to appreciate your symptoms of OCD as they pertain to your anxiety disorder—and CLAIM THEM! Because look how it's made you successful and kept things in order! There are plenty of corporate jobs out there in the field of Disaster Management which require a bachelor's degree. Disaster Managers "prepare emergency plans and procedures for natural (e.g., hurricanes, floods, earthquakes), wartime, or technological (e.g., nuclear power plant emergencies, hazardous materials spills) disasters or hostage situations!"[5]

I've been able to be a one-woman business most of my life (yes, even at BuzzFeed, we did pretty much everything, from shooting, editing, and publishing, by ourselves) because of my obsession for detail and need for order and control. I think, in this case my symptoms of OCD due to my high anxiety, work in my favor as a producer. **However, it's important to note the symptoms when they become unhelpful.** For instance, I don't think my OCD tendencies would serve me, say, if I were ever to choose to become a mom. That shit is messy, and I imagine it would cause me so much pain to see the chaos that a small child can create with their bare fucking hands that I can't control. I shudder at the thought, and my vagina tightens like a gas station sign flipping over to signal that it's "CLOSED." That is a level of "letting go" I have not achieved yet. Bravo to all moms out there! Y'all the real ones.

Watch where you are exerting your perfectionist or OCD energy.

5 Inc., MTR at CareerPlanner.com. "Emergency Management Specialist Job Description." *Emergency Management Specialist Job Description, Duties and Jobs - Part 1*, job-descriptions.careerplanner.com/Emergency-Management-Specialists.cfm.

What areas of your life do the symptoms of OCD with high anxiety serve you positively?

_____

_____

_____

_____

_____

_____

_____

_____

What areas of your life do those symptoms debilitate you?

_____

_____

_____

_____

_____

_____

_____

_____

_____

(Of course, some OCD disorders can be so evasive that they require more attention from a psychiatrist, psychologist, or even medication. So ask your doc, please!)

CONSIDER YOURSELF TO BE CONSCIENTIOUS INSTEAD!

There are ways to transform those nagging OCD symptoms from high anxiety into a positive! It starts with a simple mind shift to consider your "annoying repetitive thoughts" as a much kinder label of:

Your mind being COURTEOUS to, or CONSCIENTIOUS of, YOU!

You can still be proud of your work ethic and thoroughness, and be sure to give yourself credit for managing a healthy lifestyle while reducing the need for perfectionism. That's a mouthful! And a tricky Catch-22! How do I remain conscientious to myself without stepping over the line into perfectionism? First, we gotta be okay with failing, my friend. Failure is scary but a completely necessary part of life. BUT, WHY?! I LIKE BEING PERFECT AND ON TIME AND SCHEDULED AND LIKED AND...BUT...BUT...I CANNOT FAIL! SOCIETY HAS REJECTED FAILURES! I HAVE LEARNED TO DO EVERYTHING IN MY POWER NOT TO FAIL!

Okay, hear me out.

I like to remind myself that there are two ways of looking at life: as an adventure or a destination. When we see our life existence as an adventure, then we are living a life that gives us the freedom to grow, to learn lessons, make mistakes, break some hearts, experience pain, find joy and suffering, and, most importantly, we can FAIL and not be ashamed. IT'S JUST LIKE AN ADVENTURE YOU SEE IN THE MOVIES! AND YOU ARE THE MAIN CHARACTER! *Shit happens* in movies, right?! Good, bad, ugly, funny. Mistakes are made, lessons are learned, and we watch the main character grow (and usually, they finally get to screw the popular guy, too!). Otherwise, it would be one boring ass movie. Life should be full of ups, but more IMPORTANTLY: DOWNS! A down means there is a chance to have a ~glow up~ moment. To look at yourself and think, "Oh shit, I never thought I could do this thing, and now that I've done it, I wonder what else I'm not letting myself accomplish because I'm afraid to fail!"

But when you live life as a destination, you're looking at life through the eyes of judgment.

- Did I pass?

- Did I fail?
- Do people like me?
- Do people respect my work?
- Am I loved?

There's a judgment that happens in these questions. It's a critique rather than an earnest question that gives us room to grow. We're self-shaming, even if it's unintentional. In this mode of thinking, life can't be entertaining. It's like getting stuck on a one-way road: stagnant and unchanging, promoting a cycle of self-blame. "Why didn't I get off at that last exit?! I never pay attention! SHIT! I'M A BAD DRIVER!" Getting wrapped up in that thinking cycle makes it impossible to live and be present in the HERE and NOW. It drives us back to ANXIETY. And remember this: Anxiety is simply thinking too much into the future or too much into the past. We want to live right here. Right now. Don't ignore the life that is happening now because you are too focused on getting to the finish line of some ambiguous societal destination.

When you look at yourself as the main character, what climactic moments do you envision for yourself?

_____

_____

_____

_____

_____

_____

_____

MAKING MISTAKES

So now that you're cool with the idea of failing and making mistakes without disturbing your anxiety disorder (and you've given yourself practice, since it's not going to happen overnight!), let's talk about how we can do this shit the HEALTHY WAY! Making mistakes can be fucking EMBARRASSING. And there's nothing more shameful to a person with high anxiety than experiencing embarrassment that throws us into self-criticism. But mistakes are an inevitable part of life, and in fact, I'm going to encourage you to fail. It's going to take a bit of vulnerability. Brené Brown, my personal STAN and author of five *New York Times* best sellers about shame, vulnerability, and imperfection, says,

> *"If you can predict the outcome, you're probably not being vulnerable. Vulnerability takes courage."*

B.B. is calling us out! She's telling us that in life, work, or relationships, you could be doing some baller shit, but that doesn't necessarily mean you're being *courageous*.

Courageousness means vulnerability, which means learning how to be okay with making mistakes.

After all, how the HECK are you supposed to learn what you like and don't like if you never make mistakes? How can you grow? During my time at BuzzFeed, our managers would often ENCOURAGE us to make mistakes. They rewarded video producers who took a chance on a crazy video concept. For example, the time I made a sketch video about women asking for tampons in the workplace that devolved into chaos. The video starts with women whispering to one another, "Do you have a tampon?" Then it evolves to employees encouraging other women to not be embarrassed about asking for an essential item. By Act 3, women were proud to ask for a tampon, while it literally started *raining down tampons and pads from the ceiling*. Look—the numbers didn't do well, but BuzzFeed praised the intention of the message: *Women shouldn't be ashamed to ask out loud for a tampon. A period is nothing to be embarrassed about.* While the video was a dud, I was actually praised by my peers and respected by my bosses for taking a chance on such a taboo topic. We were able to look at the video, identify what we would've done differently, and start focusing on a Facebook page for women-centric content that blew up from two million likes to six million in no time! We discovered women wanted a space that would talk openly about that taboo shit.

I learned to let go of some of my perfectionist expectations and balance a sense of control on set by directing and editing the video myself. I learned to stand by my ideas and have confidence in my execution, which always led to a greater goal of connection and impact with other people of the world. Even if no one really watched *that* video, I kept the same mentality and learned I absolutely HAD to fail to learn and become a better filmmaker. Not everything you do or work on has to be better than the last thing you made. GROWTH IS NOT LINEAR! Learn to fail, and have fun doing it!

Boss Bitch and Vulnerability Queen Brené Brown goes on to say,

> *"Those of us with an obsession with perfectionism need to determine who we are on the inside vs. who/what other people say we are. Whether it be your job title, relationship position, sexuality—any labels society has given us—and stop looking for outside affirmations that you are doing it right or perfectly. Instead, we need to give those affirmations to ourselves."*

Which labels in life do you identify with and/or strive to be the "perfect" example of? What role would you like to play to perfection?

Example: The perfect stay-at-home-mom? The exemplary student?

_____

_____

_____

_____

_____

_____

What do you think "society's" version of this label is? What do you think society expects from such a person?

Example: Perfect Instagram aesthetic? A straight A+ student?

_____

_____

_____

_____

_____

_____

On a scale of 1-10, how closely to do you meet the societal expectations of this label? (*10 = I AM the perfect example of said label, 1 = I completely defy the status quo.*)

RATE YOURSELF: _____

How do you fear making mistakes will affect your image or how others in society will perceive your image?

_____

_____

_____

_____

_____

_____

That old saying rings true: "It's not how many times you fail, but how many times you get back up." I can't read this quote without thinking about all the times I wore heels to the club and fell down, but, goddammit, with all that Red Bull mixed with that vodka, I was always able to get back up, shake my ass, maintain some confidence, and maybe even get laid. Success.

REMEMBER: MAKING MISTAKES MEANS YOU'RE TRYING.

Fuck this box up. Make it imperfect:

ANXIETY & CONTROL

(OR LACK THEREOF)

"WHAT IFS?!" MEET YOUR NEW FRIEND…"THEN WHATS?!"

Repeated feelings of being "out of control" are a huge factor in anxiety disorders. We are led to believe we can't have an anxiety disorder and still enjoy life, because every thought and feeling comes with the back-up generator of "BUT, WHAT IF?!" We are constantly sharing our thought process with self-doubt, worries, and fears, which all stem from lack of feeling in control of our emotions or environment…but rarely do we think of the follow-up question to "What if?": "…then what?"

Recently, I found myself doing this when my doctor gave me the option of going back on birth control—not only as a safety precaution against having children, but to regulate my periods and get rid of this hormonal acne. I can give you a million WHAT-IFs about why I thought this was a horrible idea: What if it fucks with my mood, what if I gain a bunch of weight in my problem areas, what if I'm allergic to the meds, what if I get worse periods…? But I never thought about the "THEN WHATs" of the situation. The THEN WHATs are what you would do if the WHAT IFs happened. Ex: WHAT IF my mood DOES get funky on this birth control… THEN WHAT??!! Well…the answer was actually pretty easy, actually…I'd get off the birth control!!!! EASY SQUEEZY LEMON PEASY, right?!

Looking at your THEN WHATs actually gives you *a lot more control* than the un-hinged chaos of coming up with so many WHAT IFs. Discovering that you're even "what-if-ing" in the first place is a big step toward recognizing that your disruptive anxiety is popping up to say, "Hey, girl, hey." If you're like me, you'll begin to wonder WHY you're this way. Like, WHY, UNIVERSE, did you give me the brain that constantly fears LIFE!? Why can't I just be chill and LET GO, like everyone else seems to do so naturally!!!??

So, I ask you to dive a bit deeper into that thought.

What would be the first thing you would do if you could fully "let go" of your anxiety, of having the need for constant control of your thoughts, emotions, or environment?

_____

_____

_____

_____

_____

_____

_____

"Letting go" doesn't mean you need to "beat" those feelings of anxiety, or even get rid of them; we just need to learn _how to not fight with them._ You can put your dukes down and walk out of the ring for a little bit (this is my attempt at a sports reference, LOL), but that means you've got to let go of control a little bit. We learned on the last page about perfectionism, that the way to succeed is to fail and grow from it, right? RIIIIIGHT? There are people in society that brag about the grind, the hustle, and the exhaustion Olympics. As if getting less sleep, not taking care of yourself, and CONSTANTLY BEING STRESSED OUT means they're... better than you?? Instead of suffering from it, try living with it. Alongside it. Let it take up the seat next to you—but only that seat. Don't give your anxiety the whole couch.

Otherwise, the need for control will start to cyclone into thought, and you'll start to naturally feel the physical symptoms of high anxiety (or, LAWD FORBID, a panic attack!). So... LET'S GET THOSE WORRIES AND FEARS OUT OF YOUR BRAIN SPACE! And into your physical hands and feet. Because so much of anxiety disorder is focused on THOUGHTS, it's easy to end up exhausted from all that thinking and, before we know it, we've been laying on our couch in the fort of blankets we've built as a defense from the world, having a full-on slumber party with our high anxiety. Ruminating. Procrastinating. What most people who SUFFER from anxiety don't know is that simply putting some of that swirling thought-hurricane into PHYSICAL ACTION can lessen the hurricane into more of a light drizzle. Anxiety symptoms are a biochemical response; your body is turning thought into actual physical chemicals in your body, creating energy.

Typically, our bodies would then use or store that energy. But when you're just a stressed out li'l bean tryin' to amalgamate with your couch, that energy is not useful! GET THOSE THOUGHTS PHYSICALLY OUT OF YOUR HEAD. It doesn't always need to be EXERCISE *per se*, but staying stagnant is room for more thinking. Get your blood pumping. Go for a walk. Stand while you play your video games for all I care. Movement is at least MOVEMENT. If you need to get something off your mind, you can text a friend and tell them what's wrong/what's going on in your mind/ask for their help. (BTDUBS, reaching out for help is one of the hardest and most brave things to do; it's crazy how easily anxious thoughts could be solved if we asked for the opinion of another person we trust.)

An example of going from <u>thoughts</u> to <u>action</u>: Your laundry is piling up, the bathroom sink always has dried toothpaste stuck to it, and the windows have so much grime on them Elon Musk tried to get them pregnant. HOW CAN YOU GET PHYSICAL so your mind doesn't create energy that creates anxious symptoms that aren't useful?

Answer: Put on a podcast or blast a ~good vibes~ playlist and DANCE your way into cleaning! RELEASE THAT BIOCHEMICAL ENERGY!

How about a more extreme example? If you hate your job, you could technically... quit! Walking away from a job is, of course, a more privileged and dramatic example, but the *physical act of walking away* is more useful than the uncontrollable feelings of misery you experience while sitting inert and sluggish at your cubicle. What a release that would be, huh?

What are some anxious thoughts you can't control in your mind but could use your physical body to solve?

MENTAL ANXIETY:

_____

_____

_____

_____

TURN IT PHYSICAL:

_____

_____

_____

_____

※ W. O. W. ※

THE ANXIOUS
ANTICIPATION IS ALWAYS

WORSE

THAN THE THING ITSELF.

I CAME.
I SAW.
I GOT ANXIETY.
SO I LEFT.

!!!

Go for a walk alone without headphones and try to be as present as possible.	Order food at a restaurant or fast food without practicing it in your head first.	Ask a stranger for the time.	Call a friend on the ACTUAL PHONE, or better yet, FaceTime them without telling them!
Try to purposefully fail at something.	Try eating in public for all three meals today (can someone say dollar menu?).	Find a concert venue or comedy show in your city and get a ticket for TONIGHT!!!!	Bake something and share it with a neighbor you may not have met yet or don't know very well.
Spend an entire afternoon (or an hour, at least) without looking at your phone. In fact, TURN IT OFF! *gasp of millennial horror*	Ask a friend or coworker to lunch or coffee (or tea, if caffeine makes you anxious, like me!).	Ask that cute person out for drinks! Or a movie! Or to do a picnic in a park! It's cute as shit!	Improvise your entire day. Don't make any plans or use GPS—just see where the wind takes ya!
Take yourself out on a date in public.	Visit a museum in your area you've never been to. Try to stay for at least THREE hours. Get lost and learn some shit!	Pick an event in your neighborhood (check Eventbrite or Airbnb experiences) and do it!	Take your city's public transportation! Try striking up a convo with your seat neighbor [unless they're wearing headphones].
RSVP "Yes" to a Facebook event in your area or a Facebook invitation to a party you wouldn't normally go to.	Head to a local bookstore and ask a worker for a recommendation. Read a few chapters for free at the store in a comfy chair.	Download the app MEETUP and choose a FREE group event to meet up with (EX: South Asian book club, beach cruiser bike rides, etc.)	Browse books, movies, or music you might not be familiar with at you local library. Check out at least 3 things and have date with yourself enjoying them.

SOCIAL ANXIETY CHALLENGE

Up for a challenge? RIP THE PREVIOUS PAGE OUT OF THE BOOK!! YEAH, YOU HEARD ME! The one with all the boxes! Tear it out! WHEW! Didn't that feel good? Now, cut out, fold these boxes, and place them into a bowl for random selection. (*Okay fine, if you don't actually want to rip your book you can take a pic and print it out... or draw it yourself...or, hell, we even have a printable version for you! See the Resource Index.*)

The challenge is simple: You draw one piece of paper from the bowl, and whatever you pick—you do it! Unless you're having a good emotional day and feeling ballsy—then go for TWO!!!!! Or, read them all and pick the one that scares you the most, you wild bitch!

☼W. O. W.☼

Here's a tip if you're feeling anxious: Ask yourself if you're doing this to "see" or "be seen." Social anxiety causes us to feel like all the eyeballs are on us. It can feel like everyone is looking at you when you walk into a room and that you are "being seen." However, we can flip the switch on that thought to become the one who does the "seeing." YOU are the one looking. The energy and anxiety go in the opposite direction. When you become interested in others or the social situation, it gives you more control.

BONUS WRITING: How did that challenge make you feel? Would you do it again? Which box on the list scares you the most? Why?

_____

_____

_____

_____

_____

_____

_____

WHEN YOUR ANXIETY COMES "OUT OF NOWHERE"

The cause of your interruptive anxiety might not always be super clear. It's like having a zit pop up when after you've been hella good at your skin routine. Mindfully, you're doing everything you can to keep the zit (anxiety) at bay. You're not touching your face (you're not having coffee past 2PM!), you're using a spot treatment (you've done your breathing exercises! yay!), BUT THAT BITCH KEEPS ON FINDING A WAY! "Perhaps then," my dermatologist would say, "we need to look at outside factors." My derm pointed out some great suggestions that revealed my villainous zit's retaliation had nothing to do with me!

- Have I been changing my pillowcases every week?
- Am I allergic to any of the ingredients in my makeup?
- Am I eating dairy that's causing hormonal acne?
- Was I giving my face time to adapt to the pollution in the LA air?
- Did I know switching my birth control can cause hormonal changes beyond my control?

SEE! WTF? My skin had taken it upon itself to react to outside factors. It's good to notice and practice accepting the things we cannot change. And when it comes to anxiety, we can use the same thinking:

FEELING THAT YOU CAN'T PINPOINT YOUR ANXIETY?

Consider the following environmental or outside factors:

What's been on the news lately?

_____

_____

What time of year is it? Does it bring up any feelings of stress for you?

_____

_____

Birthdays, holidays, Mondays, death anniversaries?

_____

_____

When was the last time you ate?

_____

_____

When was the last time you ate something green & full of healthy shit?

_____

_____

When was the last time you had coffee or caffeine? How about the last time you chugged a glass of water?

_____

_____

Check in on your screen time usage in the settings of your iPhone…is it higher than usual?

_____

_____

How's your family? When's the last time you checked in on them? Would it serve you to do so?

_____

_____

Have you changed your medication recently?

_____

_____

When was the last time you went for a walk or got your sweat on?

_____

_____

Have you taken on the burden of a friend's feelings after they've vented to you about a specific matter?

_____

_____

What's going on at work? Are you able to leave the issues at your desk when you clock out?

_____

_____

Is there an event or social gathering on your calendar coming up that you feel a type of way about?

_____

_____

Has a song or show you've listened to or watched triggered something (for me, watching *Grey's Anatomy* ALWAYS peaked my anxiety even though I LOVED me some Callie on-screen bisexuality!)?

_____

_____

ANXIETY TRIGGERS LIST

Making a TRIGGER LIST can be super helpful in identifying things outside of the normal daily stress a human is meant to feel that flares up our high anxiety. When you are able to identify the things that sound the anxiety alarm bells, we can better prepare for the symptoms so they don't creep up on us! Check off all that apply. There's also a space at the bottom for you to add your own!

- ☐ conversations with strangers
- ☐ caffeine
- ☐ bad weather
- ☐ traffic
- ☐ driving
- ☐ bright lights
- ☐ schoolwork
- ☐ small spaces
- ☐ boats
- ☐ airplanes/airports
- ☐ upcoming travel
- ☐ your ex popping on the timeline
- ☐ certain words on your social feeds that are triggering
- ☐ smells and sense memory (for me, fog machines bring up bad childhood memories)
- ☐ a certain song that brings up feelings
- ☐ financial issues, or conversations about money
- ☐ feeling out of breath after exercise or sex
- ☐ being embarrassed publicly
- ☐ alcohol and hangovers

- ☐ having to call someone on the phone
- ☐ waiting for a text
- ☐ going on a date
- ☐ big meetings
- ☐ shopping
- ☐ crowds
- ☐ oversleeping
- ☐ talking to family
- ☐ having no choice but to interact with a coworker, neighbor, or family member who stresses you out
- ☐ drugs or withdrawal
- ☐ to-do lists
- ☐ a messy home
- ☐ loud sounds
- ☐ being touched
- ☐ repetitive noise you can't control (dog barking, neighbor power washing, cars honking)
- ☐ _____
- ☐ _____
- ☐ _____
- ☐ _____

OUR ANXIOUS SPACES

CALL 'EM OUT! CALL 'EM OUT!

Let's identify some specific things that cause your high anxiety to poke its li'l head up to say HELLO! Use the chart below to write your own, which you've identified in the previous section. I've included some personal triggers for examples, and so you can get to know my weird li'l brain a li'l better. :) (Cause, remember? You're not alone in this!)

Situation	Scale 1-10 How Anxious It Makes You Feel	Mental Symptoms What's In Your Head?	Physical Symptoms How Does Your Body Feel?	Emotional Symptoms How Does That All Make You Feel?	Things That Make Me Feel Better
hangovers	7	Guilt, rumination	Headache, claustrophobia	Sadness, self-shaming, anger at myself	Showers, staying in bed for a nap, cuddling, ordering in
airplanes	10	Worst-case scenario thinking, dread	Heart racing, panic attacks, sweating	It makes me feel stupid, like why can't I be calm like everyone else on the plane?	Medication, breathing techniques, taking a train instead
Parties where I don't know anyone	4	Racing thoughts, brain farts	Inability to talk, shaky hands, tendency to be jumpy	Self-doubt	Bringing a friend, keeping the party low-stakes

Situation	Scale 1-10	Mental Symptoms	Physical Symptoms	Emotional Symptoms	Things That Make Me Feel Better

My therapist, Kim, explained it best when she said that "living with an anxiety disorder can feel like there is a spotlight on you when you don't want it to be...like you're oddly standing out more than everyone else." There's a lot of "WHY ME, THO?" that ruminates in my head. She explained to me one day, over one of our many video sessions, "I tell my clients, 'Imagine two cars that look exactly alike. Same year, same body, same color, etc. But one car is automatic and one car is stick shift. People without anxiety disorders are automatic cars. When something stressful happens to them, their function switches automatically to manage their problem. With anxiety disorder, you have to take extra steps shifting your functions into gear. And you have to take that extra thought, that extra time, that extra step to switch gears."

WENT OUTSIDE TODAY.

SAW PEOPLE.

ZERO STARS.

DO NOT RECOMMEND.

☆☆☆☆☆

Coloring Page

CANCELING PLANS

Truly, is there ANYTHING BETTER IN THIS WORLD than being freed from the bounds of social responsibility, unexpectedly? Sure, you could argue:

"A warm cinnamon bun!"

"A kitten who purrs like Lana Del Rey!"

"Five million dollars?"

...AND YOU'D BE WRONG. NOTHING IS BETTER THAN WHEN SOMEONE CANCELS PLANS FOR AN EVENT OR MEETUP THAT YOU WERE HOPING WOULD GET CANCELED. AUUUHHJGGHHHHHKFJDLSFJKSDL Just thinking about it makes my arm hair stand on its ends (and my chest hair, but that's another conversation)! If I could open a brick & mortar storefront in the middle of town whose entire biz-nas is CANCELING PLANS, then I'd fully take out a loan to do so, make back the investment plus millions, buy the dopest couch that ever existed, sit on it, and never go out again. A socially anxious person's shooting star wish will always be: "Please let that stupid 'coffee hang sesh' with that third-string acquaintance from high school who reached out for help (and you didn't say no in the first place because you're a people pleaser who is still learning the value of your own time) BE CANCELED!" WOOOOW, what are we going to do with those two whole free hours?! ANOTHER EPISODE OF *90 DAY FIANCÉ?!* DON'T MIND IF I DO!!!!! But, alas, the stars don't always align in our li'l anxious favor. Sometimes WE have to be the one to Pull the Plug on Plans—or PPP, as I call it. And unless it's a wedding that you're canceling on (seriously, don't do this unless you are deathly ill or you have an absolute fucking EMERGENCY. Like, poop-is-leaking-out-of-your-eyeballs-and-you-couldn't-possibly-get-on-a-plane-with-poopy-eyeballs kind of emergency), I can guarantee that the anxiety you are experiencing about canceling can be more overwhelming than the cancellation or reaction of the person you're canceling on itself. LET ME REPEAT THAT: THE ANTICIPATION OF THE THING IS ALMOST ALWAYS WORSE THAN THE THING ITSELF. My friends will tell you two things about me. I am the queen of: 1) Irish exiting; and 2) canceling plans, but doing it in a way that will still make you want to be friends with me. After all, how could you resist this adorable smile?? Lucky for me, I've been pretty open about my mental-health struggles, and most of my friends know that if I say I need to cancel because I'm having high anxiety, they don't even question it. I don't take for granted that my friends are so chill and educated about this! I've also learned how to say NO to things I don't really think I'll go to. Saying "NO" is your superpower. We do not apologize for saying "no" to things we don't want to do, and we do not need to give an explanation as to why we are saying no. I also TRY TO SERIOUSLY not cancel on things that I know mean ~*something*~ to ~*someone special*~. I'm not a dick about this cancellation super-power. I try to wield it lightly. After all, you don't want to be labeled the FLAKY friend, unless that's the nickname your circle gave you because you make the most delicious buttery, flaky, crispy croissants anyone's ever had.

I could use examples of a million scenarios where I've canceled on people, and I could go over every state of mind I was in for doing so: exhaustion from the day, anxiety from too much coffee, diarrhea, sadness, meh-ness, my cat was sick, BLAH BLAH BLAH. But for the sake of the length of these pages and saving some trees, let's read the rest of this chapter with the assumption that sometimes *you just can't do it*. Doesn't matter why! And that's the emotional point I'll continue this chapter on. You just simply cannot go. To the thing.

SO!!!

There are various levels of CANCELLATION STATION or PPP'ing you can visit depending on the relationship with the person and event you're canceling on. I have a few rules of thumb:

- **You can't cancel on a wedding.** It's the most dick move ever. Funerals? BLAME THE GRIEF!!! Birthday parties? EASY!!! I JUST DON'T WANNA!!! But weddings? Sorry, nope.

- **If someone paid money for you to come** and you cancel at the last minute—say, for an event or ticket to a concert—you absolutely have to pay them back the full price PLUS A DRINK OR TWO (depending on how late the cancellation is) as reimbursement. When money is involved, don't be a dick. Pay up the $15 to that shitty comedy show you agreed to see. In rcturn, just DON'T order pizza that night. You'll be hungry. But at least you'll be under your warm covers, far far away from that smoky, two-drink minimum improv show.

- **If it's a group thing**, the same rules from above apply, except it's easier to get off the hook because there will be so many distractions with others that your friend might give you shit to start, but once the event is actually taking place and there are more people to distract them, they won't miss you. EXCEPT FOR WEDDINGS!! THEY WILL NEVER LET YOU LIVE THAT DOWN. AND THEY WILL BRING IT UP IN EVERY SOCIAL SETTING FOR THE REST OF FOREVER. But seriously, most people are thinking about themselves, not YOU. Which is GOOD NEWS! People don't care about us as much as we think they do (sad, yet, RELIEVING, RIGHT?!).

- **If you cancel and you actually wanted to go** but *just couldn't* at that time, you have to be the one to initiate the rescheduling. Don't put it on them; they're already dealing with your cancellation. Don't just ask for a rain check; give them concrete dates and times that you are available.

- **If you NEVER INTENDED TO ACTUALLY DO THE THING**, and you know this person will keep reaching out over and over to hang, be direct. Tell them you've decided to put your social calendar on a back burner to focus on ***insert thing you're more interested in here*** and have found yourself exhausted from overbooking social events. If you're able, tell them you'd be happy to chat about their thing over email or a FaceTime chat while you sit snugly in your Snuggie. FaceTime chats have saved me a lot of time and energy.

Now that we've established the basic rules of PPP'ing, here are some tips:

1. **Commit to the cancel.** Before you reach out, COMMIT TO THE CANCEL. You're going to give them a response that, hopefully, they will accept, and not shift the blame and guilt you into coming. Be direct. Avoid phrases like "I think..." or "If it's okay with you." Practice your dialogue in your Notes app and have some backup lines written down to look at if they're being pushy. **Examples:** "I'll let you know if I change my mind." "I hear you and it's not something I can commit to at this very moment." "I'm not emotionally/mentally available for this."

2. **Over-explaining can lead to suspicious behavior.** Am I telling you to lie? SOMETIMES. But the more details you tend to give, the more OBVIOUS it is you're lying—and how much harder is it to remember those li'l details when you have to recount the tale come Monday morning at the coffee cooler?! (Wait, coffee cooler??? What am I talking about?)

3. **If you've known the person fewer than three months**, they are allowed one or two jabs about cancellation. One GIF exchange or cry emoji. In this instance, you *can* use the words "rain check" and "something came up" without further question.

4. **If you've known them six months to two years**, they are allowed to pry a bit about the "why"-ness of your cancellation. You have the choice to be honest or lie, depending on how close you are, but my gut always goes with truth. Just mention you're taking a mental-health break.

There's always a caveat to this conversation worth mentioning. Sometimes, we find ourselves having friendships with emotional terrorists. "Friends" who will put you through emotional fucking trauma when you've decided to put your emotional well-being first. The assholes who lecture you upon cancellation about you being a bad friend who "always does this" and "yadda yadda yadda." These people ARE. NOT. GOOD. FRIENDS. TO. HAVE. IN. YOUR. LIFE. They tend to be younger or more lonely, when EVERYTHING feEls SoOOoo fUckING DRAMAtic!!!!!! AND THE WEEKEND IS THE ONLY TIME TO DO ANYTHING!!!! As you get older, it just kinda becomes a rule of thumb that you're not allowed to get mad at people for canceling plans 'cause we're all miserable, busy, and our backs hurt. This usually happens around age 25. BUT! Be careful of the manipulators, the ones who try to make you feel bad about yourself to an UMPTEENTH unreasonable degree and use your cancellationship as ammunition for future friendshipping time. The best kinds of friendships are the ones who text you at 8:45pm like this: ⟶

These are the friends you want to hold close and never let go of.

YOGA & ANXIETY

If I had a dollar for every time someone told me I could cure my anxiety if I "just took a yoga class," I'd be hanging out with Cardi B on a mega yacht, eating caviar off her butt. I'd been incredibly resistant to doing yoga because of the stereotype of what a "yoga person" has turned into in America: the green juice, crunchy, crystal-humping OHHMMMMers who shove their lifestyle down your throat. YOGA had seemed to be just another thing white people stole from Eastern culture, put a LuLuLemon price tag on, and flipped into another "trendy" wellness cure-thing. I would've never taken a yoga class unless I was FORCED to...which I was. In college, for theater acting, we were required to take one yoga class a week for eight weeks to help us "get into our bodies more." As someone who feels like their skin doesn't even belong to their own body sometimes, this was the OPPOSITE of what I was trying to do. I'd like to get as far away from myself as possible most days! But at the beginning of the first class, something happened that changed my view on yoga forever (how white-girl-cliché of me, right?). The yoga instructor told me to put away my worries, anxieties, and fears just for one hour as we practice, and that I could always come back to them after class was over.

Whoa, I had never thought of it that way! My anxieties and tensions instantly materialized in my head to look like a heavy backpack that I'd finally been given permission to set down. And when the practice was done, I could always pick those worries, anxieties, and fears back up. **They weren't going anywhere...so, why not just set them aside for this one hour?** And with each beginner's stretch and pose, I began to set down some more of myself and to "KEEP BREATHING!" as she adamantly reminded the class over and over and over. Of course, as mentioned many a time in this book, the last thing I want to do when confronted with anxiety is think about my own breath. The idea of purposely thinking about my breathing makes me feel like I'm going to die. My yoga teacher pointed out that my belly always seemed so tense when I was mindfully breathing. It was an unintentional safety switch my body turned on and took some practice to hardwire my body to relax my stomach. My instructor told me to think about my body being a giant stick of cold, hard butter...melting against the mat of heat like a cast-iron skillet. MMMMM, butter...pancakes...I thought to myself...ooooozy warm...French toast and a side of fatty bacon...deeeeelish—"AS WE COME TO A CLOSE," I heard the instructor say. "WHAT!? It had already been 45 minutes?" Holy shit. I didn't realize that the time had passed so quickly. I realized that, because of my rapid, ruminating, and cycling thoughts, time had always seemed to go by so slowly, so cramped with ideas and tasks that were undone....The second I put those away, the clock seemed to move so swiftly. And that makes sense, right? When you're staring at the microwave, waiting for your popcorn to finish, it feels like its taking a fuckin' lifetime!! But!! If you walk away, let your mind get carried by something else, before you know it, that sweet, sweet buttery smell coincides with a BEEEEEEEEP, and you're pleasantly surprised by how quickly that went. (Look, I could've just said the "a watched pot never boils" reference and saved us, like, four sentences of reading, but I WANTED TO PUT IN ANOTHER FOOD METAPHOR OKAY????)

ANYWAY:

If I caught myself in the middle of class, trying to lift that backpack of anxiety off the floor, the instructor would remind us that it's okay to NOTICE it...but, don't give it a thought, feeling, or opinion. *Just see it. Don't judge it.* For example: If I began to think of all the work I had left to do that night, or ugh, why did I put off going to the grocery store for so many days, I need to change the cat litter, etc., etc...Instead of berating myself that I wasn't doing good enough, or being a perfect adult who gets tasks done immediately when my brain thinks of them, and punishing myself... I would just notice my brain bringing it up. "Look at that—my brain thinkin' all those thoughts. Hmpf." It does take practice to stop judging your own thoughts, and I hadn't realized how often I let my brain wander. Put simply, it was hard to concentrate on the present moment! But each week, for eight weeks, I began to look FORWARD to yoga. I craved that hour where I could give myself permission to feel the awesome stretching and body positions I contorted into. I felt my body really moving, letting things flow, concentrating on the joy of movement. Internally, I was learning how to let my mind have uncomfortable thoughts without letting it affect the current practice of putting my right leg high in the air into whatever animal position we were flowing into!

And though it's stereotypical and annoying to hear over and over from some green juice heads at the Santa Monica Blvd. flea market, it's true that yoga CAN help minimize the physical symptoms of anxiety.[6] The practice of not judging my thoughts but rather noticing them enter into my head and allowing them to take up space without giving them emotion or judging myself became more and more crucial in managing my relationship with my anxiety disorder. It turns out this was a form of MINDFULNESS...**What's mindfulness? Keep on reading!!!!!!** YOU ARE SO FUCKIN' READY FOR MINDFULNESS!!!

6 Publishing, Harvard Health. *Yoga for Anxiety and Depression.* 9 May 2018, www.health.harvard.edu/mind-and-mood/yoga-for-anxiety-and-depression.

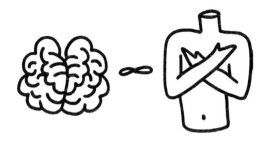

THE MIND-BODY CONNECTION

There was a decade of time where the moment my eyeballs blinked open each morning, I would get a panicky rush of what I assumed to be adrenaline (spoiler: It's not just adrenaline; it's your nervous system! Increased cortisol! Blood glucose!) and then an instant stomachache. The rush was not powerful enough to propel me out of bed like "normal" people (hi, see DEPRESSION chapter "Waking Up Really Is The Hardest Part"), but rather CEMENT me into my sheets, where my brain would suddenly cycle through all the shit I had to do that day. For example:

A lot of people wake up in the morning like this:

YAWN Yay! Another bright and sunny day! Time to get things done. Ah, life! Gotta love it!

Whereas my wake-up cycle sounded something like:

*YAWn-ooooh shit fuck another day. I'm awake. Fuck. Great. What haven't I accomplished as a human already? And why do I fail so much? Oh god, why me???? WHY ANOTHER DAY?"

This cycle of anxious morning thinking started in high school. I would wake up and immediately get that tight feeling in my stomach that would slowly travel up my chest and into my throat. The only way to combat it was by taking a cold shower. Then, I'd skip breakfast because of the stomachache, get to school right before the 7:25 A.M. bell and then—it would hit me. A wave of sweat would travel down my body, like an evil spirit was trying to pass through me. A cold, then hot, shiver would slip down my spine, and I would IMMEDIATELY...*how do I put this delicately?*... have explosive diarrhea that erupted out of my ass as if my abs were wringing out like a wet towel, sloughing off the entire lining of my insides.

I promise this story is going somewhere to mindfulness and meditation.

At 7:25 AM, students are quickly shuffling off to classes so they wouldn't be late; meanwhile, I'm SPRINTING to the most isolated bathroom in the southwest corner of campus by the auditorium, where no one had any business being that early in the AM. There, I would spend 10-15 minutes with hot fire falling out of my ass. It felt like I was peeing out my butt. Too much? Sorry.

Sometimes, I wouldn't make it to the bathroom, releasing an anxiety shart that would cause me to drag my shitty ass to the nurse's station, where I'd make the embarrassing call home to my nanny to bring me more pants. By sophomore year, I was bringing extra pairs of underwear to school in my backpack. Luckily, my first class of the day was TV Production, and because I was on my school's morning show, I could easily lie to my teacher (who loved me because I was a camera wiz and morning-show personality HAM—shout out to Mr. Lennox, you are an awesome educator!) and tell him I was off interviewing a student or developing the day's story. I was able to keep this ass issue under wraps for a very long time.

When I ran out of underwear, I finally had to tell my parents about these stomachaches. With little idea how to help me, they took me to a GI specialist, who ran a bunch of tests and told me I had IBS or *irritable bowel syndrome*. IBS is not a well-researched disorder and has no cure. Great!!!!

He sent me home with an enema and told me to bring back a sample of my shit.

Cool. Cool. Cool.

Most girls my age were worrying about which boy they should send a love note to, and I was busy fishing my own shit out of a plastic bowl, trying to figure out why I couldn't stop pooping my pants every morning at exactly 7:26 AM. I went on some meds, changed my diet, blah blah blah, and it wasn't until I was 17 and started seeing my first psychiatrist, who asked what kinds of medication I was already on, that I started to make some connections. When I told the psychiatrist that I was on antidiarrheal medication for IBS, she wanted to dive more into what had caused my mysterious morning IBS. When I explained that the first feeling I had every morning was the weight of the world, physically, in my guts, my psychiatrist was the first person to point out that the IBS and my anxiety might be related.

I'd never thought about that before: the idea that my mind had SO much power that it could physically affect my body.

It wasn't obvious to me that when I'd get butterflies in my stomach, it was because I was excited. When I felt guilty, it would feel like there was a literal weight on my chest. When I'd think about Timothée Chalamet, I'd get horny. You get the point. Your brain can do crazy shit! And this connection between the mind and body is called THE MIND-BODY CONNECTION!... yeah, that's a real term that people use in the psychology field to describe the complex interconnection between the effect our thoughts, feelings, and beliefs have (positively and negatively) on our biological function.[7] This mind-body connection that caused my anxiety disorder to arise is also sometimes called "psychosomatic." Which, at first glance, can sound a bit rude..."Who is calling me 'mind-crazy'?" But all it really means is that a physical illness is caused or aggravated by a mental factor such as internal conflict of stress. It is very real and is prescribed very real types of treatment. Which leads us to...

BODY-FOCUSED REPETITIVE BEHAVIOURS (BFRB)

- nail biting
- trichotillomania (pulling hair)
- hair twirling
- skin picking

MEDITATION & MINDFULNESS

DISCOVERING MEDITATION AFTER
SHITTING MY PANTS SO MANY TIMES

I know. I know. You were expecting a chapter like this, and you've been dreading it. MEDITATING.

> *Meditation is a practice where an individual uses a technique—such as mindfulness, or focusing the mind on a particular object, thought, or activity—to train attention and awareness, and achieve a mentally clear and emotionally calm and stable state.*[8]

7 Burgess, Patrice MD, FAAFP, et al. "Mind-Body Wellness." *Mind-Body Wellness | Michigan Medicine*, 15 Dec. 2019, www.uofm-health.org/health-library/mente.
8 Meditation. 30 Sept. 2020, en.wikipedia.org/wiki/Meditation.

Maybe you've tried meditating before and it just isn't your thing. Maybe you've tried and failed, and thrown your headphones and iPhone across the room, resulting in a broken vase and scared kitty cat. Or, like most first-timers, you find it incredibly BORING. It can get frustrating to step into the world of meditation because it can look so woo-woo-y. But there's a reason why the Western mainstream world has brought it to the forefront for solutions for managing anxiety, panic, depression, and overall well-being. More and more, we are seeing celebrities practicing meditation, posting about it on their Twitters and Instagrams. Schools across the country are starting to give kids with behavioral issues classes on meditation instead of detention. If you're like how I *used* to be and hate the idea of what this chapter is about, I encourage you to stick with it even more. As someone who came from the position of a "I'd literally rather clean Donald Trump's toenails with my tongue than meditate" mindset, I found a way to make meditation work for me. There are lots of free or low-cost meditation apps (check out the BEST GAMES ON YOUR PHONE chapter for some suggestions!) to learn the physical practice of meditation, but, in this chapter, I want to focus on what the basic pillar of meditation is all about: MINDFULNESS.

The first time I heard this word, MINDFULNESS, is when I couldn't stop shitting my pants until I was in my late teen years (as established in the last chapter), and my first therapist pointed out the mind-body connection and psychosomatic disorder. That's when she suggested I practice MEDITATION & MINDFULNESS.

"Uh, I don't even know what mindfulness means...and isn't meditation that shit monks do in the mountains and reverb their voices off rocks like OOOAHHHMMM to...idk? Summon peace or some shit?"....Clearly, I wasn't a very cultured kid. #FloridaPublicSchools

So where does this fancy buzzword, MINDFULNESS, come in to help with your high anxiety? Welp, we gotta know what mindfulness IS exactly:

MINDFULNESS is the psychological process of purposely bringing one's attention to experiences occurring in the present moment without judgment, which one develops through the practice of meditation and through other training.[9]

"So, uh, it's just like, paying super-duper attention?" I thought. "Yes," she replied. "But that attention is without judgment. It's not necessarily about trying to think about NOTHING, like most people assume meditation & mindfulness to be... rather...consciousness without judgment."

9 "Mindfulness." *Wikipedia*, Wikimedia Foundation, 30 Sept. 2020, en.wikipedia.org/wiki/Mindfulness. n.d., para 1

"Okay…uh. Thanks?" and I used my mom's debit card to pay the $40 copay and left without really knowing what the fuck this doctor was talking about.

So I went straight to one of my favorite places on Earth: BARNES & NOBLE. Something about books *just turns me on*. The peace of flipping pages. The beautiful covers that make me FEEL something. Curling up in the corner, deciding if the few first pages capture me enough to spend $20. I can't believe I'm writing one of those right now!!!!! Wow. *wipes a few tears from my eyes*

ANYWAY.

CUT TO:

Me at B&N, showering myself in self-help books about mindfulness and meditation. While I could write a whole book about mindfulness and meditation (and trust me, there are thousands), I want to focus on basic principles, tips, and tricks that will help you with your anxiety disorder.

WATCH YO MIND

"Mindwatching" is simply that: watching your mind like the way a mom watches her kid's junior-league soccer game. She's there, but she doesn't actually give a shit about what's happening on the field; she just wants her kid to be active, out of the house in a good environment, not playing with an iPad. So, as you decide to practice being mindful (you can do it LITERALLY at any moment—you don't have to be cross-legged on a Moroccan tufted pillow, drinking green tea)—just the sheer act of noticing you *want to be mindful* is EXACTLY BEING MINDFUL!!! CONGRATS!! Recognizing you are in the present and checking out where your head is in this moment without judgment—BEIN' MINDFUL AS HELL! Try to notice in what environments your thoughts feel good.

Where are you physically when your thoughts feel "positive?"

In what kind of environment do your thoughts feel "uncomfortable"?

We want to be an OBSERVER instead of a judger. So lay out your lawn chair, grab a wine cooler, and just see what thoughts run by, like a suburban soccer mom. I know it is easier said than done to simply <u>stop</u> judging your thoughts when you've been conditioned to think this way to survive your whole life. For me, whenever I start to practice mindwatching[10], I IMMEDIATELY start thinking about something else. Here's how my inner dialogue usually works:

"Okay, look at me, being mindful. I'm doing so good."

"Oh wait, was that technically a feeling? OH, wait. Shit. I just got distracted. Okay, back to just noticing that I was distracted there. No worries...letting that one float on by—fuck my nose itches. GODDAMMIT, there I go again. Okay, WHEW—here I go, back to just noticing that my nose itches. That's cool. Got no opinions about that! Bodies itch. WHY DID I RANDOMLY JUST THINK OF THAT GIRL I SAW AT THE GROCERY STORE EARLIER WHO WAS BUYING OVERRIPE BANANAS? WHAT WAS SHE GOING TO DO WITH THOSE BANANAS? WAS SHE GOING TO MAKE BANANA BREAD? SHE WAS SO CUTE!...breathe. Okay. I'm back. Noticed that I just did that. That was random. Randomness is cool. Brains are random like that. I'm always coming back to noticing that I am here. Chilling. Mindwatching."

Let's try an activity that I like to use, which stimulates me VISUALLY so I'm not so focused on the back of my eyelids when trying to mindwatch.

---

10 "Mindwatching" is an informal term used in the mental health community to describe the mindfulness practice of sitting for a period of time while objectively observing your thoughts without reacting to them. I use this term a LOT in this book, and you're about to do your first "mindwatching" exercise with me! So get ready.

MINDWATCHING

Whoa—look at this big-ass black splotch of ink! What's it doing in the middle of this page? Did the printer fuck up on this page??? NAH FRIEND! This is a fun mindwatching exercise! Try to look into it for 30 seconds, then one minute, then two minutes, etc., while trying not to judge any thought that comes by. When a thought does pop up (because it will), visualize that thought dissolving into the black splotch. Another thought will inevitably come up, but remember, this black splotch of ink has cute li'l magic powers that dissolve the thought. How do you see your thoughts? As words and sentences? Maybe pictures and action? Let whatever form that thought comes to you dissolve and break away. Then, continue until time is up!

Once you've practiced this act of mindwatching, you can take it out into the real world by using ANY object in place of the inkblot to practice mindfulness. Try it out with something now, wherever you are! A candle! Clouds! Gazing at nature! The goal is to drop those thoughts onto an object and watch the thought float by, or dissolve, or drive away or...WHATEVER! **All I'm asking is that you don't judge whatever comes up in your brain.**

The more you can mindwatch, the more you'll notice how often you do XYZ or think about XYZ. With practice, you can learn to be an observer of your thoughts. When I started mindwatching for the first time, the most prevalent thought I had was that I was never "enough." Enough of a hard worker, good enough for love, doing enough to make my parents proud. The first time I stepped back to watch that thought come in so often, I was like "Yeesh, that pops up *often!*" But I didn't know how to not feel bad about always thinking badly of myself. A vicious cycle!!

Here are some tips I used to get to a balanced spot:

BECOME CURIOUS: This might be one of the most important lessons about managing anxiety, depression, and panic. It's a phrase I want you to remember not only when being mindful, but JUST IN GENERAL IN UR LYFE! Something you'll hear quite often in the beginning stages of meditation and mindfulness is to become curious about the thoughts you are having, instead of letting the negativity creep around. Be kindly diligent about this. It can take a beat to let your inner voice say what it instinctively wants to say, taking a breath, and asking yourself…"Hmm… WHY did I think that? I'm curious about why my body feels that way. Is there more underneath this thought or feeling? Can I find out what it is?" CURIOSITY doesn't necessarily always mean analysis, but rather paves the way for space to exist in our thought patterns.

GET A LONG FOAM ROLLER: I STFG this is a fucking game-changer. Find a foam roller that is long enough to reach from your tailbone up to the top of your body so that your neck and head are supported. Lie on your back and place the foam roller in the middle of your back, so your spine, from your tailbone to your head, is touching the roller. Make sure your knees are bent, and allow your arms and shoulders to fall as far as possible to the side by making the letter "T" with your arms. Now, move your hands in the motion as if you were making a SNOW ANGEL! **Do this 10 times to open up your chest (and heart chakra, if you're into that stuff!).**

Find your balance in this position and let your chest be the star of this mindful moment. In this position, it is also easier to differentiate *diaphragmatic breathing* from *chest/lung breathing* (more about these techniques in the BREATHING chapter) as you work on noticing your breath—and look at you! You're meditating!

START SMALL: Being mindful and learning to meditate is a skill. Start with trying for 10 seconds. Then, move up to a minute. How about two?! The first time I tried meditating, I started with only two minutes for a whole week! Even if the whole two minutes I sat there thinking "This is fucking stupid," I did it. You can, too! Most meditation apps have exercises that start small, and some even provide a guiding voice—like a mindfulness teacher! You don't have practice alone unless you want to.

WHEN IN DOUBT—BREATH IS KING: If you're totally lost and close to opening your eyes, stretching out your body, and giving up (me, every day), COME BACK TO YOUR BREATH. Notice the air coming in through your nose and out through your mouth gently. Over and over again. The more I paid attention to my breathing in meditation, the smaller my fear of my own breath became. I stopped FEARING my breathing and the way it chose to flow. I let my belly get soft. I was able to pay attention to my breath without dying. And then, I didn't die again. And again, I focused on my breath without dying. I realized that my FEAR of breathing boiled down to the fact that I felt as though I never REALLY had control of my own breath—that my body just DOES it on its own, magically, all day every day! And how did I know it wasn't just going to decide to STOP on me one day?! Through meditating, I realized I could put down those worries just for the time of the practice and pick that fear back up if I needed it later. But each time I meditated, I realized the fear of my own breathing wasn't rational. Statistically, I LIVED 100% of the time I thought about my breath. My body wasn't dicking me over. I wasn't having heart attacks, and I wasn't choking. Even though it was scary as fuck in the beginning, slowly but surely, my brain came around to realizing that breathing shouldn't be viewed as a *fear*, but rather, a *friend*. CUE: "Awwww" soundtrack. I didn't need to worry so much about my body betraying me, because I was becoming friends with it. I was taking care of it and nourishing it, and not being so judgmental of it! I was finally allowing my mind and body to be friends.

SET AN INTENTION: This is another one of those tips that can feel useless until it's put into practice. If you have an anxiety disorder, odds are you are a control freak who loves goal-oriented patterns! Here's one for ya! Setting an intention is like setting a finish line for your practice. What do you want to feel connected to? WHAT MAKES YOU FEEL ALIVE?! Can you manifest it during this window of time? It can be as simple as "My intention for this mindfulness moment is to muster up as much joy as I can in my belly and chest," or "My intention for this meditation is to come out of it with a smile on my face."

Let's try it! Set an intention here and flip a few pages back to mindwatch on the inkblot for a few seconds!

MY INTENTION:

_____

_____

_____

_____

_____

_____

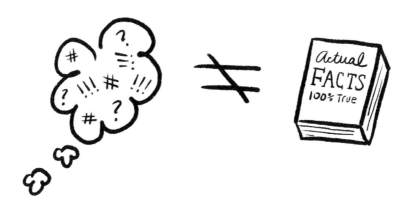

Remember, you are not your thoughts. Thoughts are just *thoughts*. Not facts.

<u>We</u> give the thoughts feeling and meaning.

SHAME & ANXIETY

WHEEWWWWW THIS IS A BIG ONE

SHAME can mean a whole-ass lotta things: embarrassment, guilt, rejection, exposure, feeling unlovable, not being "enough," being *wrong*...and I don't like being wrong...EVER!! So, shame is a really hard emotion for me to handle. And I thought I was very alone in this. But it turns out that shame is an emotional response inherited in ALL human beings in every culture around the world!

But...*WHY WOULD EVOLUTION DICK US OVER LIKE THAT?*

Why would our brains allow a feeling so MESSY & DIRTY to survive throughout history? Turns out, *shame isn't always a bad thing.* The right amount of shame has allowed our tribes, classes, and species to get along. In the time of the first humans, shame was necessary to keep some dum-dum from doing some dum-dum shit that got the tribe in trouble, exposed, or killed! Bring that into our millennium, and you'll see how it's evolved from "shaming for survival" to "shaming for civilization." For example, think about that long line for the women's bathroom at the club on a busy Friday night. We have those lines to keep order. You might not be arrested or die from skipping the line, but you will be fiercely shamed by a gaggle of drunk girls in stilettos, which, if you ask me, is way worse than getting arrested.

The first step for me not spiraling into a full-blown panic/anxious mess when dealing with shame was to recognize that shame is an *inevitable everyday part of life*. It's not the big, scary, villainous enemy that I'd made it out to be in my head. Simply, shame is the opposite of self-confidence. And there will be times throughout your day when you don't always feel 100% confident, right? When you decide to take on the feeling of shame FULL FORCE, you can actually learn a lot from it and turn it into a revelatory moment.

Sure, we could spend time breaking down how *most* shame relates back to childhood upbringing and societal standards, but that seems obvious, right? The way I see it is, let's just wrap this conversation about the history of shame up quickly by blaming it on something else! *Society! Childhood! It's not me, is the point!!!* J/k, don't blame the world for your shame; sometimes, it's actually good to feel it and learn from it. The key is to not let it take you into a shame *spiral*.

Shame does not propel us into motivation. In fact, self-shame will only hurt our already bruised self-esteem or ego.

HOW TO DEAL WITH SHAME CONSTRUCTIVELY

Get yourself out of the spotlight. Are you REALLY the center of everyone's attention right now, or does it only feel that way? Once said by a Hispano-Roman philosopher who has the same first name as Lucius Malfoy[11]: "WE SUFFER MORE IN OUR IMAGINATION THAN IN REALITY!" Remember, people aren't thinking about us, and that's THE GOOD NEWS! How are you feeling shame right now?

_____

_____

_____

_____

_____

_____

_____

Let's talk self-blame. How can we shift the feelings of self-punishment to an external explanation? Is the feeling of shame being brought on by someone else's

11   His name was Lucius Annaeus Seneca and he was a pretty big dealio back in the day.

standards of right & wrong? How about environmental? Or societal? Are you being targeted by ads? Or the hurtful words of someone you love? Even if the shame you feel comes from the idea that you did something wrong, where does the idea stem from that this thing is deemed "wrong?"

_____

_____

_____

_____

_____

_____

I used to experience this feeling of shame around being in a romantically open relationship with my partner. It wasn't until we both did some deep digging to realize that SOCIETY and CULTURE deemed relationships "unshareable" even though monogamy has nothing to do with reproductive success! And that's if you believe relational goals are solely based on reproducing which...y'all, don't even get me started. That's another book for another time. Who are these outdated anthropologists and people of power who kept monogamy normalized to maintain power and wealth to have any control over MY life now?! IN 2020, HONEY?! I THINK NOT!

BACK TO SHAME-SHIFTING!

Shame-shift into positivity: Shame is uncomfortable AF. So our brains will do some rewiring magic to spit out a different emotion that is more comfortable to feel. Like anger. Obviously, while this emotion might feel more comfortable to our brains, it doesn't help us externally to be angry when it isn't called for. So we must acknowledge the beast: Hi, Shame, thanks for stopping by. How is your mom doing? When I saw her last night, she was fine, hehehehe. Okay—sorry, back on track— let's let this shame dissipate. Like all emotions, *it can't last forever.* I give myself a rule: If this feeling of shame won't matter five years from now, I won't give it more than five minutes of my life, right now. Other feelings will eventually replace it. We can jump-start this process by actively thinking about other, POSITIVE things instead. Can we show kindness and love in the face of shame? Can we compliment the other person by focusing the attention on someone else? Can we make a joke out of it, giving ourselves the space to dissect with humor? How about *asking* for some space? Taking the time to deal with the feelings at hand in a private way? Tell me what positivity you can bring into your life right now, in this moment. (Hint: If you're stuck, you can always make a gratitude list right now in the "A Simple Gratitude Inventory" chapter!)

_____

_____

_____

_____

_____

_____

✸W.O.W.✸

HUMANS ARE MULTIFACETED.

We are capable of being completely stressed with debilitating panic & high anxiety, going through bouts of depression, WHILE ALSO being incredibly successful and outgoing and physically active!

MENTAL HEALTH LOOKS DIFFERENT ON EVERYONE!!

DISSOCIATIVE ANXIETY

AND ITS FUN COUSINS DEREALIZATION & DEPERSONALIZATION

Full disclosure: This was the scariest essay I had to write in the entire workbook. If I could make a Halloween-esque spider-web sign with blood running down it, scribbled with TURN BACK NOW, I would. But running from my fear of dissociative anxiety just gives it all that more power to fuck with me. And, IDK if you guys have gotten the vibe yet, but I'm trying to become UNFUCKABLE WITH when it comes to scary mental-health stuff. And, the truth is, the more you understand the science behind it, the less scary it can become OVER TIME. I say OVER TIME in caps because dissociation and derealization/depersonalization is such a specific type of feeling or disorder that it takes some time to understand what it is, how it feels, how to get out of it, and what science says about it.

While often experienced as a SYMPTOM rather than a disorder, anyone who has dissociative anxiety knows that it can feel like a beast of its own. This is the symptom that causes me to question my sanity on a constant basis. It's that exact feeling of "going crazy" I fear so much that I've mentioned in this workbook so many times.

Dissociation, by definition, is referred to as being disconnected to the moment. For someone who DOESN'T struggle with dissociative anxiety, they might try to understand dissociation by oversimplifying the feeling as "daydreaming" or "not paying attention." But when coupled with an anxiety disorder, dissociating can be incredibly fucking terrifying! In fact, ***party horns*** IT'S MY MOST TERRIFYING SYMPTOM! ***PEW PEW PEW PEW***. The people close to me in my life, who have helped me through high anxiety or panic, are very familiar with the following dissociative phrases:

- "Things just don't feel real."
- "I don't know how to explain it, but I feel outside my body."
- "I feel like the world isn't real."
- "My eyes don't feel like they're registering what's in front of me."
- "Life feels like a video game right now."
- "It's like I'm floating out of my own body."
- And, the classic fav, "I FEEL LIKE I'M LIVING IN THE TRUMAN SHOW!"

Any "regular" person (LOL WHAT IS A "REGULAR PERSON") might hear these phrases and think this person is losing their mind. The "regular person" might think you are having some sort of psychosis or a drug trip. And, although this is by far my scariest feeling to write about, the reason behind *how* and *why* dissociation is presented by your brain is actually very, very sweet. GET THIS: **Your brain is actually trying to *protect you.***

Like, WHAT?! How cute is that?! MY BRAIN PROTECTS! MY BRAIN ATTACK! My brain flips a switch like, "Nah, man, this shit is too intense for my person, I'm just going to propel her into a LALA land so she don't have to experience this."

SOUNDS SWEET, RIGHT?!! But come on, brain, READ THE ROOM! While I try to appreciate the kind gesture my mind is trying to create, I would rather not have it. AT ALL. It's like when a toddler comes up to you with a sweet smile and dirty hands and presents you with a peanut-butter-and-crayon sandwich, and you're like, "Ohh mmmm delicious! Thank you!" when you'd rather be like "NO THANK YOU, you idiot kid, you're causing me more issues and cleanup than your mom is paying me for."

Diving deeper into dissociation, we have to meet its close cousins, who close out our 3 Ds: Depersonalization and Derealization.

Often, these 3 Ds are intermingled, and they all kinda sound the same, so let's break it down.

Depersonalization is when your mind feels disconnected from your thoughts, feelings, actions, or body[12]. Examples of this include feeling like you are watching a movie about yourself, or that you don't have an identity. Some of the symptoms experienced as a result of depersonalization include the following:

- Alterations in your perceptions
- Distorted sense of time
- Feelings of yourself being unreal or absent
- Emotional or physical numbing[13]

I tell depersonalization apart from its similar-looking cousins because these symptoms are connected to a PERSON's physical body, and the word "person" is a part of it.

Derealization causes a sensation where the world does not feel real[14]. Examples of this include seeing the world all in shades of gray, or having tunnel vision when looking at the world. The symptoms involved with derealization include:

- Feeling like the world is not their own reality
- Seeing the world as flat, dull, or gray
- Having tunnel vision when you look at the world
- Feeling like things are not real around you[15]

The first time I experienced the 3 Ds was the first time I got high smoking the ol' Mary Jane. I was a freshman in high school (I was actually much younger, but for the purposes of this book and trying to set a good example, I'm telling you I was at least in high school). I had smoked weed one or two other times before this incident, so I thought I knew what I was doing, but, it turns out, I'd never actually been high those other times; maybe I wasn't hitting the blunt the right way or holding the smoke in long enough. But...this...incident...was...DIFFERENT.

It was a school night at my friend Steph's house. Steph's house was the place to party because she lived with her hot aunt, who didn't supervise us and let us do anything we wanted. So Steph, myself, and our third musketeer, Tara, decided we were going to smoke weed on her patio, just the three of us, to try to "get better at it." We didn't want our older and more experienced guy friends to make fun of us, or the way we rolled our blunts, or left too much spit on the spliff...we needed to practice!

12,13 Gentile, Julie P, et al. "STRESS AND TRAUMA: Psychotherapy and Pharmacotherapy for Depersonalization/Derealization Disorder." *Innovations in Clinical Neuroscience*, Matrix Medical Communications, July 2014, www.ncbi.nlm.nih.gov/pmc/articles/PMC4204471/.

13,14 Cuncic, Arlin. "An Overview of Dissociation Anxiety." *Verywell Mind*, 8 July 2020, www.verywellmind.com/dissociation-anxiety-4692760.

I felt much safer with just my close girlfriends—safe enough to take some pretty big pulls. I remember the exact moment it happened. Steph had asked me what time it was. I remember looking down at my phone and seeing that three minutes had gone by since I last looked down at my watch. HOLY FUCK?! THREE MINUTES?! I FELT LIKE I WAS SITTING HERE FOR ONLY TWO SECONDS!!!! I looked down at my hands, and they felt and looked like a mannequin's hands. "These aren't my hands, are they? Oh fuck, they are???" The time warp and perception vortex hole had begun. And, well, that's kinda the point of weed, right? It puts you in a fuzzy headspace that's hard to explain unless you've experienced it before. As you can imagine, my brain and body DID NOT APPRECIATE THIS NEW ALTERED STATE. And went into an INTENSE MOMENT OF PANIC. Like, LOSE MY FUCKING SHIT PANIC. I JUMPED UP in a state of shook-eth-ness and immediately started rambling, trying to tell Steph and Tara what I was feeling. I couldn't explain it, and my words were not coming out as making any sense. Steph and Tara—who were also pretty high at this point—couldn't help but burst into laughter. I'm not here to expose them, but one of them laughed so hard she peed her pants (it was Tara). I wasn't getting help from these two stoned idiots, so I BOLTED inside and banged on Steph's hot aunt's bedroom door. At this point, I felt like I was "STUCK" in this feeling. That I had lost complete control of my body. Steph's aunt, who was just like Amy Poehler's character in *Mean Girls,* made me a frozen pizza and sat with me in the kitchen doing breathing exercises until I was tired enough to fall asleep in her arms, like a giant fucking baby.

I tell you this story because, even though I eventually got the hang of the smoking-weed thing (like, *really* got the hang of it), that first experience of feeling "out of the body" is something I MOST DEFINITELY DID NOT GET THE HANG OF! And that same feeling that I had getting high for the first time is the closest I've felt to when I experienced dissociation, sober, for the first time. I thought I had been DRUGGED. "Did someone put an edible in my food?" "Did I ingest some crazy chemical that the government never intended humans to find out about that unlocks the next stage of their consciousness?" I even stopped eating mushrooms for a whole year because I developed an unhealthy avoidance tactic, fearing that I was going to get poisoned by a mushroom and experience dissociation again. It got so bad, I was even sneaking around restaurants, WATCHING waiters and cooks make the food when I would go out to eat, out of paranoia (this happened as recently as 2018). The experience I felt during a dissociative spell would always cause me to have to excuse myself, to reach out to someone on my support contact list and repeat those words, "I don't know how to explain this, but I was sitting at lunch with a client, then, all of sudden, my body felt like it floated outside of itself, and I was experiencing the meeting from another angle. Am I going CRAZY? Do you think the waiter has some weird vendetta against me and put poison mushrooms in my soup? Should I take myself to a hospital?" And I'm here to admit to you guys that I DID take myself to a hospital a few times during experiences of depersonalization and derealization. I thought each time it happened was *THE* time. *The* time I was going to get stuck this way forever. Of course, in the ER, a nurse would give me an IV and tell me to go get a therapist. Even now that I have three regular therapists, I can still recognize those signs that my body is trying to dissociate. So, what are the triggers and signs and how have I learned to cope (and start eating mushrooms on my pizza again)?

While the medical community is still working hard at trying to understand the brain and how the 3 Ds work beyond your brain activating trauma prevention, we can point to some basic ideas of WHY the brain tries to protect itself from something you are confronted with in the physical world:

1. **Stress:** From the example above, when I was at lunch with a client, I didn't realize the pressure I was putting on myself to make a good impression and close the deal. I was ruminating on deal points in my head, preparing the next thing I wanted to say, wondering if the tank top I wore without a bra was too nipply. I was nervous, and my brain saw the anxiety of not closing the deal as a threat. So! It put me into dissociation!

2. **Lack of sleep / exhaustion:** Your brain is like, whoa, I'm tired. I cannot function at my full capability. I need sleep! Time to shut down! SNOOZEEEEEE ZZzzzZZZZ

3. **Eating habits:** Have we been overeating or skipping meals? When your body needs fuel, it can set off the alarms that it feels unstable and needs sustenance.

The best way to come back from the 3 Ds is with GROUNDING exercises. Basically, we're going to try and get those feet back on the ground, in the present moment... literally and metaphorically.

To begin, sit in a comfortable position with your feet on the floor. If it feels better to close your eyes—do so! You can try wearing sunglasses, fixing your eyes to a soft gaze, or staring at something that makes you smile. Wiggle your

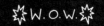

⚡W.O.W.⚡

A TRICK I FOUND ON REDDIT (SOMETIMES A GREAT SOURCE FOR FINDING MENTAL HEALTH BUDDIES!):

A random user told me that he uses sunglasses to ground himself during the 3 Ds. Something about adding another layer of depth perception helps his brain to focus on what's in front of him. It also creates a barrier from the public and allows him to manage his D (lol) in a more private manner. Try it!

toes. Really feel the ground and the connection of your skin hitting your sock or shoe or the ground, and what that feels like. Try to visualize it. The way that the bottom of your foot touches the earth. How does your body grow from this root-ed point? Where does it get stuck? Can you reach all the way to your head before experiencing the dissociation? Let's move on to identifying your surroundings. If you have a support partner around, ask them to tell you things about yourself. I tell my boyfriend to remind me of his favorite memories of us together while holding my hand. It helps me remember who I am and that I am, in fact, KELSEY DARRAGH, a person who is alive and well and managing my mental health. That this, too, shall pass. Perhaps looking through your phone at photos of yourself and your friends can remind you of who you are and how precious your life is here on this earth! What a miracle it is that you exist! AND YOU DO! YOU EXIST!

What do you need from others when experiencing the 3 Ds?

_____

_____

_____

_____

_____

_____

Another simple grounding technique is connecting with your five senses[16] to bring you back to a place of familiarity.

- **What is something you can see right now?**_____

- **What's the closest thing you can touch?**_____

- **Is there something you can smell?**_____

- **How about something that you can taste?**_____

- **Finally, what is something you can hear?**_____

---

16 For a longer, focus-breaking five senses exercise, check out the "How To Manage A Panic Attack Right Now" exercise in the Panic section.

Remember how, in the intro of this book, I told you that, hopefully, there could be at least ONE little tidbit that sticks to your brain walls and helps you get through the next tough time? Something you remember and are able to regurgitate, maybe to a friend, even? Well, this type of light bulb moment happened to ME after something my partner had told me the very first time I "came out" to him about my dissociative anxiety. I thought he was going to run. I figured he'd think I sounded fucking crazy and call my mom and tell her to come get me (from where? idk? adulthood?). But I used the example during a moment of high anxiety that "sometimes, things don't feel real...like this is all a made-up land...and this is like a government experiment, like *The Maze Runner* or something..." and then waited for his response. And the tidbit he responded with has stuck with me so much that I think about it every time I experience the 3 Ds to bring me back to reality. He said:

"Well, if this is all a made-up world...it's a pretty good one!"

...WOW. OKAY. TRU!!

As easy as it is, of course, to remember all the shitty stuff—what kind of "fake" world would give us puppies??? Or the smell of lavender?? Or cinnamon rolls?? And, more personally, what government experiment would have given me Jared, my sexy partner? I mean, like, THANKS, FBI AGENT WATCHING ME ON THE 24-HOUR CAMERAS!!!! And he's right—at least if this world is all a simulation or whatever, it really is good. It's entertaining. My cats are derps who always make me giggle, there's endless comedies on Netflix to laugh at, and hundreds of thousands of hours of TikToks to make me spit-take my drink at. I AM AMUSED!

When I learned to...appreciate?...the idea that this could all be made up...and "unreal," as I always described it as, I remembered that it could be a lot worse of a world to be stuck in. And it usually, if not always, brings me back to a place of happiness. I remind myself that there are tons of people out there in the world who also experience this feeling. Maybe I'm not that "crazy" after all. So, next time you experience any of the 3 Ds, write a gratitude list, and see how great your life really is when you take a moment to focus on the good.

Srsly tho, healing should not be up up up all the time...if that were the case, you'd just keep soaring on a cracked-out high that would eventually propel you into outer space, where you would lose touch with the realm of this Earth and have to create your own dimension where EVERYONE IS HAPPY ALL THE TIME and that's a no from me, dawg.

IF YOU HAVE HIGH ANXIETY, STAY AWAY FROM COCAINE.

(just...trust me on this one)

OKAY, FINE—LET'S TALK ABOUT ANXIETY, DRUGS, AND ALCOHOL

I've put my entire 20s on the internet via BuzzFeed, my own podcast, and doing comedy. I have very few secrets that a couple hundred thousand people haven't heard. One of those not-so-secret things about me is that I went to public school in Florida and experimented with drugs and alcohol. Yes, they are related, lol. We've all heard the reputation Florida has about drugs and alcohol: someone eating someone's face off, kids smoking "spice," the rampant opioid problem, drunk Florida Man throws an alligator through bar window (actually happened in my neighborhood)—my point is, it was never that hard to find a group of teens doing something illegal in town that you could join in on. It didn't feel so dangerous to us as much as it just seemed...FUN!?????? Like a rite of passage for putting up with all the mosquitoes and heat.

I never did the "hard stuff..." But, look, I was bored and anxious and always trying to fit in with the older and cooler kids in my high school, who were doing drugs in the school bathroom and drinking Parrot Bay through a straw on weeknights in an empty parking lot. I'm lucky in that I don't have an addictive personality (I was able to get sober in the writing of this book, actually! HOLDS FOR APPLAUSE), and I've always been able to quit my vices fairly easily and without stress. But, boy, do I miss cocaine. I'm not going to lie to you all!!!!! I was terrified of it until I tried it, and then, *I fucking loved it.* I knew that I liked it *too* much, and that *was exactly why I needed to quit.* It made my already outgoing personality more outgoing, but it also made my already high anxiety...MUCH MORE HIGHLY ANXIOUS. My anxiety got anxiety, and before I knew it, the sun was coming up and I was crouched in a tiny ball under my bedsheets, FaceTiming anyone who could talk to me to sleep at 6 A.M. (it was usually my sister, MEGAN, who I would now like to take the time to THANK for ALWAYS answering my phone calls. No matter what time it was. Even if she had work the next day. Megan, I don't know what I did to deserve you as a sister, but LORD KNOWS, I consider you my very cool, very nonjudgmental guardian angel. I love you. Thank you.) Cocaine has the worst comedown of any drug I've taken. Sure, it's fun when it's taken (again, why lie about this???!???!!!???), but, just like anxiety, you can spiral down into it if you don't catch yourself. It's never enough. And it always gave my socially anxious self something to do. Something to do with my hands physically, and a task that helped me make friends at parties. It was always acting as a Band-Aid on the bullet wound that was my *social anxiety*. The fear of showing up somewhere with nothing but myself *terrified me*. So, instead, I'd make friends by offering them a line and some good old-fashioned high-ass conversation in the bathroom. But once they'd run off to their friends, I'd feel like someone had SMACKED candy outta a baby's HANDS!!! AND I'M BABY! All my internal alarms would start SCREEEEEEEEAMING, like in the movies when there's a fight and the scuffle leads the bad guy and good guy tumbling down a staircase, and one of their feet knocks the giant canister of DANGEROUS GAS on HIGH and all the pressure builds up until it inevitably EXPLODES!!! It's me. It's my internal feels after cocaine use.

The same feeling went for alcohol. I'd made an entire CAREER out of being the girl who could out-drink ANYONE I knew. How did I get so good at drinking? Well, I wasn't the hottest girl in my friend group (according to society and Abercrombie & Fitch ads), I wasn't good at flirting, and one plus one equals two! I got really good at drinking and drinking *games* so people would like me. Then at least I'd be seen by my peers as SOMETHING, even if that came at the expense of my health. And who was I to care at 13 years old about my body and mental health when, at that age, you could bounce back from a hangover like nothing!? Beer Pong Champ, Flip Cup Queen, and Presidents and Assholes UNDEFEATED. These were all titles I was given at some point or another in my life. While friends and strangers saw me rise to the occasion every party I went to, they didn't see the crippling anxiety I battled with when I was sober and hungover.

Alcohol and drugs are an incredibly <u>easy</u> way to cover up all those anxious feels. But the problem is that it's <u>only temporary</u>. And 100% of the time, I end up worse after a night of binge-drinking or using than where I started. And HANGOVER ANXIETY is REAL. Hangovers, with any substance, fuck with your physical brain chemistry.

Not to mention all the physicalities that come with the worst hangover—you know what I'm talking about—the dry mouth like you blew an old dusty ghost the night before, the POUNDING HEADACHE like those li'l Keebler Elves got evicted from that magic cookie tree and moved into your skull and they've exchanged their baking tools for CONSTRUCTION HARDWARE, the sour acid from black swamps in *The Lion King* rumbling in your tummy. And the blues. OoOooOooOO, those Scary Sunday Blues! The feeling of waking up and your brain (that's been altered by chemicals or booze) is SCREAMING for water and screaming AT you about your choices from last night, the future you have, the mistakes you've made in the past 10 years…it's a bingo-ball cage of negative thoughts. Worst of all, the impending doom of MONDAY coming up gives your broken, hung-over body and brain a timeline to work against. It's absolutely crucial to lie in bed all day and recover, yet you'll feel like a failure if you do. It's a lose/lose situation.

While re-reading this chapter, it comes as no surprise to me that I got sober after 14 years of *hard, daily, chronic* drinking. My personality and booze just couldn't be friends anymore, not that they were ever *really* friends, to begin with. More like frenemies.

No one listens to a drunk control freak. In order for me to function at my full capacity and have everything in order, and be that boss-bitch type-A leader that I know I'm BRED to be, I can't be drunk all the time, and I need to admit that I don't always have my shit together when I'm drunk. I had a realization as I got older: Why was I so proud of the amount that I could drink? What did that prove? And to whom? It's like being proud that you can function after a few hours of sleep. And we hate those kinds of people, remember? SHOWOFFS!

I know that I'm lucky, in that quitting drinking for me was relatively easy, and we could have a whole discussion about addiction and genetics, but, remember, I'm not a doctor, so I'll just say this:

Toward the end of my drinking, I started to keep a drunk sailor's journal. A log of every time I got drunk, how many drinks I bought, why I got that kind of drink, what I was dealing with in real life, and how I felt after each drink. I challenged myself to drink water in between each glass, and would always set a bottle of water and two aspirin at my bedside each night. Because drunk Kelsey was trying to keep Sober Kelsey as happy as possible about being an abuser of alcohol. This was a slow process to reexamine my relationship with drinking. I didn't "cold turkey," and I'd quit many, many times before. I was always able to quit for 30, 60, even 90 days at a time. But I always ended up right back where I started. I thought that I should quit drinking for a very. long. time. It never seemed like a real thing I could do—just like the idea that I could ever live a happy life while managing my anxiety, panic, and depression. LOOK AT US! HEY! LOOK AT US! Who would've thought?! NOT ME! (Side note: Paul Rudd compilations on YT will make you *instantly happy*.)

If you've ever had thoughts about quitting or cutting back on alcohol, I can tell you from firsthand experience that your brain and body are TRYING TO TELL YOU SOMETHING. SO LISTEN!

For funsies, next time you have that recurring thought, try a drinking log. Or suggest to try this exercise out with a loved one and cross-examine results! This can apply to substances, too! Just replace the word "drink" or "alcohol" with your preferred drug (LOL, this makes it sound like a preferred airline? Like my choice is DELTA COCAINE!...anyway...)

MINDFUL DRINKING JOURNAL NIGHT OUT

See the Resource Index for a printable version you can keep in your bag or take a pic on ur phone!

Date/ Time/ Place

_____

Who are you with?

_____

What are you drinking?

_____

Why are you drinking that drink?

_____

What's going on emotionally for you today?

_____

_____

_____

_____

How do you feel after one drink?

_____

Why do you want another?

_____

What time, ideally, would you like to go to bed tonight?

_____

How many drinks have you had? (circle or color in)

How much money have you spent tonight?_____

How do you feel the next morning?

_____

What would you have done differently, if anything at all?

_____

_____

_____

_____

SUNDAY SCARIES

Sometimes, no matter how hard you try, you still end up with the Sunday Scaries at some point in your using adventures. **Remember: This is your brain pulling tricks on you like the smart li'l sassy hoe that is it, and thoughts are just thoughts—not facts.** That headache that you have? It's actually your brain being dehydrated. Your muscles, which are craving water, SHRINK and pull away from the skull, causing a headache. So, first things first: DRINK SOME WATER. GOT IT? Good. **More tips:**

- **Sometimes CBD can help calm the hangover.**
- **Write out all your fears & how realistic they are.**
- **Sweat it out.** You can try to find a cheap spa with a sauna, or sometimes your gym membership comes with a steam room! Hell, create your own steam room in your bathroom by shoving a towel under the door to trap the steam.
- **Shower!** A long, hot shower with a drop of lavender oil can do wonders. If you don't have any essential oils, or EOs, as I like to call them, you can PEEL AN ORANGE IN THE SHOWER TO GET THE SAME EFFECT[17]. This one is weird, I know. But it works. While you're there, ravage into that orange for some vitamin C. Let the peels fall to the shower floor and squish them around to release their full aroma.
- **MASTURBATE**—Y'all already know how much I preach about this one, but flip on over and give it a good jerkin'. Flooding that brain with some serotonin will help combat those blues.

Disclaimer: *Doctors all over will tell you that you should never mix certain types of mental-health medication and alcohol and substances. So, be honest with your primary or psychiatrist about your usage. They'll never judge you, and if they do—get a new doc ASAP, honey booboo.*

17 For more tips on showers and anxiety, refer to the "YOU PROBABLY NEED A SHOWER" chapter.

CONFIDENCE & SELF-COMPASSION

If you've ever been on the Internet, you've seen that quote that says "IT TAKES 45 MUSCLES TO FROWN AND ONLY 10 TO SMILE! SO SMILE!" I bet someone just made this shit up while in denial of their own depression. It was probably the same chick who invented those rotted-wood signs that say "live, laugh, love" on them. As someone who lives with daily anxiety, depression, and panic, I can confidently say that it feels much easier to be mean to yourself than kind to yourself. It feels like autopilot. As the self-compassion QUEEN Brené Brown says, "Confidence is a SKILL. It is a learnable trait and something that you can learn at any time."

Learning self-confidence doesn't happen overnight. It's not like you watch one TED Talk and learn how to do it. It's more like using the daily language app, Duolingo; it's something you have to practice every day and learn bit by bit. I wish my brain would send me as many notifications to be kinder to myself as Duolingo sends notifications to remind me I haven't practiced my French in six weeks. J'Y TRAVAILLE!

SO!!! STOP trying to "push through it" or "SUCK IT UP!!". You can't "walk it off" with anxiety disorders. It's not something that you're going to "grow out of," but rather GROW INTO!!

Surrounding yourself with positivity is a first step! What does that mean, exactly? Well, it can apply to MANY parts of your life:

1. **Use stick-it notes to put positive self-mantras all over your house or places where you are frequently.** (I use a dry erase marker and write on my bathroom mirror! I read, "She believed she could, so she did," every day while I brush my teeth to remind myself that I'm a WOMAN who GETS SHIT DONE!)

2. **Get rid of toxic people in your life.** Dump them. Put yourself first. You don't have time for anyone that doesn't treat your relationship, friendship, or presence as a fucking GIFT. If you get a stomachache when you think about them, they aren't good for you, babe!

3. **Bright colors and bright lights can bring an unconscious sense of happiness into your life.** I have a whole loft covered in Christmas lights that give me a warm and fuzzy feeling every time they turn on. My room has lots of natural sunlight, and I set my Alexa to play a fun song as my alarm (might I recommend "Calabria" by ENUR feat. Natasja?); as soon as I hear this beat, my ass wants to shake and I have to get out of bed. When I grow out of the song and it starts to feel like an alarm—I CHANGE IT!

4. **Start to notice your body language around other people.** Are you looking people in the eye when they talk? Can you try? What about your arm positions? Are they crossed? Crossed arms tend to look like a sign of someone who doesn't care, even though it means I'm scared or protecting my space. A common trick is to mirror the person you're talking to and their body language to make yourself and the other person feel more comfortable. Don't mirror them like a mime does. That would make everyone uncomfortable. Another trick I learned when I started public speaking (check out my video about managing panic attacks I did in front of a bunch of teens on YouTube! YIKES! SCARY!): If you start to nod slightly when you are talking to someone, they will nod, too! It's like a magic trick!

5. **Losing the words "just" and "sorry" from your vocabulary can enhance your confident appearance to others.** "*Just* checking in" or "*Just* wondering if you could..." minimizes your power and authority. Instead, replace "just" with "I WANT" or "I AM". What do you want, actually? "I AM checking in with you" or "I want you to do...". Instead of "*Sorry,* I can't do the thing you need me to do", replace it with "*Thank you,* for thinking of me, however, I am unable to...".

6. **A big part of confidence comes from knowing who you are and owning every bit of it, even the messy or "bad" things.** Some people scoff at

astrology readings and labels, but even those silly "tests" can be a simple way to understand yourself better, why you do the things you do and react the way you react. If the stars aren't your thing, look into the Myers-Briggs personality test, the Enneagram* tests, and even further—know your love language.** All of these "results" give insight, no matter how much you choose to believe in them, and can be good markers for places you might want to work on in your life or personality! For me, I'm an ENFJ, described as a Protagonist, which falls under the Diplomat category. However, catch me on a depressive wave and I'll be a Consultant, which thrives on security.

*For the Enneagram tests, I strongly identify as the "Achiever" and someone "Attracted to success," which helps in the way that if I find myself judging someone else, I try to look inward and ask why. Do I find them valuable to have in my life based on their own personal successes? Is that a shitty and judgmental trait to have? Or, is my brain trying to keep the company I aspire to be like? According to Reddit—yes, I'm citing Reddit as a source—Draco Malfoy and Rita Skeeter are 3s. Great company, huh?

**For love language, I am a STRAIGHT-UP "Words of Affirmations" girl, which means I want to be liked and I need you to tell me that. This is helpful for my partner in our "fighting style," because he knows I need WORDS to resolve conflict. I need him to tell me that everything will be okay, even if we are fighting right in this moment about who didn't clean the cat box. We are not going to break up and he loves me. That's HELPFUL! FOR ME! TO ALSO KNOW! SO THAT I CAN TELL HIM! HOW TO HELP OUR RELATIONSHIP! STAY COMMUNICATIVE! I can also recognize when I'm exhibiting these traits and be more confident in my emotions, observing my behavior rather than judging myself.

Obviously, you are someone who is interested in self-improvement if you've picked up this workbook! So, it's important to give yourself the space and goal of gaining your confidence. It's okay to feel like Wonder Woman one day and Debbie Downer the next. Debs get a bad rap. Debs is just trying her best.

Take the test every year. After all, we are ALWAYS learning and growing (#neuroplasticity babyyyy).

REMEMBER:
BRAVE PEOPLE GET SCARED ALL THE TIME

No matter how confident someone might appear outwardly, we all have our shit. Even stuff we're not able to admit out loud. Hint: A universal need most people share is that we all want to be liked! AND THAT'S OKAY TO WANT TO BE LIKED!!! Why would you want to be hated?! Not even Hitler wanted to be HATED. He wanted to be liked!! Specifically by blond people! If you WANT to be hated… you're usually one of those trolls on their computers, hiding behind a fake picture, and you just want someone to show you attention. And those people could probably use some therapy (I mean it. This isn't a joke). Don't feed the trolls; rather, shower them with kindness. In THIS instance, it really is easier and does feel better to be kind.

Want more on self-compassion during periods of depression? Turn to the "MEETING LITTLE YOU" exercise in the Depression section.

> "IN LIFE, THERE IS NO GOOD OR BAD. NO WINNERS OR LOSERS. ONLY THINGS HAPPENING, ALWAYS AS THEY ARE, EXACTLY AS THEY SHOULD'VE ALWAYS BEEN. SO THE WORST THING YOU COULD DO, IS TAKE LIFE TOO SERIOUSLY.
>
> —Alan Watts

SENDING LIGHT

During my worst trials with anxiety, I was recommended HYPNOTHERAPY. Yeah, I know what you're thinking. Hypnotherapy = Hypnosis? Like the guy on stage who swings a watch in front of people's eyes and then makes them act like a chicken? Not exactly. This was in a therapist's office, with some dim lights and a comfy couch. No watches were used, but rather his voice guided me through a meditative/hypnotic practice. With hypnotherapy, the idea is to get your body to relax so that the therapist can get into the subconscious mind. While this could sounda li'l scary, to let someone into your brain, it's important to note that you are in control. The therapist is simply there to guide you to the state of relaxation. We hold SO MUCH anxiety in our bodies. Women especially do this in their shoulder and jaw.

Right now, check in with your body to see where you are tense.

Mark the following figure to point out areas of tension in your body you have now or usually have pain in.

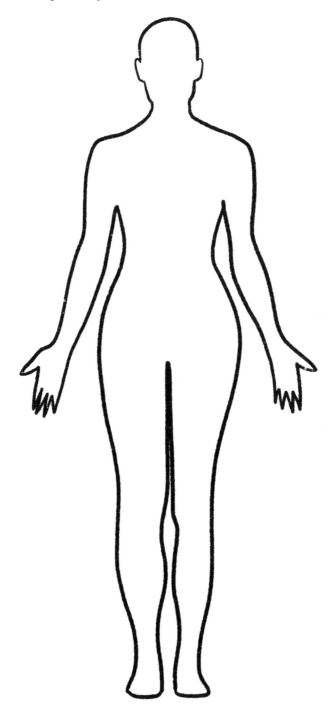

Not to get too "woo-woo" about it, but, scientifically, it's been proven that parts of our bodies can hold trauma in them. Our muscles have memory and can store physical feelings of tension and pain, keeping us locked in a certain state longer than we want to, even when our brains are feeling good. The mind and body are sooooooo connected. Have you ever gotten a stomachache because you're so stressed? That's the mind/body connection! I'm going to teach you an exercise that I learned in hypnotherapy that is used in many instances to help a person clear that negative emotion or feeling out of the body. The best part is, it can be done anywhere at any time! **It's called: sending light.**

We are going to get a li'l magical Harry Potter up in this bitch and create your own bright light that you're going to send into your body, to the tense and tight parts that are keeping you from ridding yourself of that stored anxiety and trauma. Ideally, if you have a partner or friend that can help you with this exercise, have them read the following out loud to you. If you are alone, read this over, taking in each word, completing the entire exercise.

If you can, lie down in a comfortable position. If you can't lie down, sit or stand in a position that allows you to feel balanced in your body—so, uncross those arms and legs. Let your jaw fall open. Relax every muscle in your face: your eyelids, nostrils, eyebrows, and even see if you can relax your earlobes (lol wtf, right??). We're going to do a quick body scan. You can even imagine a laser beam or scanner going over your body, up and down. As we scan, take notice of what part of your body feels tight or impatient. Don't worry if you have multiple places that feel out of whack. **Once again, mark this image to show where you're feeling unbalanced:**

Now, we're going to conjure that wizardly spirit and create a fiery, warm ball of light. If heat doesn't sound good to you at the moment, make it cool and airy. It can be any color or shape. It's yours to make.

- What color is it? _____
- How big is it? _____
- What does it smell like? _____
- Can you touch it? _____
- Taste it? _____

Make it right in front of your eyes. Put it in your field of vision. For me, I like to make my light neon pink that tastes like frosting...smooth and creamy. I'm hungry.

Anyway, take that fiery ball of light in front of you and let it float down to your feet. And, when it touches your feet, FEEL the warmth. Feel that fire; it's nice and cozy—not too hot, but just enough to give you that feeling of getting into a Jacuzzi, the kind that takes your breath away a little bit. Let that light hit your toes, your toenails, and the space between your toes. And let each muscle that it touches completely dissolve. I like to imagine that my body is a cold stick of butter and that bright light is a hot country skillet, and when that butter touches that hot frying pan, it completely melts and sizzles away into buttery froth. Let that be your body. Start by letting those toes completely dissolve away. Then that bright light starts to travel up your body, touching every bone in your ankle, bringing positivity and radiance. It's only bringing good feelings. Let it travel into your calves, melting your shins completely apart. Your knees—oh, how that light loves your precious knees. Those knees that carry you all day long, that never get enough light. Let the light BURST through all those ligaments and joints, floating up to your thighs. The meaty, strong thighs. The blood that pumps through your thighs, letting your legs be your guide, is being fused with the warm bright light. Remembering to send the light from a place of love, we move into the hips. Let that butt relax. We tend to hold a lot of stress in our butt cheeks and don't even realize it! Let those butt cheeks melt away. Fart, if you need to!!! In fact, I RECOMMEND A NICE TOOT NOW! As that positivity wave is filling you up to 50%, you're letting your stomach and gut become overflowed with light, relaxing every muscle that holds all those organs and bones together. Into your lungs now; we breathe nothing but sparkle and divinity into our air, the precious air that keeps giving is now glistening from our light, like snow in the sunshine. Into the chest and shoulders now, we let the light split in two, remaining just as powerful, if not becoming MORE charged with your body's connection, moving into the arms, elbows, and down into the wrists. Let the light flow through each and every finger, into the fingernails and little creases in your palm—the light can't help but BURST through every seam now. Back at your throat, the light is warm and inviting. It's filling your veins, and with each inhale, it gets higher and higher, gaining more and more strength, getting brighter and brighter somehow. We let it fill out the jaw bones and into our mouth. WE GOT A MOUTH FULL OF LIGHT NOW, Y'ALL. Into the back of our skulls, with the light replacing all that space, you are becoming a damn LIGHTHOUSE. Finally, as the light hits your nasal passage, behind your eyes, spurting hot light out of your ears, it can't take it anymore with how much love and happiness it carries and it FUCKING BURSTS OUT THE TOP OF YOUR HEAD, all your strands of hair are on fire right now!!! And you are one giant, beaming, hot light. You let the light carry itself as high as it can go, out of your body, out of the room you're in, into the sky, higher than an airplane, into the clouds and beyond. You take another inhale, letting the light slowly dim, not to lose it, but to hold that light in spaces where, before, you were tense. You can hold this light, within yourself, as long as you need it. And when you feel it pop up again, you are SO familiar with this light, so close and intimate with it, that you can pull it out of the air when you need to send LIGHT to those tense places. Let your light shift as your mood changes. Perhaps it changes color, or smell, or size. Each time you need it, it's always there. You never need permission. **It is your light.**

MOTHER FUCKING BAM!!!!! How did that feel?!? Maybe you felt silly? Maybe you got stuck? Tell me about it here:

_____

_____

_____

_____

_____

_____

_____

_____

_____

_____

MILK MILK MILK

Milk Milk Milk is surprisingly NOT an underground Spotify indie band you've never heard of. Rather, it's a technique from a type of therapy called ACT (acceptance and commitment therapy). This technique has been around for quite some time and involves *lessening the fear of the meaning of a word through word repetition.* The idea is that, eventually, with repetition, your brain will no longer react in a negative way (even unconsciously) and just hear it as a sound! Therapists would introduce the exercise to clients using the word "milk" as an example, which is what gave this exercise its weird long name. (Also, I have questions about galaphobia [fear of milk]. Is it ALL milk? Or just cow's milk? Are they afraid of the cows themselves? What about hamburgers? What about oat milk?)

Let's try this exercise as it pertains to ANXIETY. The idea is to gather some words that trigger unwanted symptoms in your mind and body.

Check out the Word Bank chapter if you need a li'l help thinking of some words. I'll pick mine!

If I were to use my claustrophobia as a theme for this exercise, I'd pick a word like: *Suffocating.*

What words are you choosing for this exercise?

_____

When you think of these words, what images or memories come to mind?

_____

_____

_____

_____

Use your smartphone, clock, or watch to set a timer for 30 seconds. You're going to say the word out loud (or in your head, if you're in public and can focus without being interrupted) as fast as you can. Give yourself permission to allow any thoughts or memories to come to the surface as you say these words. Try to just notice it, then focus back on the trigger word. **For 30 seconds.** Ready? GO!

How did that feel? Anything come up?

_____

_____

_____

_____

Now, we'll do the same thing again, but for 60 seconds. Ready? YOU GOT THIS! GO!!!!!

How did that feel this time around? Any different from the first?

_____

_____

_____

_____

STICK WITH IT! **Next, set your timer for 90 seconds and repeat!**

Tell me once more how you're feeling. If you're exhausted or annoyed, write that. Losing your attention? Do you feel differently about the word?

Finally, we'll do this one last time, but for a whole 120 seconds. I'm proud of you for getting this far! Thank you for being willing to try it at all! GO!

After saying the word so many times, how does your mouth feel? How about your mind? Did you feel anything new? Do you feel any different from when you started?

_____

_____

_____

_____

This is just the beginning. Change it up with words that are similar to your original choice. For my claustrophobia example, next time, I might try: *stuck, darkness, or isolation*. Try this technique whenever you can: when you're in the shower, grocery shopping, or on your next work break. Let me know how this *does or doesn't* change these words and their meanings for you over time.

THE KNITTING CRAZE

Over the last year, I'd often see young millennial women carrying around balls of yarn everywhere I went. And it confused the shit out of me. First of all, it's 90 degrees in Los Angeles. Who are these people wearing knit ANYTHING? On planes, trains, at the gym, at the sushi bar...It felt bizarre. I'd always seen knitting as some old-lady shit; why knit when you have Twitter? Why knit when you can endlessly search the Internet? Why knit when you can spend hours watching a Netflix series? Why knit when you can stalk your ex-girlfriend's new girlfriend's LinkedIn account? Why knit when you can—ohhhhhhh, I'm starting to see the point here.

Ironically, the all-women's workspace that I have a membership to was offering a knitting & mindfulness class for $25. I decided, for research purposes for this book, that I should attend. I arrived early and picked my seat away from the front, and made small talk with the other women who had shown up alone...to knit with strangers...on a weekday evening. We all laughed at how silly this looked, and then ~THEY~ walked in: the ~KNITTING INSTRUCTORS~. They looked like the most relaxed, Zen, and tranquil women I'd ever seen, as if they'd been manufactured in a Free People warehouse.

When we started the class, the instructors told us that we'd be making small scarves (or snoods, as they call them) and that THEY WOULD BE TAKING OUR FREAKING PHONES. THE HELL? I didn't sign up for that! My functioning anxiety momentarily sprung up at the thought of being detached from my device...but, then I remembered that I can give my body permission to set aside my worries/ fears/anxieties for just an hour, and they will always be there for me to pick them back up. Reluctantly, I threw my phone into a handwoven basket and grabbed my ball of yarn and those beginner's stick thingys to knit with (they're called needles, LOL, but they are not sharp or scary. More like plastic kindergarten scissors). We all watched and tried to follow along, some girls picking up the move seamlessly... some...like me, ending up with a tangled spider web that couldn't catch a fly. I was pissed. "This is stupid," I thought to myself many times, imagining my cold neck with no snood. The instructors could tell that some of us were checking out (me), so they called a pause. "Now, we're going to add in some mindfulness. Everyone, put down your needles, and we'll take some grounding breaths and focus on remaining neutral about the knitting."

Well, well, well, now they were talkin' my language! The group did some MUCH-NEEDED breathing exercises, where I was able to chill my negative self-talk and encourage myself to just enjoy this time I'd carved out for myself. Who cares if I end up with a snood or not? I'm here with a bunch of cool chicks who are all just interested in calming their nerves by weaving some string together. I'm sure we have a lot in common. I thought to myself, "Sure, Kelsey. You COULD leave...You always have an exit plan. You're not stuck. But you're not in any immediate danger and I'm proud of you for trying something new. So, why not try to enjoy this?"

And, I'm sure you can guess where this went next: I started chatting with the girls more, smiling bigger, asking more questions, laughing a lot, sharing mindfulness tips with my fellow knitters, and catching the attention of one of the instructors, who saw me struggling. She pulled her chair up next to mine and walked me through the patterns like I was a baby trying to learn how to walk. And, once I got the hang of the pattern, I BECAME A SPRINTING BABY, BABY! I was knitting my BALLS off. I began to see how the repetition and movement of my fingers was so fucking calming. If a mistake was made, it was possible to go back and fix it. No harm, no foul. You bet your bitch ass I ended up with a bright yellow SNOOD by the end of the class and was proud as fuck to wear it leaving the clubhouse, almost forgetting to grab my phone. I brought it home, showed it off to my partner and roommate, who truly did not believe I had knitted the beautiful creation, and even put it on my cat, who absolutely hated it. Whatever; he doesn't know fashion. That night, I went on Amazon and ordered myself a knitting starter kit. I knitted a few more items, even started a hat, but the yarn eventually ended up on my shelf—not to be put away, but rather to be added to my anxiety toolkit. Another technique that I know I can bust out at a moment's notice if anything starts to get squirrelly.

My positive experience with knitting had me curious as to how someone had turned this old-lady trope into a thriving and booming millennial biz. I reached out to **Sophie Thimonnier,** the founder and chief coaching officer of *HeartKnit,* a mindful knitting class, to ask about the emotional & sciencey stuff of knitting.

> **Kelsey:** Hi, Sophie! What PHYSICAL benefits does knitting have on our bodies? How about the MENTAL benefits?
>
> **Sophie:** *I was giving knitting classes...I was a teacher, and sometimes, when you teach people, you touch people. People who attended my classes all had hectic lives*

that were basically run by their smartphone—and when your smartphone runs your life, it ruins your life. After one or two hours of knitting, all these super-busy people were leaving the class telling me how much better they felt, inside and out. I did more research and found out that knitting has scientifically proven health benefits. Knitting, it turns out, is full of superpowers: It's good for the heart; the act of knitting lowers your heart rate and blood pressure. It's good for the brain; like meditation, knitting keeps you focused by its repetitive and rhythmic movement. That's why it is so relaxing for the mind, and it's good for yourself because you actually create something with your hands; you can be proud of yourself and say you did it yourself! It's a clarity machine. I wanted to take full advantage of these benefits, so I created a new practice called "Mindful Knitting." It's basically a mix of mindful exercises and knitting techniques.

Kelsey: I've personally seen so many young millennial women carrying around balls of yarn in public places. Why do you think this act is catching on with so many people? And is it here to stay?

Sophie: *It is not a trend, but a philosophy of life, a way to take away stress, and this urge to go back to simplicity.*

Kelsey: Your company's slogan is "put down the phone, pick up the yarn," and when I took your class, our guides took our phones! It was so shocking and WONDERFUL! Why is this slogan important to you?

Sophie: *Connecting with your friends is timeless. When you ask people when was the last time you truly connected with someone else around you, I mean truly connected: when you felt so comfortable, you can be yourself, and not only speak your truth, but also listen, give the gift of listening. Most people don't have many opportunities to do so, even with their close friends, because everyone is busy working, traveling, parenting. We created a safe, positive, inclusive space, where you have to drop your phone and grab your yarn. It's magic to see people having fun, together, "in real life."*

CONTRIBUTE MORE THAN
YOU CRITICIZE

To yourself! Intrusive thoughts, or negative internal monologue WITHOUT examination of the thoughts, is like leaving a shitty YT comment on the video of your life, with a blank avatar and fake username, and disappearing forever. **DRAW your own thumbnail of a video you would post about something awesome about you.** Give me a title, view count, and leave a positive comment for yourself!

VIEWS:

TITLE:

COMMENTS

YOU:

CREATING BOUNDARIES

Boundaries can help keep useless anxiety at bay. Saying NO can be your biggest asset. Do you need to distance from something in your life? Maybe it's an unhealthy habit, an energy-sucking friend, or parents who ~*just don't understand*~. Use this template to help guide yourself into creating a conversation about setting boundaries in your life.

1. Express what you need without apologizing or overexposing:

_____

_____

_____

_____

_____

_____

_____

_____

_____

2. Don't try to control their reaction. In fact, let's get that out of the way now. How do you think they'll react? (If it's an object, hobby, or something that doesn't talk, tell me about what you THINK the reaction would be if this thing could talk.)

_____

_____

_____

_____

_____

_____

_____

_____

3. Sit with this feeling of discomfort. How does it feel?

_____

_____

_____

_____

_____

_____

_____

_____

_____

_____

4. _Remind yourself that the only people who disrespect boundaries are people who take advantage._

5. Don't feel bad if your boundaries change. They can. And will. As long as YOU are the one to make the change, and you aren't influenced by others' thoughts or opinions, you shouldn't apologize for being a human whose needs change over time.

6. Remember: _No response_ IS _a response._ BYE GIRL BYE

When in doubt, return to step 1.

DATING/LOVE ANXIETY

It's TOTES NORMAL to feel SOME anxiety around dating. Who WOULDN'T feel a little weird about getting totally emotionally intimate with a complete stranger who I've messaged with, like, five times before deciding they're okay enough to meet up with IRL, when I don't even like to leave my own house or waste makeup if I'm not getting laid, or at least having some interesting convo, and GOSH, *don't you feel like you know within the first 15 seconds of meeting this person in the flesh if you want to sit on their face or not?!* THEN YOU'RE JUST STUCK THERE, WITH SOMEONE WHO DOESN'T HAVE A SITTABLE FACE, PRETENDING LIKE YOU CARE BUT REALLY I'M NOT TRYING TO MAKE A NEW "FRIEND," so what are the chances of meeting someone I like vs. the chances of me having an AWESOME night in bed in my PJs, masturbating and watching *Teen Mom* on TV?... Whew. Sorry, had to get that out.

Anyway, let's say you've gotten over those little butterflies that we all get when meeting someone new and attractive that we think has a chance of getting the HONOR to date us...and then, the social anxiety kicks in. Instead of COMPLETELY FREAKING OUT AND MAKING AN EXCUSE NOT TO GO, like, "I'm so sorry, my cat ate one of my boric acid pills that I had set out on my nightstand so I wouldn't forget to shove it up my pussy before bed, please don't block me, but I'm canceling!!!!" (This is a true event that happened to me, BTW. Larry was fine. Don't worry. Larry is my cat, not the guy. IDK WTF the guy's name was.) Instead, I like to remember that they are likely nervous, too. It's fine to just call that out. And, if your date asks you why you're nervous, feel free to quote my monologue above. Another trick I've learned after being in the dirty & rough dating scene of LA for nine years is to have five questions in my back pocket, ready to be asked at any moment; things you've already thought about to ask someone AND have five answers to those questions for yourself, too. Because chances are, when it gets quiet, AND THAT'S THE MOMENT WHEN THE ANXIETY CREEPS IN HARDEST, they'll hit you with that "How about you?" response. If all goes well, and you end up wanting to see this person again, my best advice is to just be honest about your feelings. Honesty and trust are the foundation for any relationship, so might as well get it out now, right?! Skip a few steps and a bruised ego by letting the person know upfront how you feel about relationships, the anxiety it gives you, how it's affected past relationships, etc. **If they run, they aren't grown enough to handle that kind of emotion, and you don't want them, anyway!**

Let's put you in an IMPROMPTU MOMENT OF FLIRTING!! Let's say you're at a bar, and there's an attractive person you found yourself in conversation with. GOOD FOR YOU! Look at you! Then...things get dull...the spark isn't as bright as you thought it was...and you panic...NOW WHAT?!

This was something I personally struggled with. It's probably because I'm a people-pleaser and my fight, flight, freeze, and fawn response is overactive, but I tend to stay in conversations longer than I should. Afraid to dismiss myself. I had to get used to the idea that not every person I meet needs to become a lover, a friend, or even somebody I exchange Instagram handles with. It's OKAY to excuse yourself, say it was nice to meet them, and move on to the next thing. My classic cop-out is saying, "Nice to meet you! I gotta pee!" You leave on a definite, but low-stakes, emergency. And, you've said a nice closing statement. OFF TO THE BATHROOM TO CATCH YOUR BREATH!

Let's come up with your five questions to keep in your back pocket! Most people enjoy talking about themselves, unless they are introverted and shy, or maybe even anxious themselves! So, try to keep the questions short, interesting, and easy to answer.

Avoid the obvious and bland questions like "what do you do for work?," but also don't ask something super fucking weird, right? We've all had that happen before, when someone says something ~*totally random*~, and you're sitting there like, "Bro, I know you use this line all the time. This is *totally* your 'line.'" OR when they ask "What's your life story?"...UM. How exactly am I supposed to sum up 30 years of mental health problems, rehab, unpacking the trauma that caused it, oh and what I like to do for fun on the weekends?

To prepare, here are some of my own back-pocket questions for people dating with anxiety:

- Instead of "What do you do for work?" try "What do you do for fun?"

- "What's your favorite drink?" is a good one that you might be able to contribute to by telling a fun memory attached to why this is their/your favorite drink, or ask where the best one in the city is. Maybe you go there on a second date?!

- Pretend you got a notification on your phone and say, "Have you seen XXX on Netflix? It's the thing everyone is talking about! I keep seeing it on the trending page!"

- Is there anything in the next year you want to do that you've never done before?

- How bad is your screen time average? (Then, you guys can compare screen times and see who is a worse millennial.)

SILENCE IS GOLDEN

SILENCE IS OKAY. This is something we want to get comfortable and confident in: your silence. Give yourself permission to experience silence as a *positive* rather than a negative, anxious thing. When you look at silence as being negative or awkward, it translates into more work for yourself; a job to fill the silence. **Remember, conversation is a two-person job.** Silence, when you're dating for a while, actually shows COMFORTABILITY!!!!! When you reach the step of silence in a relationship...it's A GOOD THING! It's a milestone to *want to* hit. You're going to be warmed by it and not freaked out by it! So, in the beginning of dating, if you can remind yourself that silence is actually something you want to achieve, even if it starts out as awkward silence, it becomes easier to think of it as a good thing. Practice sitting in that "awkward". Time warps when we are anxious, so chances are, it's not as awkward as you think! A question that I get asked often in my DMs, from people of all ages, is when they should tell the person that they're tryin' to get freaky with about their anxiety disorder. My advice, and it might not be popular, is TO PUT IT ON THE TABLE AS SOON AS YOU FEEL COMFORTABLE ENOUGH ADMITTING TO YOURSELF THAT YOU EXPERIENCE HIGH ANXIETY. For some of you, that might be right now! And within the first five minutes of a first date! For others, those still trying to be diagnosed or who are ashamed of their feelings, you might want to set aside time with a therapist or with yourself to not only OWN the words, but to know the language to use, when and if, you decide to talk about it with a partner.

When you can bring it up, no matter how soon or far into a relationship, coming with confidence and NO APOLOGIES about your mental health is THE SEXIEST THING I'VE EVER SEEN ON A PERSON. It shows how HUMAN they are. They are not perfect. No one is. And they're not afraid to admit that. And, I promise you, seriously, there will be more people who can relate than not. And if they can't, or refuse to understand, or think of it as some nightmarish horror story—OR MAKE FUN OF YOU BECAUSE OF IT—you don't want to date that person, anyway. THE RELATIONSHIP WILL NEVER BE AS SUCCESSFUL AS IT CAN BE IF YOUR PARTNER IS NOT SUPPORTIVE OF YOUR MENTAL-HEALTH JOURNEY. PERIOD. POINT MOTHERFUCKING BLANK. Sorry if that was harsh. But it's true.

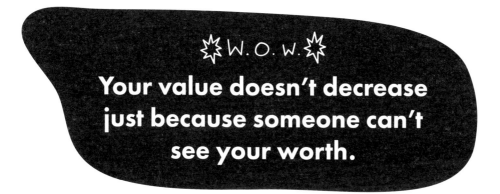

✴ W. O. W. ✴

Your value doesn't decrease just because someone can't see your worth.

And remember, EVERYONE has mental-health issues. The varying levels of intensity or disruption can change at all points in life. What is dope about partnership and mental health is that you have someone who can be an extension of you; they will learn your needs and wants. It won't happen overnight, but if you keep an open mind and open heart, I believe everyone can find that type of supportive partnership in love. Love! Just the fact that it exists at all is amazing! How is it even possible?! It's so fucking crazy to think about these feelings that...propel the world forward?! Caring enough about someone else above your own needs—it's pure. It's thoughtful. And you're striving to be the best person you can be. And when it's meant to be—godfuckingdammit I hate that this is cliche but true—it will be. As much as I wish I could say, **"There's no point in getting anxiety about dating because the person who is right for you to date will like you with your anxiety and all,"** but we just know our brains won't accept such info easily, huh? 'Cause we are impatient and taught by society that we'd be happier with a partner, no matter how immature they are about mental health, and the sooner the better (untrue). But! What I said *is* true! What will be, will be. So, focus on what you can control. Like what cute-ass outfit are you going to rock on this first date?!

A LI'L LOVER HISTORY WITH KELSEY & HER ANXIETY DISORDERS

High-school lover: He was a jock. Came from a very tradition-ally conservative family. Did not speak about mental health with his friends or family. Ever. When I started to have panic attacks, he would hug me...but never asked any questions. How could he help? Did I need anything? We were both too young to under-stand how this diagnosis works. No shade to him. He tried his best.

First Big Adult Love: You know, the one that makes all the other lovers look like crushes or infatuation. This relationship was a great relationship, but easily the most ups and downs with my mental health. I was on over 20 different medications in our time of dating, having regular panic attacks, going to therapy, drinking a lot to hide the anxiety. I felt like a burden. They didn't understand what I was going through and couldn't relate in any physical way. They were already pretty pessimis-tic in their world views, so my depression didn't freak them out or seem too severe to worry about. That is, until I was spending DAYS at a time in bed, sleeping, too afraid to leave—they started to feel that I wasn't handling the diagnosis "the right way". They blamed it on my age, my job choice, my drinking...pretty much everything EXCEPT the chemicals in my brain. Any time I spoke with them about it, the relationship became more strained. It was in this relationship that it became clear and clearer that it was NEVER going to work, no matter how much I tried or offered to bring them to therapy appointments...It was like trying to mix oil and water. I had to FLOW FREE, BABY!! When we broke up, I experienced a severe depres-sive episode that I speak more about in the Depression chapter. This person would often tell me that the support and love I was looking for "only existed in the mov-ies," and that I needed to get realistic about how much one person could care for another. I thought about this statement for years. It haunted me. It made me feel unlovable, and it took me a long time, until I met my current partner, to believe that everyone, no matter where they are on their mental-health journey, is capable of being loved. FULLY. ALL the "messy" or "dramatic" or "sick" parts. Thinking back on this relationship, I hope this person is able to feel more. And I know that's a big ask, to think deeper about their own emotions and find the room to make space for the person whom they love's emotions. I want nothing but the best for this person. I feel very lucky that I am in tune with my body and now, at age 29, am capable of identifying and communicating my needs and finding healthy partnerships. That only happened with growth, time, and the bravery to dive in deeper, into the thoughts and feelings that scared me most. And most importantly, not falling into a codependent relationship where my happiness depends on what another person thinks of me and my mental health. How someone treats you is more important than how you feel about them. Looking back now, the biggest flex I've had on all of my exes is LOVING MYSELF THE WAY I WISH THEY DID! And, if any of that resonates with you and you're ready to keep reading this workbook, know that *I am so fucking proud of you...*

The Soulmate: I didn't really believe in soulmates...I thought the idea was cute... but I, after 10+ years of dating around—and y'all, I mean DATING AROUND—I didn't think I could find anyone that I could t*ruly speak every word, honest thought, and fear that came from my soul with. Unashamed. Without being judged.* And then, I met Jared.

On our first date, we went to a Halloween event being thrown by Universal Studios— it was free drinks, free food, and a walk around the theme park. Jared and I surveyed the chicken finger line, found crispy curly fries...aaaaaand the open bar. We began taking shot after shot, beer after beer, and with each sip, we found ourselves spilling every secret about ourselves. Things we'd never told anyone, thoughts that I thought I'd be ostracized for, dreams and nightmares. I finally found the courage (liquid courage, let's be honest) to spill about my "disordered" past. The amount of meds I'd been on, the rehab, the ER appointments, the "crazy" brain, the feeling "unreal." ALL OF IT. He soaked it all in, asked tons of questions, and smiled a lot. He made me feel comfortable and praised me for sharing such deep and, what I considered embarrassing, thoughts about myself. I learned about his "baggage," too. That he had trauma, he had experienced tough times, and, though he'd never had a panic attack, he had his own mental-health struggles. He wanted to know more about how he could help if I ever had a panic attack in front of him, or any resources, books, articles, or podcasts he could listen to about the topic. This was our foundation. We let it all out on the first night of knowing each other. Yeah, maybe we have the vodka lemon drop shots to thank a little bit, but, at our core—this is who we were together. We were two honest people who were looking for support in the right person. We both WANTED each other but didn't NEED each other. While our brains and anxieties were not the same, our hearts were traveling on the same path. Three years in now, and we are still learning. We keep an open mind and dive deep into the subjects that scare us—TOGETHER. We've done couples therapy, we do neurofeedback appointments together, we pick up each other's prescriptions at the pharmacy, we know when to back off and give space, and, most importantly, we both know that this will only continue to work as long as we are open and honest with each other about ALL our feelings.

LARGE CROWD ANXIETY

& AGORAPHOBIA

I've never been to Coachella. Full stop! I'm a white bitch in LA who loves to party AND I'VE NEVER BEEN TO COACHELLA. And I probably never will. Not only because I need a place to pee and sit in the shade at all times, because that just doesn't exist there for my beautiful, pasty, Nicole Kidman-like swan skin—but, mainly because I have a fear of large crowds. It's a mix of my debilitating claustrophobia (I was locked in the trunk of a car as a prank when I was a kid, and, boy, did THAT follow me into adulthood) and my mild AGORAPHOBIA.

Agoraphobia is a disorder involving anxiety about situations from which escape would be difficult or embarrassing. Or places where there might be no help if a panic attack occurred. I often think about where I would go, what I would do, how I would survive if I had high anxiety in a large crowd that I could not get out of. This agoraphobia slowly crept up on me during a depressive state, where the idea of leaving my room caused my body to feel intense high anxiety. I slowly started spending more and more time in my room, bringing a mini-fridge to my nightstand, eating only takeout, doing therapy appointments over the phone...and, before I knew it, I hadn't left my room in WEEKS. And it was hard to tell, because I had kept the room super clean. It wasn't giving off those hoarder vibes. I was comfy there. But...all the rest of my body parts were like, WHAT THE FUCK ARE WE DOING, YOU FREAK?! TAKE A WALK! GO TO THE COFFEE BEAN ON THE CORNER! GO SMELL A FUCKING FLOWER! ANYTHING!!! I got frustrated at myself for constantly IMAGINING the worst-case scenarios if

I were to leave or attend a social gathering or go to work even though I knew my brain was fabricating these scenarios. Even though these anxieties didn't actually exist yet, my brain told me there was only one way to find out if I'd *actually* get hit by a car and pinned under a truck that would catch fire if I left my apartment building. I NEEDED TO GO WALK ON THE SIDEWALK AND SEE!!

It started with literal small steps, but the way I was able to overcome my fear of being hit by a car outside my home was by...doing the thing...*and it not happening*. Over and over. My brain had to recognize that the scenarios it had made so real in my head did not hold any real danger.

Agoraphobia can arise from so many outside factors, like environment, genetics, symptoms of trauma, and general stress. For me, putting myself IN THE ENVIRONMENT over and over again helped lessen the feeling of being overwhelmed. I'm still working on the large crowd part (plus all those sweaty wannabe Lana Del Reys at Coachella rubbing up against me just doesn't seem pleasant from a hygiene standpoint), but when I find myself in a scenario that might cause my large-crowd fear to bubble up, I recall my EXIT PLAN...

THE EXIT PLAN

GET ME TF OUTTA HERE

I'm not suggesting you become a doomsday prepper with this chapter, but if you are coming out of a shaky headspace, perhaps try sliding out of some of that avoidant behavior by using the EXIT PLAN exercise.

Unfortunately, this chapter created itself not only in the sticky, icky paranoia cracks of my anxiety brain and agoraphobia, but also because of the way the world has shown its darker, uglier side in the last decade. I think the world has ALWAYS had a dark and ugly side, but with social media, it's become easier to witness the shootings, global pandemic disasters, and troll behavior.

The idea with the exit plan is to tell your brain that you are safe and never physically or mentally "stuck" in any scenario. Ever. **That you have control, but you are actively choosing to not exert the control. The exit plan is just in your back pocket, in case you need it.** In that case, when your brain KNOWS this, it can chill out a bit. Brain be like: OKAY, WE CAN USE THIS IF WE NEED IT, BUT WE DON'T SO...I'm...safe? Not in danger? I can actually enjoy the thing we came here for for a minute?? All right! WE PASSED THE VIBE CHECK!

Often with anxiety, we get stuck in the "what-ifs" of life. Us anxiety-ers go down every which worst-case scenario rabbit hole for anything that sets off our anxiety antennas. (I feel like a cute li'l anxiety caterpillar.) The exit plan consists of a <u>physical and mental action plan</u>. If you need to leave, you know how to get out of there and what to say. OR, if you can't *physically* leave, you have the tools in your tool kit to *mentally* safeguard yourself.

Physically—due to my agoraphobic behavior—I limit myself to doing activities that I know I could *physically* leave if I felt uncomfortable. It doesn't cost me a penny to pick the seat closest to the door in a restaurant, or avoid the mosh pit happening at the club. At a movie theater, for example—if I leave, I may lose the $10 that I spent on the ticket (although AMC once refunded me the ticket when I told them I felt sick halfway through *A QUIET PLACE* when I actually had a li'l panic attack), but the safety net of knowing I can PHYSICALLY GET UP AND WALK OUT AT ANY TIME is worth it! Same for parties. Yeah, some people might ask where I'd gone and why I'm so fabulous at Irish exiting (sneaking out of a party without saying goodbye to anyone), but my ability to put my comfort first so that I don't slide back into an anxious state makes me feel empowered, usually to a point where I won't *actually* have to leave the party, but just knowing *I could leave if I wanted to* makes me feel better.

There are a million and one scenarios that you could find yourself in that you can't physically leave: airplanes, boat rides, buying tickets to something where you just couldn't afford to leave the experience because of anxiety...so, having a "mental exit plan" is helpful, too.

Something that I *can* control is carrying my AirPods on me wherever I go, in case I need to put on a meditation track. I also spent years carrying my emergency meds in a small pill case that fit in any pocket to every place that wasn't my bedroom. If I experienced high anxiety that got out of hand, I could pop one in, which definitely was strong enough to mentally take me out of reality and into Zzzzz DREAM LAND. And, to my serious surprise, eventually, I found myself tapping my back pocket, checking for that pill-exit, less and less. I eventually could leave my pillbox at home, feeling confident enough that I could handle the drive back to my house to get them if I really found myself freaking out. Even today, I'll pack the pills if I'm going far from California, but just having that "mental" exit plan, knowing it's there, allows me to *take the damn vacation* and experience the fun trip with friends that I otherwise would've missed out on.

What are some things you could do to make an exit plan, physically and mentally, for your next outing?

PHYSICAL EXIT PLAN:

_____

_____

_____

_____

_____

_____

_____

MENTAL EXIT PLAN:

_____

_____

_____

_____

_____

_____

_____

IF YOU ARE ANXIOUS ABOUT THE FUTURE RIGHT NOW, DON'T BE. IT LITERALLY DOESN'T EXIST. How often are you right about predicting the future with your anxiety? Do you manifest it? Try not to conjure up any unnecessary incidences. Unless you're a witch, then, practice on, my sister.

HANGOVER ANXIETY

Me, most mornings in my twenties: UGHHH...HAANNNNGGGGGGG-NNNNN...bleehhhhWAAAAHHHHHH...FuuucckkkkkinggggCAAACAAAAA!!!!! It's like a desert in my MOUTH. The DADS (day after drinking shits) are in town. I am FRAGILE—THIS END UP. Which way is up???

Is there ANYTHING more horrendous on this PLANET than HANGOVER ANXIETY??? A.K.A. hangxiety, the Sunday Scaries, the emotional hang le over, REGRAT, or, in Norway, they actually have a word to describe all of this: *Fylleangst.* Despite the confusion you may feel hungover, the fancy brain science behind hang-over anxiety is pretty easy to understand. Think of it as, *what goes up must come down.* AND IT COMES DOWN HARD, BABBYYYYYYYYY.

That headache you feel? That's the thin muscles around your skull, dehydrated as FUCK because of the alcohol, and they are physically shrinking a bit, pulling the muscle away from the bone...a la HEADACHE. Look, that imagery alone is enough for me to remember to drink WATER WATER WATER in between each cocktail, but, of course, sometimes we all get lost in the sauce and just wanna have fun. So, I've compiled this list of tips to lessen those tough, unforgiving mornings:

1. **Put a big glass of water next to your bed BEFORE you go out.** While you're doing your hair and putting on your makeup, reach in that medicine cabinet and snag two Advils for your bedside as well.

2. **Keep Pedialyte packets in your nightstand.** In the AM, chug one of those down while you sit in bed and MEDITATE over last night's actions, instead of letting them swirl into intrusive thoughts in your head. Don't avoid the memories; they'll only come back stronger later.

3. **Try taking charcoal pills the night before drinking.** They are supposed to help absorb the alcohol in the stomach, lessening its effects, yes, but keeping your tummy happier!

4. **Shower immediately.** The sooner you can get last night's crud out of your armpits and netherbits, the better! In the last minutes of your shower, slowly start to turn the nozzle to cold—it won't feel like such a shock if you do it gradually—and sit in the coldest stream you can tolerate.

5. **Have some caffeine**, like a coffee or soda, BUT NOT TOO MUCH, because too much caffeine can exacerbate those nasty feelings or destabilize that peace in your brain we just worked so hard at meditating on. Caffeine, however, can help blood flow, which will lessen headache tension.

6. **Worst-case scenario, hair of the dog, but only one or two.** Seriously. We're just putting a Band-Aid on a bullet hole at this point. But I won't judge you.

Try to plan the heavy drinking. Don't go on a spontaneous binge (although they happen, and for me, it's usually weirdly at Disney World??). You'll tend to make yourself feel LESS guilty if the drinking is planned (a.k.a. around holidays or birthdays); you will give yourself permission to have a long morning in bed the next day. Find out if you're good at day-drinking (spoiler alert: most people are not). And if you're not, sip on a bubbly drink that isn't booze (my go-to is ginger beer—despite its name, it's a non-alcoholic gingery fizz delight—with soda water and lime!). I promise, no one will care as much as you think they're going to, and IF THEY DO, it shows more about their character than yours. People peer-pressure usually because they don't want to drink alone.

And last, but MOST EMPHASIZED: Always call an Uber, or have someone sober drive. [18]

---

18 For more drinking exercises, see the "Mindful Drinking Journal" in the resources index.

GROCERY STORE
& FOOD ANXIETY

This chapter isn't going to be telling you what foods you should or should not get at the grocery store, because we *shouldn't* SHOULD ourselves! Ah, fucking dammit. It's HARD, RIGHT?! Food, eating, and our emotional relationships can be super intertwined with anxiety and cause stress for a lot of people. So, the goal of this chapter is to make the act of buying or consuming food a little less stressful...

...OKAY, BUT I WILL THROW IN ONE OR TWO LITTLE THINGS ABOUT EATING FOOD. In 2018, I started seeing a nutritionist. Not because I have dealt with an eating disorder, but, as she put it, I had "disordered thoughts around eating." I found myself using food as a reward or as comfort, which distorted my routine around meals. I didn't realize it immediately, but when it came to stress, anxiety, or depression, the first place I would look was to the golden light in my fridge. I got so close with food. Watching all those Netflix food-porn shows, keeping snacks in my bedside drawer. My boyfriend says often, "Food makes Kelsey cum harder than I ever could," and I'm sorry, Mom and Dad, but I HAVE TO LAUGH BECAUSE IT'S TRUE. Food is the emotional connector of people! It knows no language, age, or gender! It can be an overwhelmingly wonderful pillar in important moments and memories of life: Birthdays! Weddings! Hangouts with friends! On the flip side, it can also have an overwhelmingly negative emotional affect vs. effect when co-occurring with a mental-health disorder.

The exercise I found most helpful that my nutritionist gave me was mindful eating. AND WHILE SOME PEOPLE MIGHT ROLL THEIR EYES AT THIS IDEA, I WANT TO REITERATE THAT I DON'T THINK THERE IS SUCH THING AS A "bad" OR "good" FOOD. WE SHOULD (and "should-ing" myself doesn't apply here) BE ABLE TO EAT WHATEVER WE WANT, WHENEVER WE WANT...with the caveat that we *should try to* simply...*notice how we feel about it.* Be curious! You might start to recognize patterns you weren't aware of before. (Anyone who has experienced an abusive relationship with food or an ED[19] [eating disorder], let it be known that this exercise is encouraged to be FREE FROM JUDGMENT!!) Write truthfully about how you DO feel without using triggering words. (*Check out the Resources Index for a printable version.*)

MINDFUL EATING

DATE & TIME AM/PM

_____

WATER INTAKE THUS FAR:

WHAT I'M EATING

_____

WHY I'M EATING IT: (meal time, craving, social, bored)

_____

HUNGER SCALE: (not hungry) 1–10 (growl!!!) _____

MOOD BEFORE EATING: 🙂 😐 🙁

MOOD AFTER EATING 🙂 😐 🙁

NOTES:

_____

_____

19 For more info on ED resources, check out *The Intuitive Eating Workbook* by Evelyn Tribole.

The act of acquiring food itself is a privilege in many ways, so the guilt that can come up when experiencing GROCERY STORE ANXIETY can be confusing AF.

I need food to live

+

I can't go where the food is without
experiencing more stress

=

?????

However, there are some small things you can do to prepare for the grocery store trip so that your anxiety levels stay chill.

1. **THERE ARE TOO MANY CHOICES!!!** So, go in with a list. Try to avoid those moments when you're driving home and think you should just SWING BY the store on a whim to pick up a few things. It never goes as planned. We go rogue in the bakery; we start buying plungers and chip clips that we don't need…it's just a mess. I bought a magnetic notepad & pen that sticks to my refrigerator so that I can always add things and rip off the paper when I'm planning a grocery trip. Some people like to use their phone, but I find a physical piece of paper a lot more formal and official. Plus my roomie and BF can add to it that way, too.

2. **When in doubt, Cuties are your friends.** You know, those little miniature oranges? They are a great snack at a good price that are just tart enough, with a bit of sweetness, to grab on the go. When I find myself emotionally snacking, I always try to reach for a Cutie—that way, when I have the inevitable four or five oranges, I don't feel sick to my stomach the way I would've if I'd had four or five of ANY OTHER TYPE OF SNACK (a.k.a. five spoonfuls of Funfetti frosting or Kroger Sugar cookies, which I have a severe addiction to)!

3. **Combine errands.** I like to shop at a store that sells groceries and all-life items, like TARGET. That way, the food shopping part of the trip just feels like part of the bigger picture of getting a fun Target run in.

4. **Don't go in hungry.** Make sure your blood sugar is regulated, and bring some water to chug if you notice yourself getting handsy with some snacks you don't need.

5. **If you just can't keep ya hands to yaself**, grab a banana from the produce section and eat it. Pay for it with the peel at the counter. Grocery store workers won't care. They see it all the time. Bananas are rich in potassium, which can help reduce symptoms of anxiety.

6. **If the store itself is triggering for you**, try food delivery apps that bring your groceries to your front door, like Instacart or Amazon Pantry (Use the "Prime Day" option to cut down on cardboard waste), which seem to be all the rage with the way that all errands are turning to digital services in our day and age.

7. **If you have a roommate or BFF**, **trade off duties** of grocery shopping, or go together and hold each other accountable. Ask them to take notice of your mood and offer to step in with finding certain items if you're starting to get irritable. For me, twirling my hair or pulling my eyelashes is an obvious sign of self-soothing, and my boyfriend will know I need an extra hand with whatever is in front of me—and it's usually deciding WHICH KIND OF OAT MILK TO BUY I MEAN MY GOD THERE ARE SO MANY CHOICES!!!!!!!!

There are a lot of studies being done about how gut health is linked to *preeeeetty much* everything that has to do with our mood. Johns Hopkins has even gone as far as to say your gut has its own kinda brain[20]! It's capable of communicating back and forth with our upstairs brain! A lot of chemicals in our bodies are produced by our gut, and if you think about it, even our medications get broken down in our guts and carried through to the rest of the body! So, it would make sense that a lot of SHIT is going down in there! Like the mind-body connection, doctors are just starting to scratch the surface about this connection, so it's an important subject to pay attention to as the research evolves! I'm not here to tell you what to eat, but I WILL tell you that the more I looked into the gut/mental health connection, the more inclined I was to put less sugar and more leafy-ass greens into my meals! Eat your food as medicine!

---

20 "The Brain-Gut Connection." *The Brain-Gut Connection | Johns Hopkins Medicine*, Johns Hopkins Medicine, 2020, www.hopkinsmedicine.org/health/wellness-and-prevention/the-brain-gut-connection.

WORK ANXIETY

JOBS ARE HARD. THAT'S WHY IT'S CALLED WORK.

Even if you love what you do, there are going to be days where you just want to **lose. your. shit.** I've played out many scenarios in my head during a tough day, about how I'd set a trash can on fire, dump it in my boss' office, flip the bird, and walk out yelling, "I'M OUT THIS BITCH!!!"

However, most of us are in a position where we just...can't do that. Unless you work at a trash-burning factory, then you *might* be able to pull this off without actually getting fired. But logistically, my dream scenario requires too much work on my part. For instance, how would I start the fire? I don't smoke or carry a lighter. My boss is an okay guy; it's mostly the system that's fucked up—so, does he really deserve a flaming pile of trash on his floor? Who would have to clean that? Also, unless there's a getaway car waiting for me outside, there's a high chance that security would follow me out and...arrest me? For, like, arson, right...? Since my options for this epic walk-out moment would never come to fruition without a lawsuit, I quit my job, like a regular ol' person via email with a two-week notice and decided to start working from home in 2018. This decision was thought out well over a year in advance. I sat on the anxiety of leaving my dream job at BuzzFeed, hoping things would change enough for me to want to stay. I stand by the fact that BuzzFeed was the greatest job I ever had, with coworkers who are superhumans who change the world on a daily basis. Alas, I had simply outgrown my position and opportunities at the company. I slowly transitioned out, taking more and more days to work from home, since I was my own manager and no one seemed to give a shit where we worked from as long as things got DONE. I spent about four months setting up the perfect workspace, in my apartment on the third floor of my townhome in our extra loft, before peacing out permanently. However, I quickly learned that HEAT RISES, and my loft was a small sauna during high noon. I didn't have a window or enough space to walk about aimlessly when thinking of ideas, pretending the floor is lava. I was stuck, creatively and physically, combined with the fear of venturing out on my own to become a band of...one. Myself. No pressure, right? If I suck and can't get it together, then my whole company (of one person) will suck and not be able to get it together, either. I had to learn how to reach out for help. I wasn't going to be able to manage my business all on my own after coming from a media conglomerate worth millions that provided most resources to me. Asking for help when you have an anxiety disorder can feel *hella* burdensome. I believed for a very long time that asking for help was seen as a weakness, that I couldn't do it on my own, and I wasn't good enough or smart enough or blah blah blah enough. In reality, asking for help is a sign of strength, that I know how to delegate my time, that I know my worth and where to expend my stress and worries, which turns out is a lot cuter and more manageable than worrying over every little (that turns into a big) thing in my life! I paid for a TaskRabbit moving company to help move my furniture from the third floor sweatbox/office to the first floor, in front of beautiful sunlight and French doors. I hired two part-time employees to run my podcast. I learned that cutting a small percentage of every deal to an agency that would bring in work would be slightly more helpful than keeping 100% of no deals. I utilized freelance employees (many of whom had worked at BuzzFeed prior, so we spoke the same work language) and knew that, even though I was spending more money than I was comfortable spending for other people's help, I was NEVER going to be able to do everything on my own (though I tried!) and it was an investment in not only myself, but also my mental health. Plus, my friends got to make some money so that's always a plus!

Now that I've seen the anxieties from both sides of the literal work desk table, here are some tips for maintaining your work anxiety.

1. **Make your desk your safe space.** Work can feel like a second home at times (fun fact: when I first started at BuzzFeed, I was so obsessed with the job and didn't know what work/life balance was and would stay every night past 10 PM...eventually, the JANITORS TOLD ON ME to HR, and I got a very kind but obviously stern email about leaving work at an appropriate hour to avoid burnout...WHICH IS V REAL!!!!), so keeping your space comfortable is vital. For instance:

   • I had family photos surrounding my desk.

- Bright-colored crystals.
- A small essential oil diffuser that I had approved by my close deskmates.
- Sparkly things that made me feel cozy.
- My favorite snacks in my desk drawer.

2. **Remember, the bathroom is not only a good place to flush your physical shit out, but also your emotional shit.** Cry in the stall, collect yourself in the mirror, use cold water on your wrists to shock your vagus nerve system and calm down. Don't be afraid to let out some steam during the workday; we tend to hold it all in and wait till we're home to dump that negative shit all over our space. Leave it at the office, in the bathroom where it belongs with the other crap!

3. **Find a panicky friend!** At BuzzFeed, I started a Slack channel (which is basically like a group text) for the company called #HAPPYPLACE. It was for anyone who wanted to talk about mental health, whether it be someone living with a disorder or wanting to know more about it (say, for a video or article idea) to come into the space and speak freely, without judgment. No HR or professional status held court in this chat. We could pop in and ask if anyone wanted to go on a walk together, grab lunch, or meditate in one of the open conference rooms. We did that as employees, without any help from the company, and they took notice. They then hired an outside company to come in and pump up the mental-health culture and support. They put in meditation "quiet rooms" and classes about multitasking. They listened because we asked, and you can do the same at your company if you know your employee rights. Which brings me to:

4. **Learn your mental-health rights as an employee!** The Americans with Disabilities Act (ADA) DOES protect employees with mental health. It doesn't hurt to also schedule some time with your HR to ask questions you might have. Remember that mental health is HEALTH, and you should treat your disorder the same way someone with a broken arm might ask to work from home for a little while.

5. **For work-performance anxiety, accept that having a job means having ups and downs.** Not everything will be perfect all the time. Learn from your losses and mistakes. Company culture is an important factor in keeping your mental health in a good place. Chances are, if the employees don't pass the vibe check, you're going to have a bad time.

6. **Have a big meeting? Set an intention.** Intentions are a great way to give purpose to work that feels mundane or scary. Take a few moments to find a space where you can set a clear goal for yourself. It can be as simple as, "In this meeting, I will communicate as clearly and effectively as I can. I am a boss-ass bitch." Repeat this phrase over and over for at least one minute, focusing on each and every word.

What is your intention for a work event coming up in the future? Remember: You can't control how people respond, but you can control how you react to it.

_____

_____

_____

_____

_____

_____

_____

A visual list of all the things you need to do at work can be very helpful in quelling those nighttime worries that keep you from being able to fall asleep. Don't think of it as a "to-do" list; rather, a "list of ways to be less anxious in the future!" And when things pile up: TAKE ADVANTAGE OF YOUR SUNDAY!

TAKE ADVANTAGE OF YOUR #SELFCARESUNDAY

OR TUESDAY, FRIDAY, OR WHENEVER
YOU FEEL LIKE YOU HAVE THE MOST DOWNTIME.

Use the time wisely, knowing you are doing FUTURE YOU a favor :)

Ahhh—Sunday, "the day of rest"...MUWHAHAHAHAHAHAHAHA HAHAAAAA LMAOOOOOOOOOOOOOO!!!!!!!!! NOT WHEN YOU HAVE DEBILITATING ANXIETY! For us, every day can feel like the most important day of your life while simultaneously feeling like nothing matters and there's no reason to leave bed. Our job is to find a balance! I've discovered scheduling out one day, or even half of one day, to reset and restock for the week ahead has become a mandatory part of my self-care routine. Here are some suggestions on how to make the most of those days off without feeling like you're doing extra work:

1. **Plan out five outfits for the week**. That's right! I said FIVE! Not just the next day's outfit! This way, you will have five options if the outfit you originally picked doesn't fit your "vibe" for the day. Plus, one night of planning for five days free of wardrobe anxiety just makes sense, mathematically.

2. **MEAL PREP.** Don't worry, I'm not trying to recruit you into some protein/ CrossFit food plan—you can meal prep CAKE for all I care. (I have done this.) My favorite? Overnight oats are truly the easiest thing to meal prep.

Ten minutes of prepping can make you breakfast for *a week*. Here is my very own recipe!

- Start with a mason jar (I can't help it; I'm a whyte millennial) and stack:
- Two parts dry oats (you can buy a big-ass container of one-minute oats at the store for three bucks!).
- One spoonful of chia seeds.
- Two parts oat milk (or regular cow's milk, whatever).
- Fill to cover oats.
- Shake the jar so the dry parts are all covered.
- Add one scoop of yogurt (or dairy-free coconut yogurt, in my case!) on top. Let it be a big ol' blob on top.
- Add strawberries, blueberries, bananas, walnuts, granola, WHATEVER TOPPING YOU WANT! If you switch up the toppings, you won't feel like you're having the same thing over and over. One jar might be flavored more fruity...the next can taste like a PB&J!
- Add local honey (local honey can help with allergies!).
- Put this shit all together in a mason jar, x7. Seal it and store overnight in the fridge. Enjoy breakfast for seven days straight! No hassle! And the jars are recyclable!

3. **Post-it Notes are your friends.** I used to keep a Post-it Note next to my bed to write down any last minute thoughts/ideas/reminders I had for the next day. I'd stick the note on my phone so that when my alarm went off, I could see it first thing in the AM. Or I'd leave it on my doorknob so I see it before I leave the house for the day.

4. **Get outside.** Most of us spend our workdays indoors at a desk, so Sunday is the perfect time to catch some D...vitamin D. But don't forget that sunscreen, of course! Even if you have work to do over the weekend, pull up a chair in a nice bit of shade and do it right in Mother Nature. In the complex that I live, we pulled together some funds and bought a daybed for our shared outdoor space. I even put a hammock up with my own two hands! Maybe you can finally get around to visiting that community park you've always seen but never had reason to stop in. Why not set up a comfy patio chair at your local community garden? OOO! You can even download an app called DayPass, which gives you access to the best hotel pools for a small usage fee. It helps

to create multiple outdoor sanctuaries for yourself, so that if one spot doesn't feel right energetically, there's another space available that you might feel more comfy in.

5. **MASTURBATE.** I won't stop pushing this one, y'all. If you're sexually active, you know that sometimes you just gotta scratch that itch—and sure! Sex is cool! But self-pleasure (if you do it) and alone time with your body can be a vital part of self-soothing. The way to turn off your brain to the desires and completion of a partner and turn ON…well, yourself! Orgasms release oxytocin, which may help to relieve stress. My partner might kill me for writing this in a worldwide published workbook, but, hell, I want to share as many tips and tricks as I can to help you guys get some ideas! So, when he moved in, we realized alone time was a little…ahem, hard, to schedule. There was also a shared fear that if one of us DID get that alone time, say, if the other person ran out to the store, that we'd be racing against some kind of clock to finish or have that potentially embarrassing moment of walking in on a loved one in a very personal and vulnerable position. To solve this problem, we agreed that the pressure would feel less intense if we just let the other person know we were having personal time by texting each other the BANANA EMOJI. LOL. I know, we're like 13-year-olds. We don't need permission to self-pleasure, and we don't need to feel the shame of scheduling out time for ourselves. The other person acknowledges it by "liking" the emoji in the text chat, and it's up to the other person to notify them if they discover they would like the other person's "help."

MAKE A SELF-CARE CALENDAR FOR YOUR DAYS OFF!

Here are some ideas to get started:

DAY 1	DAY 2	DAY 3	DAY 4
Start your day with 5 mins of stretching.	Download "time block" worksheets and see if it helps you prioritize your day.	Watch the sunrise!	Watch the sunset!

DAY 5	DAY 6	DAY 7	DAY 8
Spoil yourself and order postmates for dinner.	Mail a letter to someone you love (yes, like the old days, HAND-WRITTEN!).	WASH YOUR BEDSHEETS YA LI'L NASTY!	Try a new, random, YouTube workout.

DAY 9	DAY 10	DAY 11	DAY 12
Take a nap today!	Try baking something (and share it with a friend when it's done!).	Watch a classic film (let's say Disney Channel originals count as "classics."	Drink a LITER of water today!

DAY 13	DAY 14	DAY 15	DAY 16
MASTURBATE... TWICE!	Start a bucket list and write down WHY you want to do those things.	Watch a documentary to educate yourself on a new subject.	Create a "feel-good" playlist on Spotify.

DAY 17

Try making home-made body scrub and use it in the shower.

DAY 18

Browse etsy and get yourself something under $10.

DAY 19

GAME NIGHT! Might I recommend Ticket to Ride or Settlers of Catan.

DAY 20

Have a photo selfie-session with yourself today. Find some good light and a comfy outfit to slay in.

DAY 21

Clean our your inbox. Use a system like unroll.Me to receive a list of all your subscription emails in one place.

DAY 22

Clean your bathroom. It never gets enough love! LIGHT A CANDLE!

DAY 23

Try being vegetarian today! Your farts are gonna smell!

DAY 24

Try making a home-made face mask.

DAY 25

Journal for 15 mins without stopping! Write ANYTHING that comes to mind.

DAY 26

Do something you've been putting off.

DAY 27

Call your local shelter and see if they need any donation items. Bring them some!

DAY 28

Scroll TikTok to your heart's desire.

DAY 29

Go to a tea shop and discover a new flavor to bring home with you.

DAY 30

Unfollow some unhealthy profiles on your social media accounts.

DAY 31

TAKE A HIKE! Jk, you can just walk if you wanna. Exercise is nature's mind-altering drug.

A SIMPLE GRATITUDE INVENTORY

Write every single thing you can think of, no matter how big or small, that you're grateful for. Write all over this page. It can even be a drawing, or just a word. Add to it whenever you think of something. ANYTHING. A full sentence. A song lyric. A doodle! Anything that makes you feel GOOD. Even the "simple" stuff, like having your life, food on the table, or the ability to walk pain-free is worth acknowledging!

NEWS/SOCIAL MEDIA ANXIETY

WHEW LORD. This is a big one. In the next year or so, I bet we are going to see a lot more self-help books about social media and news addiction. Is it just me, or does there seem to be a freaking SCREEN in every establishment I go to?! Airport restaurants! My dentist's office! PRESCHOOLS WITH IPADS, FOR GOSH'S SAKE! My job is literally to be on the internet 90% of my time, so I'm guilty as fuck when it comes to being a stereotypical "millennial" who is attached to their phone. Even as I type this chapter, my phone is sitting between my two wrists that are stretched out on the keyboard, leaving my eyeline with just enough room to see my screen. WHY?! I have all the messaging apps and such on my COMPUTER, WHICH IS RIGHT IN FRONT OF ME! It feels like a third arm, right? I ain't sorry. I feel that I am a much smarter and more complete human with my phone attached to my hip. I can Google anything, reach out to someone in a second's notice, and, most importantly, look at photos of my cat anytime and anywhere.

There comes a time when I get a li'l notification on my phone that tells me my screen time is up compared to other days, and I know I need to put the phone down. There are so many news apps that are constantly pushing me notifications, and while it's *informative* to know what's going on in the world at all times, it's not always *helpful* for me. I don't necessarily need to know every traumatic thing that is happening, from the environment, to the economy, to the sales at Forever 21 AT ALL TIMES via drop-down notifications on my watch and phone!!!

It happens slowly, too. You'll find yourself discussing world topics with friends, becoming more aware, recognizing the different traumas in the world...You'll feel smart and informed...and then, you'll start to take on the emotions, anxieties, and stressors...of ALL OF THOSE ISSUES. You'll wonder how you can exert your help in the best way. Where can you volunteer? Where can you donate? How can you repost for visibility? HOW CAN I CARE ABOUT SO MANY THINGS AT ONCE WHILE ALSO MAKING SURE I FEED THE DOG AND MYSELF AND DO THE LAUNDRY?!

The best thing you can do for your anxiety is to turn off those notifications, bb! Another way to change your relationship with your phone is to check the "pick-up" number in your settings (how often are you "picking up" the phone each day?). Notice the times you pick up your phone most often. Which apps are you clicking on? What does your brain GET from viewing this app? Is it a hit of serotonin? A jolt of anxiety? A wave of calm?

Are you someone that picks up your phone first thing in the morning when your eyes flap open (GUILTY!)? I'm not going to try to convince you NOT to pick up your phone first thing in the AM, because we need it for things like our alarm clock or calendar reminders, HOWEVERRRRRRRRRRR, can we *try* ONLY using it for those necessary things in the morning? Can we avoid clicking through our feeds? Can you get your news from a different source in the early morning hours? How about through a podcast (I LOVE ABC's Start Here w/ Brad Mielke [Brad Mielke feels like my best friend who talks to me every morning])? Watching the news on TV? READING A NEWSPAPER THE OLD WAY?! Give yourself a moment to check in with how YOU feel today before taking on the emotions of how the world is doing today.

Once upon a time, I did a seven-day social media detox. AND IT WAS A ROLLERCOASTER ride of emotions. It really made me look at how much I depend on social media for things like validation, income, news notifications, etc. I realized I couldn't remember what life felt like PRE-SOCIAL MEDIA! And that scared me!!!! HOW DID I CONNECT WITH HUMANS?! HOW DID I KNOW WHAT TIMOTHEE CHALAMET WAS UP TO?! WHAT DID I DO FOR AN ALARM CLOCK?! I wondered if after seven days, I'd revert back to an ignorant, uninformed cavewoman. Jokes aside, I was curious how I'd feel mentally after this detox. I don't want to spoil it, but I felt fucking awesome...but not without struggling at first!

SO CONGRATS, YOU'VE REACHED THE PART OF THE WORKBOOK WITH A SEVEN-DAY SOCIAL MEDIA DETOX CHALLENGE!!!! (plz don't throw this book in the garbage now).

THE DETOX INCLUDES:

Deleting the major social media apps off your phone for seven days. I'm talkin' Twitter, Facebook, Instagram, TikTok, *BUZZFEED, NYT*, Amazon…etc.

When the instinct to open an app comes up, you become mindful of it and ask yourself what are you looking for emotionally right now. Find a backup activity![21] Use the WORD BANK to write down how you feel if you find yourself feeling the same way each day.

DAY 1-7 JOURNAL

DAY 1:

YOU'VE DONE IT! You've committed to the detox! I'm proud of you.
What are you worried about today starting this detox?

_____

_____

_____

What app on your phone do you miss the most already?

_____

Why?

_____

_____

_____

Is there something else you can do right now to alleviate those feelings of discomfort?

_____

_____

---

21 Check out Self-Care Bingo in the Depression section or Self-Care Calendar in the Anxiety section for ideas!

DAY 2:

How did you wake up today without your social media?

_____

_____

_____

Has any part of your routine changed?

_____

_____

_____

If you were going to post a tweet today, what would it be? Write it here:

_____

_____

_____

DAY 3: You're amazing!

When you have the instinct to reach for your phone, can you replace it with a physical activity instead? Maybe ten jumping jacks, a new craft (I like gardening and making stickers!), or some stretches?

_____

_____

_____

Do you feel like you're missing out on anything from the social media apps?

_____

_____

_____

DAY 4: You're more than halfway there!

How do you feel about your relationship with social media? How has it changed in the last five years?

_____

_____

_____

Can you make a list of pros and cons about social media here?

PROS: CONS:

_____   _____

_____   _____

_____   _____

_____   _____

_____   _____

Could you imagine having all the time back in your life that you spent on social media? What would you do with that free time?

_____

_____

_____

DAY 5! ROUNDING THE FINISH LINE!

What's the first thing you're going to do with your social media when the detox is over?

_____

_____

_____

Can you use the time today that you'd normally spend on your phone to

CALL someone and have a convo with them? Who are you going to call??

_____

_____

Have you noticed any physical differences now that you've been off social media for five days? Does your hand hurt less? Your neck? Less eye strain?

_____

_____

_____

DAY 6

Wow. Look at you. Your mind must feel so REFRESHED!

Pick up a newspaper or magazine today and read an article, or read a chapter from a good old-fashioned book. Tell me what you learned here:

_____

_____

_____

Are you ready to go back to your social media life? Or do you think you could hold out even longer?

_____

_____

_____

What's been the hardest part about this detox?

_____

_____

_____

DAY 7—YOU FUCKING DID IT!!!!! YOU ROCK!

HOW DOES IT FEEL!?

_____

_____

_____

Did you check your social media yet?

_____

_____

What are your feelings about resuming use of these apps? *

_____

_____

_____

Set a limit moving forward for how much time you spend on each app.

What was the easiest part of this detox?

_____

_____

How about the hardest?

_____

_____

What friend could you recommend this detox to, and could you do it again with a partner?

_____

_____

If you're not up for a detox (it's cool, baby steps, baby!), try using these tips to limit your social media time:

APPS ARE UR FRIEND

- Download f.lux, an app used to control your screen's color settings to put less strain on your eyes.

- Use TIME OUT, which is an app for your computer that will send you notifications after every 50 minutes of work to take a 10-minute break.

- EyeLeo app has a mascot that comes out to tell you that you should take a break. Then, it gives you a RANGE of different eye exercises to try!! Something as simple as looking at objects that are a different distance away from your computer helps to take the stress off your eyeballs.

- Set a limit on your phone using the Screen Time app for iPhone users. You'll get a notification when it's time to put the phone down!

- TALK ABOUT HOW YOU FEEL ABOUT THE NEWS AND SOCIAL MEDIA! Get it out. Don't let your emotions come out in tweets and troll-y comments. Talk to a real person about how you understand, feel, and process the info coming at you a million miles an hour every day.

- Remember that, even though the Internet is an infinite hole, growing every millisecond, you have limited information; you are only getting one side of the story in that moment with the news and social media. We are complex people, but social media narrows us down to be one person. The news can affect your opinion of an event more than you realize. So choose your sources wisely! Do your research!

How do you think evolution is going to change the way our thumbs grow out to hold our phones? **Draw one of our FUTURE FINGERS here:**

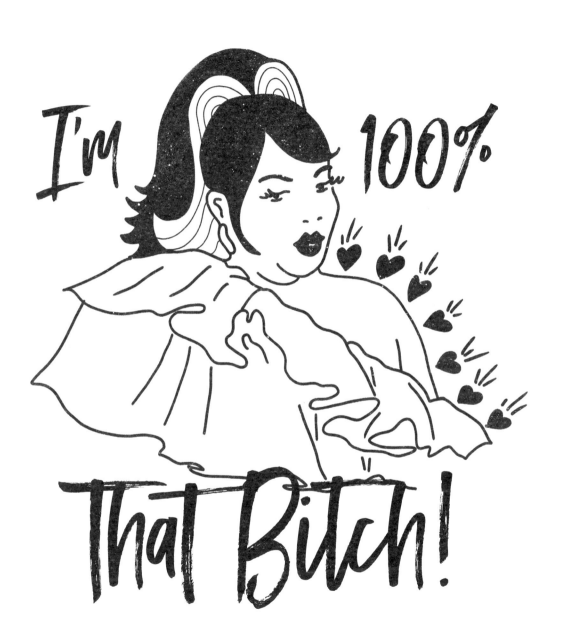

I'm 100% That Bitch!

— LIZZO

NEUROPLASTICITY

(THIS IS A BIG WORD DON'T BE AFRAID)

I know, this sounds like some shit Elon Musk invented in his giant underground spaceship basement, right?

But don't let this sciencey page make you turn away. The easiest way to explain neuroplasticity is that WE KNOW OUR BRAINS CAN CHANGE! Which was a big-ass revolutionary find that came along only in the last two decades! Scientists thought the brain was fully developed by adolescence and early adulthood. It's not that scientists didn't know we could LEARN past that age; rather, they didn't know that:

- you could generate and regenerate NEURONS
- your brain can change its physical structure
- your brain could repair its own damaged regions after stroke, concussions, or other traumatic brain injuries
- your brain can grow new neurons and discard neurons not in use, like bye girl bye, making room, movin' on up

Why does this matter for us who are anxious, panicked, and depressed??

Because you can CHANGE your anxiety, panic, and depression!!! I REPEAT: Your brain is OPEN to learning new ways of managing these disorders. It's not STUCK in your DNA!!

THIS IS THE BEST FUCKING NEWS IN THE WHOLE GODDAMNED WORKBOOK!!!!!

People don't inherit anxiety disorders.[22] Disposition is about 30-40%, but inherited predisposition does not equal disorder. That other 60-70% is about how you relate to those worries/anxious feelings.

Remember: THIS IS GOOD NEWS! You get to be in control of how you relate to anxiety. You can be the COACH of your own brain, body, & emotional team. And it's NEVER TOO LATE TO CHANGE YOUR BRAIN. No matter how fucked-up you might think you are, no matter how many therapists, medications, or meditations that have or haven't worked for you—it's not too late. In fact, the brain MUST change. It's ALWAYS CHANGING!

I interviewed a very smart man who just LOOKS like he knows shit about the brain named Dr. Hill, who explained to me alllllllll about neuroplasticity, because, listen—I wanted to know how to change my brain, but I also didn't want to have to sit through a bunch of boring-ass medical lectures on YouTube I didn't understand. I'm very preachy about learning more about your body so that you are less afraid of it, but when it comes down to the micro-sciencey words and shit, like "NEURONS" and "EKG" and all that mess, my brain straight-up "nopes!" out. So, let me try to break it down, like, in a way that doesn't sound too obscure.

Dr. Hill is the founder and lead neurotherapist of Peak Brain Institute (which I have visited many, many times for neurofeedback therapy!!!), which is kinda like a gym for your brain. What is neurofeedback therapy? Dr. Hill says, "It's not like you're sitting around doing puzzles and Sudoku and solving riddles... We're working on the physiology of your brain. We do something called BRAIN MAPPING, in which we record baseline brain activity and compare it to a database of a few thousand people and see how unusual you are. And people are unusual! Being weird is normal! So we don't go, 'Why aren't you average?' We say, 'Ooh, where is the statistical sore

22 Sorry, you can only blame your parents so much!

thumb?' And sometimes, that means 'X,' so its hypothesis generation process is not really a diagnostic process."

Which makes what Dr. Hill does at the Institute sorta like being a dope cartographer, but instead of world maps, he's helping you read and understand your mind's map! What intrigued me about neurofeedback therapy was, as Dr. Hill mentioned, that it doesn't *really* matter what someone has been diagnosed by a doctor or been labeled by society; with the thousands of brain maps that Dr. Hill has studied, he's able to look at any map results and make a hypothesis about the person without knowing much about their mental-health history. The type of brain waves that Dr. Hill can read give information about everything from sleep, mood, addiction, focus, and creativity, to name a few.

Once the results of any abnormal frequencies are identified, Dr. Hill uses neurofeedback therapy to induce associative learning. Neurofeedback is a type of biofeedback that uses real-time displays of brain activity[23]—most commonly EEG (electroencephalography...I know, big word; it just means they put magnets on your head that can read brainwaves and then project it onto a TV screen where you can watch your brain activity!)—in an attempt to teach self-regulation of brain function. It's not invasive; *it's your brain changing itself.* It's based on a rewards system, so when your brain does something good, the screen will give your brain a reward with a positive sight and sound. If it does something "bad," it won't reward it. So, it becomes an exercise, because they are working to change those brainwaves. All while you sit in a chair and watch a screen because YOU are not changing your brainwaves...the BRAIN ITSELF IS! Fuckin' meta dude, whoahhh.

Neurofeedback therapy isn't the only way to induce your neuroplasticity. Simple things like getting good sleep, reading, and challenging your brain to learn new hobbies—all of these things are like exercise for your head!

If we've learned that the brain can change in only the last two decades, imagine how much more we will learn in the next two. That's why we can't give up hope on ourselves. I think of this often in my deepest bouts of high anxiety, depression, and panic. The times where I most feel like saying, "FUCK IT! I'M OUT! I'm throwing in the towel," I convince myself to believe that perhaps TODAY will be the day that science breaks through the barriers of the unknown and finds some incredible treatment to make my life more manageable! I'd be ROLLIN' IN MY GRAVE (or tbh, laughing from hell) if I chose to "check out of earth permanently" the day they come up with a "cure". I'm certain that we will find out more and more every year to manage our disorders! So, stick with me!!

23 "Neurofeedback." Wikipedia, Wikimedia Foundation, 4 Sept. 2020, en.wikipedia.org/wiki/Neurofeedback.

UNDERSTANDING TYPES OF THERAPY

While there are TONS of types of therapy out there (hello, goat yoga can be considered a form of therapy!), these are the most commonly used for anxiety and panic disorders.

 **ACT**—Acceptance and commitment therapy is a form of psychotherapy and a branch of clinical behavior analysis. It is an empirically-based psychological intervention that uses acceptance and mindfulness strategies mixed in different ways with commitment and behavior-change strategies, to increase psychological flexibility. The objective of ACT is not elimination of difficult feelings; rather, it is to be present with what life brings us and to "move toward valued behavior".[6] Acceptance and commitment therapy invites people to open up to unpleasant feelings and learn not to overreact to them and not avoid situations where they are invoked. Its therapeutic effect is a positive spiral where feeling better leads to a better understanding of the truth.[7] In ACT, 'truth' is measured through the concept of 'workability,' or what works to take another step toward what matters (e.g. values, meaning).[24, 25, 26, 27,28]

 **CBT**—Cognitive Behavioral Therapy is a psycho-social (how environment influences behavior) talk therapy that aims to improve mental health. CBT focuses on challenging and changing unhelpful cognitive distortions and behaviors, improving emotional regulation, and the development of personal coping strategies that target solving current problems. I've done CBT before and would say this is the most common style of therapy used for anxiety disorders.[29]

24 Plumb, Jennifer C, et al. "In Search of Meaning: Values in Modern Clinical Behavior Analysis." *The Behavior Analyst*, The Association for Behavior Analysis, Inc., 2009, www.ncbi.nlm.nih.gov/pmc/articles/PMC2686995/.

25 Hayes, Steven. *Acceptance & Commitment Therapy (ACT)*. contextualscience.org/act.

26 Zettle, Robert D. (2005). "The Evolution of a Contextual Approach to Therapy: From Comprehensive Distancing to ACT". *International Journal of Behavioral Consultation and Therapy*. 1 (2): 77–89. doi:10.1037/h0100736

27 Freeman, Arthur (2010). *Cognitive and Behavioral Theories in Clinical Practice*. New York, NY: The Guilford Press. p. 125. ISBN 978-1-60623-342-9.

28 "Focused Acceptance and Commitment Therapy (FACT): Mastering The Basics." contextualscience.org. Association for Contextual Behavioral Science.

DBT—Dialectical Behavioral Therapy (DBT) is a *type* of cognitive behavioral therapy. DBT aims to help patients identify how their feelings, mood, and behavior all influence each other, just like CBT, but with greater emphasis on *validation* and *mood stability.*[30]

Hypnotherapy—Hypnotherapy is guided hypnosis, or a trance-like state of focus and concentration achieved with the help of a clinical hypnotherapist. This trance-like state is similar to being completely absorbed in a book, movie, music, or even one's own thoughts or meditations. In this state, clients can turn their attention completely inward to find and utilize the natural resources deep within themselves that can help them make changes or regain control in certain areas of their life.[31] I've done hypnotherapy before, and it was like taking the most INSANE WELLNESS NAP of my life! I would recommend starting with free YouTube hypnotherapy sessions to see if it's for you.

Mindfulness therapy—Mindfulness-based Cognitive Therapy (MBCT) is a modified form of cognitive therapy that incorporates mindfulness practices such as meditation and breathing exercises. Using these tools, MBCT therapists teach clients how to break away from negative thought patterns that can cause a downward spiral into a depressed state so they will be able to recognize depression before it takes hold.[32]

EMDR—This one is pretty cool! It's rather new in the world of mental-health treatments, and there are tons of YouTube videos where you can see the processes happening IRL. Eye Movement Desensitization and Reprocessing is a form of psychotherapy developed by Francine Shapiro in the 1990s in which the person being treated is asked to recall distressing images; the therapist then directs the patient in one type of bilateral sensory input, such as side-to-side

28, 30 Association, Author: Canadian Mental Health. "What's the Difference between CBT and DBT?" | *Here to Help*, 2015, www.heretohelp.bc.ca/q-and-a/whats-the-difference-between-cbt-and-dbt.

31 Hypnotherapy. *Psychology Today* in Reference to APA, SCEH, ASCH, www.psychologytoday.com/us/therapy-types/hypnotherapy

32 Abbott, Rebecca A., et al. "Effectiveness of Mindfulness-Based Stress Reduction and Mindfulness-Based Cognitive Therapy in Vascular Disease: A Systematic Review and Meta-Analysis of Randomised Controlled Trials." *Journal of Psychosomatic Research*, vol. 76, no. 5, 2014, pp. 341–351., doi:10.1016/j.jpsychores.2014.02.012.

eye movements or hand-tapping. EMDR therapy facilitates the accessing of the traumatic memory network, so that information processing is enhanced, with new associations forged between the traumatic memory and more adaptive memories or information. These new associations are thought to result in complete information processing, new learning, elimination of emotional distress, and development of cognitive insights.

TLDR: lights in your eyeballs + therapist = can help you alleviate traumatic memories.

Immersion therapy—Immersion therapy (also sometimes referred to as exposure therapy) can help address very specific fears and phobias. I'm sure we've all heard of arachnophobia—fear of spiders, right? Immersion therapy could help with that! First! A fear hierarchy must be created for this therapy to work: The patient is asked a series of questions to determine the level of discomfort the fear causes in various conditions. Can the patient talk about the object of their fear? Can the patient tolerate a picture of it, or watch a movie that has the object of their fear? Can they be in the same room with the object of their fear, and/or can they be in physical contact with it?

Once these questions have been put in order, beginning with least discomfort to most discomfort, the patient is taught a relaxation exercise. Such an exercise might be tensing all the muscles in the patient's body, then relaxing them and saying "relax," and then repeating this process until the patient is calm.

Next, the patient is exposed to the object of their fear under the conditions with which they are most comfortable, such as merely talking about the object of their fear. Then, while in such an environment, the patient performs the relaxation exercise until they are comfortable at that level.

After that, the patient moves up the hierarchy to the next condition, such as a picture or movie of the object of fear, and then to the next level in the hierarchy, and so on, until the patient is able to cope with the fear directly.

Although it may take several sessions to achieve a resolution, the technique is regarded as effective. Many research studies are being conducted with regards to achieving immersion therapy goals in a virtual computer-based program, although results are not conclusive.[33]

---

33 Lamson, Ralph. "Patent for Virtual Reality based Immersion Therapy." U.S. Patent Office.

My therapist had me try this for my fear of small spaces. I was locked in the trunk of a car by some neighborhood kids as a "joke" when I was a kid, and from that moment on, I would always avoid elevators, hiding under the cabinets during hide and seek, and sleeping bags during Girl Scout trips (What if that bitch BRIELLE zipped me up in my sleep?!). I thought it was something I would grow out of, but, even in my late 20s, when I tried doing a FLOAT TANK for my anxiety, I totally panicked 20 minutes into a two-hour session and ended up in the lobby in my swimsuit, looking for any of the workers to double-check that nothing in the room outside of the float tank could fall or be pushed in front of the tank, trapping me in there forever. I know this logic doesn't make sense, but anxiety has no room for logic when we have no tools to LOGICAL-IZE WITH. When I couldn't find any of the workers (because I panic-looked for a whole 25 seconds), I left in my bathing suit and sandals and never went back for my dress. LOL WTF IS WRONG WITH ME? After talking with my therapist about this fear, she had me write a list of 10 things I considered to be claustrophobic, from the easiest things that I could try to do (ride an elevator by myself with no cell phone) to the WORST—which I determined, for me, would be cave diving. Somewhere in the middle was "getting in the trunk of a car," and we decided to work up to that. After riding elevators and spending a lot of alone time in my walk-in closet, well...

(Conversation between my therapist Kim and I, summer 2019; she was VERY proud of me.)

KELSEY: *Hey there! Guess what! I GOT IN THE TRUNK OF THE CAR YESTERDAY!*

THERAPIST KIM: *WHAAATTTTTTT!!!! You go girl!!!! You cannot just tell me that...what are the details! What happened? How are you feeling now? I am so proud of you!!!*

KELSEY: *It was CRAZY. I started with just sitting in the back with a friend of mine. I couldn't get in so I just kinda hung my legs out the sides of the doors. It was pretty funny and must have looked crazy to any passersby. Then when my boyfriend got back into town, we used our car which has a very spacious trunk. We tried about 15 different methods before actually closing the trunk—we tried with my hands out, with the doors open and the seats laid down, with the flashlights, etc. The closest feeling I got to the discomfort was when I was laying on my back looking at the top of the trunk and I was instantly transported back to childhood— and I could remember the exact feeling and what I was doing pounding on the door of the trunk and screaming and kicking my little legs. I got super nervous but I think the wading into the water rather than jumping right in right helped. Finally, I was able to shut the trunk all the way and use the emergency hatch to get out! It* *was super freeing and awesome to have my boyfriend there to see it happen. He's been with me on so many plane trips where I've freaked out so it was great to see some progress made. I was SHOCKED to see how big of a deal it WASN'T!!*

THE "GOOD THINGS" JAR

Grab one of those mason jars that they seem to sell on every fuckin' block now (SIDEBAR: How do farmers feel about the gentrification of mason jars????), cut up a piece of paper, and write down some really dope moments in your life. I'm talking about BIG ACCOMPLISHMENTS (Babies! Weddings! Pets! Job success!), little accomplishments (Nailed your winged liner! Didn't shit your pants when you farted earlier! Finished something on your to-do list!), happy memories (First time you met your best friend! A great holiday or vacation! Last day of school!). How about even writing down times you were anxious/scared/unsure, but things worked out!?

Next time you're having a rough time, pull one slip out of the GOOD THINGS jar and read it. Read it again. Read each word. Try to remember the moment as vividly as possible.

Who was there?

_____

_____

_____

What did it feel like in your body during this moment?

_____

_____

_____

What did it smell like?

_____

_____

What about it made you so happy?

_____

_____

_____

_____

Feel the slip of paper until you can recognize that small tiny little feeling in your gut, butt, or brain that is *happiness*. Then, try to expand on that happy feeling! Do a little dance in your room! Treat yourself to a delish snack! Watch a funny TikTok compilation!

If you can muster it, take a blank slip and write down a new dope thing to replace the one you pulled.

I can tell you from personal experience that it will feel so good to pull out an older "good thing" slip and remember how dope you are and how far you've come.

DIGITAL GOOD THINGS JAR If you're not looking to add a *tchotchke* jar full of good memories because maybe it doesn't match your decor...?? Try using FutureMe.org, which is a website that allows you to write a letter to the "future" you. It's not necessarily readily available at a moment's notice for when you need it like the good things jar, but it's a very cute idea that is a wonderful little reminder of your progress. On the website, you can choose what date you want to send the letter to yourself, or the automatic option of one year, three years, or five years. I did one to myself last year and had totally forgotten that I had filled it out. When it popped up in my inbox, it completely brightened my morning and made me LOL about the things that I thought that were stressful in my life a year prior that had worked out or that I'd totally forgotten about!

ANXIETY TIPS
FOR PARTNERS

Before you pass this chapter to your partner, I have a couple things to say to you, lovely reader:

> Remember that *you can choose your support system.* You are in control. It doesn't need to be biological, relational, or even IRL. You can find someone you feel comfortable with, and maybe that's a social media friend, a pet...etc.

SUPPORT does not mean:

- Feeling like you're walking on eggshells talking about mental health with this person.
- Lying about your feelings to them.
- Being afraid of their reactions.
- Them defending unhealthy choices.
- Remaining loyal to your old patterns because they say so.
- Sacrificing your own needs to save or fix someone else!

With that said, the most important part of having a support system starts with your own acceptance. **In order for your significant other to be accepting of your mental health, YOU have to be accepting of yourself.** It doesn't mean you're supposed to have it all figured out, or be in a "good mental headspace," but you do need to recognize that you are in a place of being able to accept help. Asking for help is hard, and it takes a lot of bravery to put yourself out there like that. But **YOU are the only one who can manage your mental health**. Therapists, loved ones, self-help books—it's all great SUPPORT, but YOU and only you have the power to accept the help and find peace. Know that you ARE ALLOWED TO ASK FOR HELP! Humans aren't meant to do this "life" thing all by themselves. You are allowed to ask the universe for what you want and identify your needs.

If you don't like who you become during high anxiety/panic attacks/depressive episodes, give that version of yourself a name! Then, you and your partner can talk like you're speaking about someone else. It deserves a separate name because it's *not who you are*. It's a heightened or lowered version of yourself. Just a part of you. Some might even agree that it's, chemically, a different version of yourself in these moments. Maybe your medication (if you choose to take that) is giving you unhelpful side effects. My anxiety/stress/panic/depressive ego's name is RILEY. In an example with my current partner, Jared, if I am feeling insecure, I can say "Right now, Riley (a.k.a. my anxiety brain, panic rush, depressive episode) is telling me you don't love me, and please know that you can't personalize that info right now." It's a more understandable way of telling him what my needs are in this moment and being VERY VULNERABLE about it! I'm admitting I need help and, even more specifically, I'm letting him know I need a certain type of help (love, reassurance, physical touch, etc.). It is helpful for the other person when you can give them a task or end goal. If you are able to acknowledge that it's anxiety outside of the relationship, then we're able to blame the <u>anxiety</u> and not <u>each other</u>. Even though all this anxiety, panic, and depression is PART of me, it is not ALL OF ME.

Also, make an A, B, and C-team for yourself. The same way we have emergency contacts for regular life, make an anxiety/panic/depression emergency contact list. Your A-team can consist of the people closest to you, the ones you feel comfortable admitting all your feelings and thoughts to in times of crisis. Your B-team can be your acquaintances, or perhaps even an online support group or Facebook page that you can go into and talk with others. Your C-group can be the last resort, but usually involves spending a little bit of money if your A & B team don't work out, if they're busy, or they don't pick up the phone, or they are not in an emotional space to help right now, etc. I'm talking about the C-team as a therapy appointment, an emergency panic trip to urgent care, maybe even a yoga class... etc. C-team should be your last resort.

Go over your emotional needs and appropriate times to reach out with the A-team (maybe they have a tough working schedule, or they have kids), and protect those boundaries. Ask them if there are specific times they are not able to help you (maybe

Tuesday nights are date nights with their partner and they won't have their phone on volume), or create a code word that they can use to let you know they aren't emotionally available for you.

We can ALL work on giving ourselves a little bit of grace when we are able to separate the disorders from ourselves. Your anxiety is not who you are; it's a PART of you. It's where you ask yourself questions that, if you didn't have anxiety, you wouldn't ask. "Are you sure you love me?" "Am I annoying you?" "Are you sure you didn't look at that other girl?" Doubts and insecurity don't *just* come from low self-worth or self-esteem; anxiety disorders can act like a fuel to the fire that might be stress, past trauma popping up, a tough day, or chemical imbalance.

Remember: Everyone has baggage. Our goal is to make sure your baggage is just a carry-on and not a big-ass duffel full of bricks that you need to check in and pay an overweight fee for. The best way to receive help is with *honest* and *positive* support, and we can do that here by learning about attachment style, personality types, and fighting style.

I have to remind myself often how much Jared really has been there for me without expecting anything in return. I try, as much as I can, to find a way to show him how grateful I am for his support (blowjobs) without OVER apologizing or making the relationship's "scales" feel unbalanced. Here are some ways I say "thank you for being there" to a partner who has shown unwavering support without being repetitive or apologetic (besides lots of blowjobs):

- "It's an honor that we found each other and the universe didn't choose to separate us by space and time."
- "My world is better with you in it."
- "Laughing and smiling with you is the best cure."
- "You know me as well as I know myself and sometimes I need that second perspective to heal."

FOR PARTNERS

Hiiiiii. Thanks for reading this. *It probably means more than you know or realize* to the person who gave it to you.

THAT BEING SAID: **You cannot fix someone else.** You are there to support them, not fix them. Fill your own cup first, then give from the overflow. So, take that weight off your shoulders. It's been scientifically proven that the warmth of our relationships across life has the greatest impact on life satisfaction. CONGRATS! You're a big deal in someone's life. The more social support someone has, the better their chances of living longer are! So, helping your partner while coming from a positive and supportive place is not only helping them manage their daily lives, but helping them live longer!

However, relationships can also be one of our biggest struggles and causes of stress.

As a partner, when experiencing shitty times in this relationship due to mental-health struggles, are you:

More over-involved or uninvolved? _____

Do you listen or lecture? _____

Shut down or attend to? _____

We want to figure out what we can do or NOT do that will positively impact the relationship. **Check in with your partner during a rough time by first assessing the H.A.L.T.:**

- **H—Are they hungry?**
- **A—Is there anger in their actions or dialogue?**
- **L—Do they feel lonely in their struggle?**
- **T—Are they tired?**

Assessing the HALT can help you to get past the stuck points that everyone deals with. When the HALT is addressed, we can move into MENTALIZATION. Mentalization is the ability to understand the mental state of oneself or others that underlies overt behavior. Can you put yourself in your partner's shoes and really feel what they are feeling? Are they able to communicate those feelings to you clearly? If not, can you empathize with their frustration that they CAN'T communicate to you right now?

Be cautious about GIVING UNSOLICITED ADVICE. Especially if you don't deal with chronic mental health issues yourself. It can feel demeaning and belittling. Unfortunately, how they decide to balance themselves isn't up to you but you can be there to give gentle suggestions when, over time, you learn the patterns of their mental illness. YOU HAVE A CHOICE. And know that you are not a bad person if you do not think you are able to be in a partnership that requires certain emotional labor from you. Your partner deserves someone who can. So have a real come-to-Buddha convo with yourself.

Are you willing to not advise without asking first? _____

Are you willing to do some reading or listening to talks, articles, podcasts, and lectures about mental health? _____

Are you able to tell the difference between minimizing, gaslighting, and projecting? _____

HOW TO HELP YOUR PARTNER
THROUGH A CRISIS

☀ W. O. W. ☀

REMEMBER: **If your partner is in crisis to a point where you feel unsafe or feel that they are unsafe to be alone, always call a crisis hotline.** ALWAYS.

This might feel tough because your partner might tell you that they don't need the outside help or that you are betraying them by calling for help. However, you are only one person. You are doing your best. And it's ALWAYS better to be safe than sorry in extreme instances.* You always have the option to opt out during times of these extreme crises. But please, make sure there is a backup person that is capable of understanding the situation. Let your partner know that you are unable to be their primary support system if they are unwilling the get the help that they need.

*Given the current climate with the police and mental health crises, I would advise against calling 911. I do not believe police officers are as trained as crisis hotline workers to handle such intense moments of emotional distress. If there is violence or psychosis outside of your partner's control, allow the crisis hotline to make that call to emergency services. I think the world has a lot of work to do in this sector. You can also consider taking them to the ER or urgent care.

1. Tell them 'thank you' for trusting you enough to confide in you and that you acknowledge this must be super hard for them.

2. When asking what got them to this point, actively listen but don't interrupt. Nodding your head or eye-contact is good.

3. Take time to repeat back to them what you heard without judgment and ask them if you are missing anything.

4. VALIDATE THEM. Language like "no wonder you're upset" or "I can see why" is helpful.

5. Signal openness and that you are willing to offer support if they want it.

6. Tap into your own emotions to signal how and why you care about them.

7. Show trust and belief in them that they can handle anything, even if it doesn't feel like it right now.

8. Ask them to agree to a safety plan: whether that be going for a walk, calling a friend or therapist, sleeping over, anything you guys can do together while still giving them emotional freedom to react.

9. Do your best to help them enact measures of recovery when they feel ready. Maybe they just need to sleep on it. Know that the crisis doesn't necessarily need to be solved right in this moment.

10. Check in with yourself. Are you able to be there for this person from a place of peace and honesty from within yourself?

COMMUNICATIONS WORKSHEET

When my partner is _____

(anxious, having a panic attack, being difficult, angry, distressed), **I feel**

_____

(helpless, fed-up, worried, sad, disappointed). **When I feel this way about it, I tend to**

_____

(shut down, try to fix it, give in, express my disappointments, help, show love).

I do this in hopes that

_____

(it will help my partner feel better, help them take responsibility for their actions or life). **My biggest fear is that**

_____

(they won't get better, that I've failed them as a partner, we will break up).

If things are still rough between the two of you, try a VALUES exercise. Each of you will write down your top 10 values in life. That is, what do you value most out of a life that feels "well-lived"? What is a value you strive for? If you need help thinking of values, type in "values exercise" in Google and the first link will download a PDF list of values such as: peace, security, love, adventure, etc. After you've both written down ten values, share your list with each other and compare. Talk about why those values made it where it landed on your list. Did you learn anything new about each other?

My three musketeers are my sister, Megan, my mom, Kristy, and my best friend, Lacey. I don't know what I did to deserve them, but I got very lucky, in that they understood some of this crazy shit I was going through. With over 10 years of experience, it feels like *they* also live with my anxiety disorder. **So, I asked them what advice they had for partners who need help supporting someone they love with anxiety or panic disorder:**

MEGAN (MY SISTER):

When you have someone in your life who suffers from panic attacks, it's not uncommon to see their name pop up on caller ID at 3 in the morning. Always answer. You might be that person's only chance at being able to catch their breath or get into a safe space mentally. It might also feel like you have nothing scholarly, therapeutic, or intelligent to say at that hour...hell, even during normal hours of the day...but reminding your friend/loved one to focus on their breath, and telling them that you are always here for them, is ALWAYS a pretty awesome response.

KRISTY (MY MOM):

Picture a small kitten who unexpectedly fell into a rolling river and is rapidly approaching a waterfall. The panic and terror in their eyes! But you can see a clear path ahead as a parent (I also suffered from panic attacks for 20 years)...You know there is a safe island ahead and you know they will be safe. They don't know it, though. All they know is the overwhelming sense of terror...Because YOU know that it will be OK, it gives you the confidence to walk them through the ride...as it breaks your heart. Sometimes, it's just as simple as having their mind off the situation...Comforting may take many shapes. Sometimes, you have to get on the first flight across the country to them... Other times is just a simple conversation. Just let them know that they are not crazy...That this will pass...That you are there for them no matter what!

LACEY (MY BEST FRIEND):

There is only one question to ask when someone is having a panic attack: What do you need? Never: What's wrong? What happened? What are you freaking out about? Because that person usually has no idea, and the more you try to "fix it," the longer it will last. All that person might need is a glass of water, or a hug, or just you in the room, and sometimes the answer will be "I don't know," and that's okay, too. Try a bunch of stuff, and don't be discouraged if they are short with you or push you away. It's not about you*.

* I LOVE a point that Lacey makes here. Please don't take anything personally when we precious, sensitive beans are "going through it."

IF YOUR PARTNER IS AVOIDING YOU, IT COULD BE FOR MANY REASONS OUTSIDE OF SOMETHING RELATED TO YOU PERSONALLY

For instance:

1. They might be overwhelmed with work.

2. They might need to process trauma alone.

3. They might be embarrassed or confused about the way they are feeling.

4. They might be tired. It takes a lot more energy to exist with an anxiety, panic, or depressive disorder than society realizes.

5. They might just need some space. Space isn't a bad thing. Space is good! Space apart keeps a relationship healthy and fresh. Your partner might need to reset themselves in a private manner.

HERE ARE SOME ALTERNATIVE OPTIONS YOU CAN TRY WITH AN AVOIDANT PARTNER

1. Sit beside them, saying nothing. Just being there, sometimes, is enough.

2. Give them a hug.

3. Send them an edible arrangement.

4. Put their favorite movie on in the background.

5. Make them a snack or their favorite meal.

6. Remind them that they are loved and you are there when they feel ready.

7. Try writing down the things that you want to say to them and revisit the note when they are ready to read it.

WORD BANK

Here is a list of words that you can use to help describe your feelings and needs. I have a hard time thinking AT ALL when I'm panicking. Come to this page when you need help describing how you feel:

Sad, happy, *carefree*, ANXIOUS, depressed, **ANGRY**, hurt, **peaceful**, curious, *tranquil*, ANNOYED, uneasy, **DEFENSIVE**, irrational, **complacent**, *absorbed*, ALERT, shocked, **ATTACKED**, energized, **enchanted**, troubled, envious, lonely, stunned, stressed, unsupported, **disrespected**, *irate*, TENDER, warm, **EXHAUSTED**, connected, **empowered**, blissful, *unsafe*, APPREHENSIVE, serene, **JOYOUS**, afraid, **dreadful**, accepted, *foreboding*, FRIGHTENED, distrustful, **PETRIFIED**, scared, **suspicious**, terrified, *wary*, WORRIED, annoyed, **CLOSED OFF**, confused, **loving**, aggravated, *appreciated*, EMPATHETIC, dismayed, **DISGRUNTLED**, frantic, **displeased**, loved, *exasperated*, FRUSTRATED, grateful, **IMPATIENT**, respected, **irked**, enraged, *peaceful*, FURIOUS, livid, **RESENTFUL**, honest, **free**, appalled, *safe*, CONTEMPTUOUS, disgusted, **HORRIFIED**, stimulated, **secure**, hostile, *boggled*, OPTIMISTIC, dazed, **SUPPORTED**, lost, **hesitant**, self-preserving, *trustful*, PERPLEXED, appreciative, **PUZZLED**, independent, **torn**, calm, *disconnected*, ALIENATED, aloof, **BORED**, adventurous, **cold**, detached, *distant*, DISTRACTED, numb, **REMOVED**, uninterested, **withdrawn**, alarmed, *discombobulated*, DISTURBED, rattled, **FRAGILE**, vulnerable, **self-caring**, restless, *surprised*, TURBULENT, uncomfortable, **EMBARRASSED**, ashamed, **shameful**, guilty, *flustered*, MORTIFIED, self-conscious, **FATIGUED**, burnt out, **depleted**, lethargic, *sleepy*, TIRED, weary, **WORN-OUT**, pained, **anguished**, heartbroken, *miserable*, REGRETFUL, remorseful, **NOSTALGIC**, dejected, **forlorn**, gloomy, *heavy-hearted*, HOPELESS, unhappy, **CRANKY**, edgy, **fidgety**, frazzled, *irritable*, JITTERY, overwhelmed, **VULNERABLE**, fragile, **guarded**, helpless, *insecure*, RESERVED, sensitive, **UNACCEPTED**, affected, **secure**, supported, *spontaneous*, MANIC, hyper, **DISTRACTED**, triggered, **powerful**, yikes-y, *fearful*, BREATHLESS, restless, **WORRIED**, bitter, **cross**, moved, *quiet*, SATISFIED, proud, **ALIVE**, amazed, **adventurous**, (and my favorite) MEHHHH.

Also, lol, if you read this whole list really fast, that's basically what it feels like being in someone's head that lives with anxiety, depression, or panic.

(*Pssst...you can download a copy of this—see the Resource Index.*)

PANIC

The WTF World of Panic Attacks, Panic Disorder, & Emotional Heart Attacks

HOW TO MANAGE A PANIC ATTACK

RIGHT NOW (OR, AT LEAST TRY)

The first two steps are the most important. The rest of them can be skipped around or used as needed.

1. **Read this over and over, letting it sink in.** Look at EACH WORD individually and let your brain register what it means. **Start over or read it a few times through if needed:**

PANIC IS A VERY REAL AND INTENSE FORM OF ANXIETY, WHICH IS A COMPLETELY NORMAL RESPONSE TO STRESS. Even if I cannot pinpoint the stress at this exact moment, my brain and body are trying to protect me. I will not judge if it is right or wrong. I will get through these TEMPORARY feelings of discomfort. This will not last forever, and these feelings will subside. Panic attacks are a biochemical response and I am not in danger. THANK YOU, BODY, FOR TRYING TO PROTECT! I can breathe. If I can talk and sing and hum, that is sheer proof that I am breathing. I will not over-breathe, as that will make things feel more intense. I will let my body do its natural thing. I am in good health. My body and brain may not be on the same page as to why we are feeling these physical/emotional/mental feelings, but I will now find a way to connect to myself. The panic symptoms feel scary, but I will get better at managing them. THIS WILL

PASS. THIS WILL PASS. THIS WILL PASS. I AM SAFE. I AM LOVED. I WILL FEEL BETTER SOON. I WILL FEEL BETTER SOON.

REMIND YOURSELF: No one in the HISTORY OF THE WORLD has ever been stuck in the feeling of panic permanently. It's physically and physiologically IMPOSSIBLE. This WILL pass. You can prepare yourself to feel a little weird for some time after this passes (usually an hour), but beyond that, focus on just getting through these next few minutes.

2. **BREATHE:** You need to SLOW YOUR BREATHING, even if you feel like you can't catch your breath. I know, it's ass-backwards. But *hyperventilation* is hurting you right now. You probably feel like you can't get enough air in your lungs, so you are OVER-BREATHING! Yes, that's a thing! Over-breathing is going to make you feel WAY more panicked. By *over-breathing*, your brain thinks you are purposely trying to feed more oxygen into your body for a reason it isn't understanding. So, your brain (trying to be the supportive and faithful friend we all need in times of trauma) is trying to keep up with your over-breathing by turning on all the knobs and buttons it would in an oxygen-deprived situation. In turn, your brain is going to heighten your heart rate, set off the alarms for fight or flight, and perpetuate the cycle. Hyperventilation can cause chest pain, too, and we don't like that shit, do we?! **So, the sooner we slow down that breathing, the better your physical symptoms will feel, too.** If your mouth is dry, get some water if possible, or run your mouth under a sink. The quickest and easiest way to slow your breath is with SQUARE BREATHING. Draw a big square in your mind's eye, or with your finger on a surface in front of you. With each line of the square you draw, you breathe in; when you make the next line, you hold your breath. On the next line, you breathe out and hold it again as you draw the final line to make a box. Continue. See if you can make these breaths last at least four seconds each at first, then five, then six, then seven. You got this.

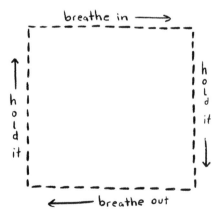

3. **Shifting focus is key for panic attacks.** We want to break the thought loops that are happening at rapid speed for you. Wiggle your toes on the ground or against your shoes to ground yourself. Perhaps you can't get your thoughts straight enough to read this sentence—if that's the case, go back to #1. Your

thoughts may feel garbled or not make any sense. AND THAT'S OKAY! THAT'S 100% SUPPOSED to happen during a panic attack! Remind yourself that your thoughts are JUST THOUGHTS. They are NOT FACTS. You are not your thoughts. You are the observer who gets to choose what you do with those thoughts. Do not feel compelled to "fix" them right now. Repeat out loud or in your head: THOUGHTS ARE JUST THOUGHTS; they are not facts. For example, I can have the thought of a unicorn butt-fucking a peanut butter and jelly sandwich, but that doesn't mean there is a real unicorn butt-fucking a PB&J right now. So, perhaps your brain right now is telling you to PANIC THERE IS SOMETHING WRONG, and even in a high-stress situation, we want to break those thought loops and look at the facts:

Remember, *facts are things that exist outside of our own feelings*. Judgments are not justified. **Tell me some FACTS**[34] **right now about your surroundings:**

_____

_____

_____

_____

THE FIVE SENSES GROUNDING EXERCISE: To break your focus on your internal symptoms and feelings, let's think about the here and now *beyond the panic attack*. Let's get out of our own way for a moment. Counting can be the quickest way to shift focus, as it doesn't require a lot of thought change. Start counting things around you. It can be anything! Tiles on the ceiling...number of snacks in front of you, etc. In the order of the five senses:

- What five things can you see?
- What five things can you smell?
- What five things can you hear?
- What five things can you taste?
- What five things could you touch?

If someone is with you, that can support you through this attack. I like to have them ask me the questions and keep going in a loop until I feel calmer. I also like to try to sync my breathing to theirs while doing so.

34 Review Facts vs Feelings in the Intrusive Thoughts chapter for more.

4. **Remember: THIS MOMENT IS NOT EVERY MOMENT.**

   Tell yourself that YOU ARE GOING TO BE UNCOMFORTABLE FOR A LITTLE WHILE. Give yourself permission to FEEL WEIRD! THIS WILL SUBSIDE! You just need to distract yourself for the next five or ten minutes and HANG ON!

   My therapist said, in order to be the victor, you have to heal the victim. So, don't "push it" by forcing yourself to "get over it" right now. Your body needs to "heal" in a sense by calming your sympathetic nervous system.

5. **Try splashing some cool water on your face, or, if you're home, jump in a cold shower.** Cool water can help activate the vagus nerve, which helps lower your heart rate. Remember, you WANT to slow the heart rate, even if your symptoms are telling you otherwise. For more info on this, look at step #2.

6. **Notice if you are *catastrophizing* symptoms.** It's true: You are absolutely feeling symptoms (heart racing, increased blood glucose, overwhelming sense of impending doom, inability to explain your thoughts, sweating, nausea), and your body is feeling something MORE THAN STRESS, but see if you can equate this rise as a *response of safety* instead of *betrayal* from your body and mind.

7. **Some people like to talk through their panic out loud.** It can feel like our thoughts are jumbled and swirling, and even just making some noises out loud can help. If you're in an environment to do so, try letting whatever sound come out of your mouth that your body needs to make. ROAR, if you need to! Scream! Laugh! Whatever you need to do to get some energy out of your body.

☀W.O.W.☀
Essential oil aromas, like lavender, can help.
I carry a roller ball wherever I go!

8. **Find something physical that makes you happy and take it out during this panic.** The key is to focus on how it feels in your hand in every aspect. Tell me every single little detail about this item. Try to draw the item from memory.

9. **If you feel it's necessary, or that it might be helpful, give your therapist a call/text or email.** Don't expect them to pick up or be able to answer right

away (another good reason as to why relying on other people to "stop" your panic might not be helpful in the long run). Let them know you had a panic attack and that you'd like to speak with them about it. Maybe it's over text or FaceTime, or, if you're still struggling with the aftershock, you'd like to come in and speak with them about it and find out together where things felt like they got out of control. Even if you calm down and cancel, just knowing you've made an appointment with a professional may calm your worry right now. Reach out to your A, B, and C teams.[35]

If you are feeling your symptoms a little less...even JUST A LITTLE! FOR EVEN A MOMENT! That's a good thing!!!! And means your brain or body understood and recognized some of the words you just took in. Try to go back to the list above and do any of the things you couldn't previously.

As UNUSUAL as you feel, remind yourself that **YOU ARE NOT ALONE IN THIS EXPERIENCE**. *There are millions of people all across the world of many different positions, ages, races, and economic statuses that have felt what you are feeling now.* No thoughts or feelings are "too crazy" to feel right now. Panic attacks fucking SUCKKKKKK. THEY SUCK. I wouldn't wish panic attacks on my worst enemy. They are the scariest, total mind-fuck, SUCK-ASS things to go through. I am SO SORRY you are experiencing them. But you are not alone. You are doing it. And you are going to survive.

The more this happens to you (as annoying and unfortunate as that is), YOU WILL GET BETTER AT MANAGING IT. You will start to recognize symptoms, and you will feel more confident and strong when you recognize what it is; it won't be so scary when you can recognize it. **The symptoms might not get easier, BUT YOU WILL GET STRONGER.**

After the attack has settled, you are going to feel completely drained. This is the aftermath of a panic attack. It's normal to feel shaky or unsteady, even nervous that the attack will return, which might leave you in a heightened state of awareness while your body deals with the exhaustion of what it just went through. This is a crucial time to be kind to yourself. To take what you need. Can you possibly leave work? Take your lunch break early? Ask for some space wherever you are? Can you get outside and go for a walk? Use the restroom as privacy if the outside world feels too big right now.

---

35 For more on building your teams, turn to page 170.

MANAGING PANIC: A QUICK VISUAL FLOWCHART

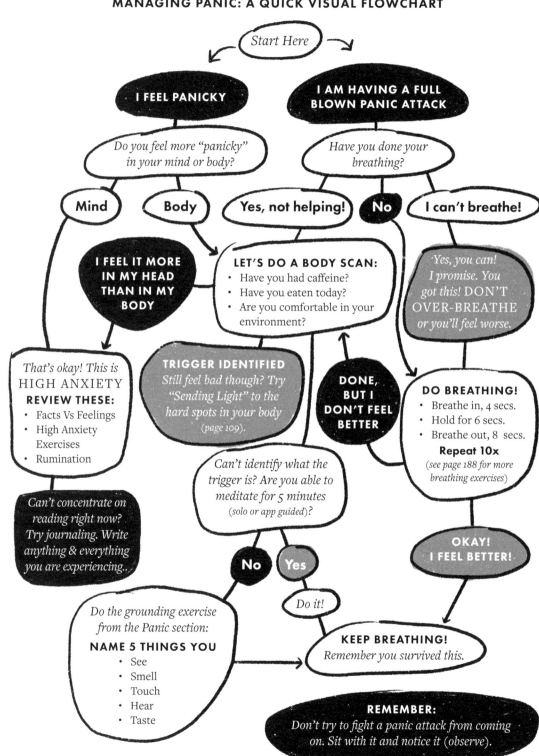

Start Here

I FEEL PANICKY

Do you feel more "panicky" in your mind or body?

Mind

Body

I AM HAVING A FULL BLOWN PANIC ATTACK

Have you done your breathing?

Yes, not helping!

No

I can't breathe!

I FEEL IT MORE IN MY HEAD THAN IN MY BODY

LET'S DO A BODY SCAN:
- Have you had caffeine?
- Have you eaten today?
- Are you comfortable in your environment?

Yes, you can! I promise. You got this! DON'T OVER-BREATHE *or you'll feel worse.*

That's okay! This is HIGH ANXIETY
REVIEW THESE:
- Facts Vs Feelings
- High Anxiety Exercises
- Rumination

TRIGGER IDENTIFIED
Still feel bad though? Try "Sending Light" to the hard spots in your body (page 109).

DONE, BUT I DON'T FEEL BETTER

DO BREATHING!
- Breathe in, 4 secs.
- Hold for 6 secs.
- Breathe out, 8 secs.
Repeat 10x
(see page 188 for more breathing exercises)

Can't concentrate on reading right now? Try journaling. Write anything & everything you are experiencing..

Can't identify what the trigger is? Are you able to meditate for 5 minutes (solo or app guided)?

No

Yes

Do it!

OKAY! I FEEL BETTER!

Do the grounding exercise from the Panic section:
NAME 5 THINGS YOU
- See
- Smell
- Touch
- Hear
- Taste

KEEP BREATHING!
Remember you survived this.

REMEMBER:
Don't try to fight a panic attack from coming on. Sit with it and notice it (observe).

Notice I didn't use the word STOP your panic attack for this chapter, eh? If the idea is to stop something, and it doesn't work on the first try, our bodies can go into even more panic and start spiraling! **Panic attacks aren't meant to be FOUGHT or STOPPED or CONTROLLED (especially controlled).** Many experts, blogs, and videos will tell you that you need to RIDE THE WAVE of panic.

Learn to become nonjudgmental about these physical symptoms, which, FUCKING TRUST ME, is a lot easier said than done. I know it can feel IMPOSSIBLE right now to imagine feeling all Switzerland about a panic attack, especially when the main symptom causes you to feel pretty much the opposite of neutral. But as someone who suffered for many, many years in many, many different ways, I can tell you that it IS possible. More to come...but, the first step to getting there is on the next pages about the fight, flight, and freeze response...

EXPERIENCE YOUR EMOTIONS

Your emotions are like waves going in and out of the ocean. Don't try to get rid of them, push them away, or ignore them. Don't suppress or block them. The opposite is also true: Don't try to keep unhelpful emotions around. Don't hold onto them. Don't amplify them. Ride the waves.

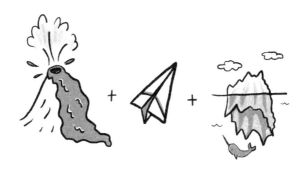

UNDERSTANDING FIGHT-OR-FLIGHT RESPONSE

AND ITS NEWEST MEMBER OF THE FAMILY,
FREEZE, AND DISTANT COUSIN, **FAWN**

Most people have heard of "fight or flight" without knowing exactly what the body is doing when it happens. Is it adrenaline? Your survival instinct? And what the hell takes control over me when this happens? That big ol' swell of panic you feel RIGHT when a panic attack starts is your fight-or-flight (or freeze or fawn) response!

The part of your brain that controls emotion (me remembering that I have a poor, poor double Gemini rising & moon'd brain) is called your LIMBIC system. The limbic system is part of an autonomic system that largely functions UNCONSCIOUSLY, so you don't even freaking have much of a choice when this system's fire alarm goes off! Which is why panic attacks can feel like they "come out of nowhere." Cause they're KINDA comin' from your "nowhere:" your mystic, self-regulating, responsive bodily function, the part of your brain where you don't have awareness of THINKING!!! This limbic system is *supposed* to keep you safe, but sometimes will sense danger, trauma, or stress when your eyeballs don't see it. Whether or not it's right (and it's a dick like that, not being able to admit when it's wrong), it will set off the fight, flight, freeze, or fawn response.

- **Fight:** This reaction can come from a place of aggression or anger while also feeling prepared, as if you have tools or weapons as a defense. You'll wanna put your war paint on and shout into the battlefield of your body. But resist, warrior. This cannot be solved with violence or anger.

- **Flight:** You, your brain, and your body have left the building and want no part of this narrative. You have straight up NOPE'd outta feeling this mess of emotion. It can quite literally cause you to LEAVE the current situation you are in. We don't want this response, either, because we don't want you to dip out every time you feel uncomfy. Those panic symptoms ain't goin' nowhere fast, no matter where you run off to *they will find you*. We gotta address the symptoms head on, baby! I am with you!

- **Freeze:** This newer term is kinda like when your body's reaction is to play possum, hoping you can play "dead," a.k.a. FREEZE, and the problem goes away. Trauma isn't just thinking about the past, but rather how it replays in our body in this present moment, so sometimes, people who freeze can even lose their awareness in the stressful environment, i.e., dissociating, memory loss, brain fog, etc. This doesn't work because...well, you have to come back eventually and face your fears!

- **Fawn:** The fresh baby of this F-Family "seeks safety by merging with the wishes, needs, and demands of others," writes Pete Walker, the therapist who coined the concept of fawning as the fourth F. "They act as if they unconsciously believe that the price of admission to any relationship is the forfeiture of all their needs, rights, preferences, and boundaries." These people tend to apologize profusely and/or over-flatter to take the stress and attention off themselves. Not putting yourself and your needs first?! I WILL NOT ALLOW IT!

In panic, you can be a combo of all four at different times! Sound familiar? You get angry and try to fight the bubbling feeling that's coming up. You may take "flight" in a physical way, such as standing up suddenly, or needing to take a walk so as to not lose your shit in front of people. You might even freeze by dissociating, or not remembering the panic attack ENTIRELY because your brain wants to protect you from it, or fawn, in the sense that you overly apologize to the people around you for what's happening to you.

A key point in understanding panic response is recognizing when the fight, flight, freeze, or fawn is happening and not faulting yourself for it. That key moment of feeling that ~*feeling*~ and, if you've had a panic attack before, you know what feeling I'm referring to. It's a micro-moment where things feel...*off*. It might be recognizable, like, "Oh, fuck, I'm about to get that WAVE of panic," or it might be a new feeling that totally takes you off your feet. **Usually, people won't know how they**

react in a traumatic crisis until it happens to them! There is no "right" way that your body will react to panic! And, as you learn more about managing your panic, you will become familiar with these responses. No one is immune to those physical responses our unconscious creates. It's about learning how to recognize when it's happening and not trying to stop or fight it. You'll know what it is because you've become familiar with it, and you'll learn how to let it pass through your body. It's not easy, and, unfortunately, it requires a type of "practice" I wouldn't wish on anyone, but, if you're having regular panic attacks, this UNDERSTANDING of what is happening to you is a KEY PART of not freaking the fuck out when a panic attack does come. Again, the more you know, the less scary it becomes. It may still happen (or may disappear completely, because you'll feel it and your brain will go "oh nvm u got this? cool"), but you'll handle it better and better each time.

I know what you're thinking, because I thought the same thing the first time someone told me that eventually, I'd be chill about having panic attacks....ARE YOU FUCKING CRAZY HOW THE FUCK AM I SUPPOSED TO DO THAT?! Well, that's what this chapter is all about!! Giving you those tools, not so that you can FIGHT your panic (it's not your enemy, remember, it's your cute li'l brain trying to SAVE you from something it thinks is scary! We should be thanking our li'l brains and saying awww, I'm okay, not now, li'l brain), but so you will have the tools to SUPPORT and COMFORT yourself when and if, your panic attacks ever happen again.

THINGS THAT CAN CAUSE FIGHT, FLIGHT, FREEZE, OR FAWN

- Stress
- Diet
- Unresolved Emotions
- Genetics
- Exhaustion
- Brain neurotransmitters (serotonin and GABA[36] are low)
- Intense physical activity mistaken as panic symptoms
- Being scared.

---

36 GABA is a brain chemical that blocks certain communication between nerve cells in the brain. Researchers think GABA may make you calm or boost your mood. Low levels of GABA may be linked to anxiety or mood disorders. KEEP AN EYE OUT FOR THIS WORD as mental health research progresses! See "Gamma-Aminobutyric Acid." Wikipedia, Wikimedia Foundation, 17 Sept. 2020, en.wikipedia.org/wiki/Gamma-Aminobutyric_acid.

PANIC ATTACK SYMPTOMS

Some of these might make you say, "duh, bitch," but, just in case you're not sure if you've had a panic attack before (usually you WILL know), they have symptoms that look as such:

- Racing heart
- Chest pain
- Shortness of breath
- Hard time swallowing
- Uneasy stomach
- Feeling of choking
- Sweaty
- Dizziness or fainting spells
- Feeling that you or your surrounding area isn't real (also known as dissociation)
- Numbness in hands or feet

- Fear of dying (fear of heart attack)
- Racing thoughts
- Inability to express words
- Feeling of "going crazy"
- Overstimulation of feelings
- Inability to separate reality from thought
- Hot and cold sweats
- Clammy palms
- Feeling physical pain
- Thinking you're having a heart attack

What symptoms not listed here do you experience during a panic attack?

_____

_____

_____

_____

_____

_____

THE BREATHING

TAKING BACK THE REINS ONE BREATH AT A TIME

The truth is, no matter how much I fucking *hate* paying attention to my breath during a panic attack (as you've read numerous times in this workbook), BREATHING is the ONE BODILY FUNCTION that we can take back control of, no matter what our physical circumstances are during a panic attack. Even in a high-stress or small environment, you ALWAYS have control of your breath. It can feel a bit backwards, because one of the worst symptoms of a panic attack can be loss of breath, feeling like you're having a heart attack, etc., etc. The energy your body is producing to power the fight, flight, freeze, or fawn NEEDS TO GO SOMEWHERE! And we should focus on putting that energy into *controlling our breath.*

For years, the symptom of a panic attack that I feared the most was the feeling that I couldn't breathe. As someone who also experienced debilitating claustrophobia, the thought of dying by "running out of air" ranked pretty high on my intrusive thought list. In fact, if I thought about it TOO MUCH, I could FEEL the sensation of choking coming on, which would propel me into high anxiety and into panic. As soon as I felt that shitty feeling bubble up, I would start gasping for oxygen, like I was a diver who'd just come up for air after their tubes had sprung a leak and water was rushing in. I was EATING the air, like I'd been starved of it my whole life. Heaving. Heavily. In and out. As if it were my first time breathing. I couldn't get enough of it, and I couldn't stop gulping it in.

WELL WELL WELL MY FRIENDS—GUESS FUCKIN' WHAT? It turns out

breathing TOO MUCH is completely the OPPOSITE of what we want to do when we feel panicked during high anxiety! OVER-BREATHING and reaching for more and more breath is the exact opposite reaction our lungs should have during a panic attack, and we actually want to SLOW DOWN our breathing! Even when it feels scary or like we can't. Have you ever seen that part in a movie where something insane is happening and the quirky best friend with glasses is in the corner, puffing into a paper bag? Well, that character is trying to SLOW their breathing to manage panic!

W.O.W.

If you fear that you're "choking" or "can't breathe," start vocalizing the fear—even if it's humming or just making noises. The fact that you are continuing to produce sound will remind you that you are not dying, choking, or having a panic attack.

A POINT TO NOTE IS THAT WHEN DOING BREATHING FOR PANIC ATTACKS, **YOU ALWAYS WANT TO BREATHE IN THROUGH YOUR NOSE AND OUT THROUGH YOUR MOUTH**. If your nose feels blocked or stuffy because you are crying during a panic attack, make sure to take extra care in noting how slowly you should breathe in from your mouth. If you're a singer/musical theater nerd like me, you'll know to differentiate the CHEST breathing from the BELLY breathing. Chest breathing comes from—you guessed it—the chest. In the upper area, where your lungs will be the only thing inflating and deflating. With CHEST BREATHING, your breath will be shallow and not useful in calming a panic attack, UNLESS you pair it with your belly breathing. You'll know you're chest breathing if, when you inhale, you can see the "wings" of your LUNGS expand. We want to move that CHEST breathing into harmony with our BELLY breathing. Technically, belly breathing stems from your DIAPHRAGM, but, for the sake of panic, focus on the area of your belly. BELLY breathing means you use your diaphragm, which is a muscle that separates your the bottom part of your lungs from your abdomen—the abs being the "stomach" part of your belly. When you use BELLY breathing, the bottom half of your abdomen will fill up like a balloon first, and THEN your chest/lungs will rise last. This technique might take some practice to master (I sang in chorus for over 12 years, so I'm Gucci on this one), but would be great to practice when you're NOT having a panic attack! How about now? With the list below, try out which technique feels right for you. They can all be used to quell that scary-breathing panic stuff!

4, 7, 8—The most popular breathing technique I've heard of to practice during a panic attack is the 4, 7, 8. You want to BREATHE IN for four seconds, HOLD THAT BREATH for seven seconds, and then BREATHE OUT for eight seconds. Try it now! I will say, the breathing-out length had me stuck at first, as I didn't think I was capable of breathing out for double the time I was breathing in, but, in fact, because I knew I only had four seconds to breathe in, I'd make them very balanced, stable, and strong. Try it! What do you think of this one?

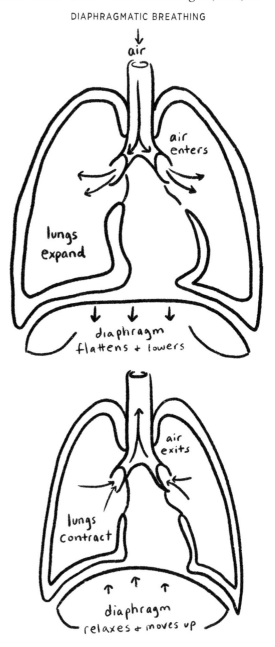

Underwater or straw breathing— I've seen some people who live with panic disorder carry a straw around with them! Some people say by blowing into the straw, or even putting the straw in water to use the liquid as an extrasensory feeling, they can slow their breathing down greatly from a hyperventilating state. Try belly breathing in the air around you and blowing out for 15 seconds through the straw. Again with the in-breath, out this time through the straw for 20. Finally, another deep belly breath in, and out through the straw for 30. Just pay attention so you don't accidentally suck in a bunch of water! Or blow it out all over the table!

The birthday candle—Imagine your index finger is a birthday candle! See the flame! Pick a color for your candle, and hell, while we're at it, why not imagine a cake under your clenched hand? You'll breathe in through your nose, because you want to smell the delicious birthday cake for five seconds, and then you gotta blow those candles out, baby, or your wish won't come true! (Lemme guess, your wish is to never have a panic attack again, right? Same.) But the only way to blow this candle out is nice and slow for five seconds. Ah, look, they're trick candles...Guess you'll have to keep trying until the candle blows out! (Hint: The candle blows out when you feel calm again.)

Box exercise—Draw a box, or, if you don't have a pen nearby, use your finger to trace a box. Each side will be a breath in, a hold, a breath out, and a hold. Each side of this box takes four full, slow seconds to draw.

PRACTICE HERE:

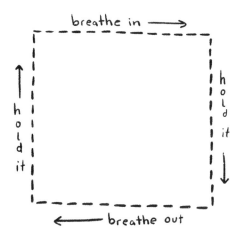

Bumblebee breathing—Doesn't this shit just SOUND CUTE AS FUCK!? You don't HAVE to imagine you're a tiny fluffy bumblebee in a gorgeous garden while doing this exercise, but I HIGHLY RECOMMEND IT! Breathe in through your nose for four seconds, and, as you breathe out through your mouth, let your lips fall together, and use your tongue to make a humming or buzzing sound for 10 seconds. Repeat. Keep repeating until you feel like a soft li'l bumblebee, flying from flower to flower, getting that cash-money nectar.

✦ W. O. W. ✦

TRY TO THINK OF IT LIKE THIS: The pain and suffering you are surviving now will be the strength you need the next time you have a panic attack. You will be able to look back on this moment and remember, "Oh, hell, that was hard as fuck, but I got through it!" Each time you suffer and live through it, it puts another notch in your anxiety tool belt.

BE LIAM NEESON

Dear reader, you are not going to love this entry. You might even hate it. But there's a slight chance that your panic will not come because of it. I need you to pretend to be Liam Neeson. That's right. You're going to embody the essence of Liam Neeson—the 68-year-old Irish GEM of an actor—as he portrayed the character Bryan Mills in the cult-classic movie, *Taken*. You're going to talk to your body as if it were his character's daughter, Kim, who is about to be physically TAKEN (i.e., abducted), only in our little role-playing game, your body is about to be taken... taken by panic.

Okay, time-out real quick from role-playing so I can explain myself. You're going to reach a point when you've had so many bouts of panic that the next time you start to feel one bubble up, you're going to recognize it and get *mad* instead of *scared*. You're going to be angry that another one of THESE fuckers is trying to run up on you at the most inconvenient moment. You're going to be sick of it and frustrated and just SO OVER IT. UGH. Instead of HITTING YOU OUT OF NOWHERE, the symptoms will start to creep up on you, and you'll notice and say, "Oh, shit. Not this fucking shit again. GODDAMMIT. Now, this is NOT THE FRIGGIN' TIME, BODY!!!" Then, instead of "coming out of nowhere" with the intensity of a loud-ass smoke detector that scares the shit out of you, the feelings will graduate to a more slow and steady rising alarm...like an old hand-crank fire truck siren from a black-and-white film. But instead of allowing the rumination of self-anger and punishment to fester up, I want you to channel that anger into READINESS—ready like Liam Neeson's character in *Taken*. The good news about being Liam Neeson is that you've reached a new level in your brain; you're becoming more and more aware and recognizing your symptoms and triggers!

Okay, time-in! Back to BEING LIAM NEESON FROM THE MOVIE, *TAKEN!*

Tell yourself that being mad at your panic is not helpful. When we get ANGRY, we release our control to the thing causing us anger. Liam Neeson (i.e., Bryan Mills) does not lose control. He stays cool as a cucumber in times of chaos. This is what he would say to his body if it were about to be overcome by a panic attack. Try saying this to yourself:

"My mind and my body will continue to be stronger than any sense of panic. When I need to, I will tell myself that I am safe right here, right now. I don't have money to solve this panic. But what I do have is a very particular set of skills I have acquired over long reads of this amazing workbook that teaches me to be kinder to myself and more aware of my emotions without judging them. If I let my panic go wild, that'll be the end of it. I will not enjoy my time. I will not pursue my goal of non-judgment. But if I don't give up, I will look at my panic and recognize this feeling. I will find it and use my skills to manage it, and I will NOT judge it. I will manage it."

...that was a weird one, huh?!

ANCHOR THOUGHTS

Let's say you've managed to get that doubt and worry under control before a big trip or event (WOO!). You've prepped, packed, and double-printed everything you need to get where you're going (HELL, YEAH). You've scheduled your Uber the night before, packed your backup meds, and downloaded your in-flight meditations (LET'S GOOOOOO!). You got to your gate early and are calmly sitting in your seat and YAS QUEEN! GO OFF! WE STAN A PHYSICALLY OVER-PREPPED BITCH!!

But...what if your body feels good, but your head's still swirling? Sometimes the brain and body just can't get in sync. We're going to use a tactic called ANCHOR THOUGHTS. You know how an anchor works: It keeps the big ol' boat from drifting too far from its intended location. We're going to use our imagination to help create an anchor for our brains.

An anchor thought is a trigger or stimulus that retrieves a desired emotional state.

Think of it as the easiest way to link <u>a thought</u> with a <u>positive emotional state</u>. You probably use anchor thoughts in your daily life all the time without even thinking about it! For instance, when you think of your pet and can't help but smile thinking of their big ol' dumb smushy face, waiting for you to get home from a long day at work?! Or perhaps it's the idea of some fresh post-exercise fro-yo that keeps you pushing through an intense workout that you really want to quit. We can use a similar idea to create thoughts in our brains when we are in uncomfortable positions or in unfamiliar places. An anchor thought can also be something you've yet to experience but are excited to get to. Don't be afraid to use your imagination to create your anchor thought! You can also think of an anchor thought as similar to what Harry Potter experiences when he's trying to produce a patronus! Remember, he says, "I'm not even sure [if this memory] is real...but, it's the happiest one I've got!" For example: When I'm flying cross-country to visit my best friend, Lacey, my anxiety will try to trick me into thinking I can't do it. When I arrive at the airport, no matter how prepared I am, my anxiety tells me that the flight will cause too much emotional stress, that I should somehow figure out a way to get a refund for the ticket and stay home. Or, if I'm actually able to make it onto the plane, my fight-or-flight response will kick in and raise intrusive thoughts about the safety of flying. In these moments, I come back to my ANCHOR THOUGHT: *Why am I going to NYC in the first place? What am I looking forward to doing?* The answer is simple: Lacey and I eating brunch in Central Park, with her big chocolate Lab, Woody, by our side. It's sunny, the breeze is blowing, and Woody has the derp-iest face, resting his massive velvety head on my lap. Spending time with my best friend in the world, and her goofy doggo. I think of the hilarious conversations we'll have about what's going on in our lives, and that we'll walk down Madison Avenue, window-shopping. THESE are the moments I'm surviving anxiety for. As a very very cheesy Delta pre-flight ad says, "Connection begins with departure." Ugh. Truuuuue.

Your trip or event can certainly get off on the wrong foot if we enter that space with worry and fear. Learning how to change your emotional state will help change your perception, and isn't that what life is all about? What WE make of it? ~*CHANGE YOUR ENVIRONMENT. CHANGE YOUR LIFE*~

Some people like to use a *physical object* to help produce an anchor thought. Perhaps a charm, a picture in your phone, or something you can carry in your pocket that reminds you of a special person. Slide your fingers up and down the object, close your eyes, and be as present in your anchor thought as possible. Even a scent can help drive memory. Perhaps a lover's cologne (I carry a travel-size version of Jared's cologne, *Chanel Bleu,* in my pocket as scent therapy that anchors my thoughts to him and how happy he makes me) or your favorite snack, which you can keep in your bag (peanut M&Ms for ya girl)? When you connect with that memory, you will know because you'll be unable to keep that smile off your face! Congrats, you've learned how to consciously change your emotional state! Look at you go!

What's the happiest anchor thought you can use to get through this uncomfortable experience or new situation?

_____

_____

_____

_____

_____

_____

_____

_____

_____

Can you associate any objects or scents to help boost that memory?

_____

_____

_____

_____

THE PANIC ATTACK ABOUT GETTING A PANIC ATTACK

AH YES, CONGRATULATIONS!

You have officially entered a very special META PANIC ATTACK CLUB! This club has no perks or a membership card. Sorry.

We're already established that panic attacks are the fucking worst, right? It's only natural that now that you know what one feels like, it's easy to fear them coming back. A very few select non-members of this club can have one panic attack in their life and never have one again. Fuckers. They are able to just say, "Huh, that was fucking weird, wasn't it?" and continue to live their lives. This happened infuriatingly on the cult-classic show *Sex and the City*. It's the episode where Miranda (the neurotic redheaded lawyer whom fans rank as the least-favorite character in the show) buys her own apartment! HURRAY! BIG LIFE MOMENT, RIGHT?! Nope, of course not—that's not good TV! In the show, Miranda chokes on her food while she's eating take-out alone at home and has to give herself the Heimlich maneuver against a cardboard box. She then realizes that getting her own apartment means she is, in fact, ALONE in this apartment (a thought you'd THINK an intelligent professional woman would've had before this near-death experience) and she has...A PANIC ATTACK. She takes herself to the ER, thinking that she's having some sort of heart attack, and her BFF4L, Carrie, meets her in the tiny medical room to save her. Miranda SIMPLY SHRUGS IT OFF, saying "Oh, the doctors said I had a panic attack." ¯_(ツ)_/¯

And she basically...takes her recovered ass home to continue living life. To never speak about it with a doctor, or therapist, or HER BEST FUCKING FRIENDS SAMANTHA OR CARRIE OR CHARLOTTE ever again. Fuckin' WOMP WOMP, missed opportunity there, WRITERS. We coulda had a full-ass story line about Miranda leaving the ER with Carrie, trying to erratically explain to Carrie what the feeling was like while hopped-up on Ativan. How she can't REALLY explain it to her—how Carrie would need to feel it herself to understand. Miranda could then spend the next 24 hours in her new apartment alone, carefully walking around on eggshells, looking over her shoulder, breathing shallowly, like she's waiting for the next panic attack to hit. How, after a week of checking her own pulse and clearing her calendar, she finally logs onto Psychology.com to find a therapist who might be able to help her. At brunch, she finally tells the girls that she's going to see a therapist. Okay, maybe that's not GREAT TV, but it's real. And if we MUST add some spice into the mix, let's have her bang her therapist. Right? I don't know. *Don't bang your therapist.*

Having a panic attack about a panic attack is completely normal. Speaking with my doctors and personal therapists, they all told me it's the most COMMON problem they hear from their patients about panic attacks. And of course we're worried! Panic attacks are fucking gnarly if you aren't in the space of managing them just yet. Overthinking the possibilities of when one might hit at the most inconvenient time could throw you into a spiral. I'm sorry I'm about to say this, but, it's exactly like that saying, "Try not to think about a pink elephant right now," to prove that your brain has something called "ironic process theory." IPT, as I've decided to call it just now, proves that the more you try to suppress the thought of having a panic attack, the more likely you are to think about it, therefore putting you in the position to have one. The same way if someone tells you NOT to think of a big pink elephant, it's the only fucking thing you can think of! And there's nothing more frustrating than feeling like you brought on a panic attack yourself. So, I'm going to ask you do to something scary:

LEARN TO LEAN INTO THE IDEA OF HAVING A PANIC ATTACK.

Yes. You read that right.

In this case, your FEAR is FEEDING more FEAR. Your mind will react the more you do—so, if you are checking your pulse, avoiding places, asking for reassurance from the internet constantly...you will train your mind to see these things as a threat associated with panic and muster up those feelings once more.

You cannot STOP fear with more fear. Instead, we want to bring confidence to the table. Confidence that we acquire by becoming familiar with our mind and body in this state of high anxiety and panic. When we find that confidence, we can face our fear with no judgment and only acceptance. That's right:

THE WAY YOU FIGHT THE FEAR OF A PANIC ATTACK...is to not *fight* at all.

In order to LEAN INTO THE IDEA OF HAVING A PANIC ATTACK!!! (!!!?!??WTF?!%&$*@&@), we gotta become friends with your panic a li'l to understand them better. I want to take this time to remind you that you are not alone in this. Nothing will sound too crazy or weird for this workbook (or its creator! Hi! I've been to really weird places in my brain, too!). Mindfulness eventually leads to acceptance when done enough to see yourself outside of an attack. By even completing the following exercise, you are already BEING MINDFUL of your attacks! LOOK AT YOU, BB! On the way to the top already! So, let's talk PANIC. Specifically, YOUR PANIC ATTACKS.

Say I have a magic genie, whom I'm letting you borrow, and she's (genies can be chicks, right? Can they be non-binary?) nice enough to grant you one wish as it relates to your panic attacks. **What is your one wish?**

_____

_____

_____

_____

If I had to take a guess, I'm going to assume your wish was that you would never have to have one again!

So, tell me, what would you do if you knew that you'd NEVER have another panic attack again?

_____

_____

_____

_____

_____

_____

_____

What's the worst you've ever felt during a panic attack?

_____

_____

_____

_____

_____

Have you ever found something that helps you manage your panic in a healthy way?

_____

_____

_____

_____

How about an unhealthy way (but, maybe it helped with the panic)?

_____

_____

_____

_____

Does anyone know about your panic attacks? Family? Friends? Coworkers?

_____

_____

_____

_____

What would you like to hear from a family member, friend, or coworker if you were having a panic attack in front of them?

_____

_____

_____

_____

How has your panic affected your relationships with others?

_____

_____

_____

_____

_____

_____

How do you feel about the future of your life, having to live with panic attacks?

_____

_____

_____

_____

_____

What makes your panic attack feel WORSE? For example: Do you want to be held, or not touched at all? Are you hot or perhaps cold? Do you like to lie or sit down?

_____

_____

_____

_____

_____

What makes your panic attack feel BETTER? (It's okay if this answer is NOTHING, or I DON'T KNOW! That's what this workbook is for!)

_____

_____

_____

_____

_____

What kinds of thoughts, if you're able to remember any clearly, go through your head during a panic attack?

_____

_____

_____

_____

What are your physical symptoms?

_____

_____

_____

_____

Let IPT (ironic process theory) do its thang, baby! Try acknowledging that you are thinking about having a panic attack. **You can say it out loud, or even write it**

down below—just get it out of your head.

_____

_____

_____

_____

_____

_____

It's okay if you are panicking about panicking. THINKING about it doesn't mean it's happening...because WHY, LOVELY READER?! *Screams like we are in an auditorium full of students repeating my special phrase* **YOU ARE NOT YOUR THOUGHTS. THOUGHTS ARE JUST THOUGHTS & FEELINGS ARE JUST FEELINGS...NOT FACTS!** Panic is just a possibility out of an infinite list of possibilities that could happen to you in your life at this very moment. You could have a panic attack, or you could find a scratch-off ticket on the ground that rewards you with $10,000 every week for the rest of your life! ANYTHING COULD HAPPEN!

You won't hear me talk about medication much in this book because I'm not a doctor!

I've been on it, off it, on it...many, many times. I've been for it...against it...been in rehab because of it... It's such a personal and important journey that only you and your doctor can decide what's right for you.

Even after managing my panic for a very long time, confronting my fear with confidence, and finding a way to create a nonjudgmental response to my body's fight, flight, freeze, and fawn, I have to accept the reality that...I still might have a panic attack. It's SO important to not see these instances as a setbacks that bring you down to where you started. PROGRESS ISN'T LINEAR! You have to build a tool belt to see what works for you. And, even when you feel that you've implemented all your tools in this tricky "relapse" attack, there is always room to grow. The brain and body are probably trying to tell you something! It's all like, PAY ATTENTION TO ME!! I NEED SOMETHING!!! LOOK AFTER ME! SLOW DOWN! I'M HUNGRY! I'M SLEEPY!...or whatever the message may be. Treat any "relapse" attack as a chance to get closer to your body's needs and wants. Pay attention to any tension in your body. Notice what time of day and where your mood is if you experience racing thoughts. Understand that you are actively working on managing this undesirable feeling—and THAT, in itself, is STILL progress!!

MAKE YOUR OWN PANIC ATTACK PREP KIT

You can make your own prep kit and carry it wherever you go! Buy a cute bag for it! Make one! Decorate it! An excuse to go to TARGET! DIY! YES!!!

1. **Voice memo from a loved one:** This was my wonderful partner's idea when I took my first international plane flight alone since we'd met. He recorded a few versions of a voice memo to keep on my phone that didn't require WiFi to listen to. One version was very relaxing and meditative, and had funny and cute details about our relationship. Another was a little more high-energy of him, gassing me up to do anything I believed in, like a dope rapper's hype-man. I was able to pull these up on my phone and play them through my AirPods as the flight was taking off. His voice made me smile, and his jokes made me laugh. Sometimes a generic meditative track won't do it for me...but, this comforted me in a way I didn't know was possible, because it was so personal.

2. **Medication:** This is not a necessity. Many cultures don't believe in using medication to treat mental-health issues, and that's completely fine. In my opinion, when used correctly, pharmaceuticals have saved my life at certain times, but have also felt detrimental during other periods of my life. So, if you believe in pharmaceuticals, make sure you have enough for home, but also one or two to carry in your prep kit. If you don't have medication, or don't believe in it, "medication" can mean other things. Maybe it's a religious relic. Perhaps it's a tiny airplane bottle of vodka! Hey! I don't judge!

3. **Phone charger:** The last thing I need when panicking is being separated from the option to call a loved one if needed. Or text. Or listen to a soothing song on Spotify. Maybe even the option to look at a funny meme. But if your phone is dead, we can't do any of this! Mobile chargers are super-easy to find these days. (I've even seen some companies give these away for free at events!) Designate this mobile charger as your prep kit charger only, so you're not tempted to use it for other scenarios.

4. **Lavender essential oils:** Only a drop will do, so as to not affect the others around you. Warm it up in your hands and sniff that shit like you're a police dog sniffing for crack cocaine.

5. **Pre-downloaded podcasts or Netflix on your phone:** DM friends for logins if you can't afford it; EVERYONE has extra room on their accounts. Distract your panic with your fav shows or podcasts (I recommend you listen to CONFIDENTLY INSECURE on any podcast platform).

6. **Fidget cube:** Have something to do with your hands, so you're not checking your pulse or creating unnecessary body movements or twitching.

7. **A photo or small object that brings you happiness!** If you can, use your phone to create an album of funny memes of videos you know will make you smile. For a physical object, find something personal that brings back a happy memory. For me, it's a small rock that's naturally shaped like a heart that I found at a lake during an amazing trip with my family. When I run my fingers over it, I think back to those memories and the people that were there, who I know would love to be there for me during this tough moment.

RECORD YOUR PANIC

You're going to get through this! IT IS AN ~ATTACK~, AFTER ALL, NOT A LIFE-LONG SENTENCE! EITHER WAY, I DON'T BLAME YOU FOR FEELING EMOTIONAL!!! I know it's scary, but let's try to get your mind off the *emotional* feelings you are having about this attack.

Let's try some *objective* note-writing as opposed to *subjective* note-writing. The difference?

Subjective recording is when you're being a dick to yourself: "Ugh, this panic attack is BAD, I SUCK, I feel like shit, this is scary as fuck, fuck this shit. I'd rather die than do this again."

Objective notation is totally nonjudgmental, factual, and concrete. "Right now, I feel unstable. I can sense my heart rate has risen from its normal levels".

Our goal here is to find some patterns in the triggers and symptoms of the attacks themselves. **The best way to do this is an hour-by-hour check-in post-attack.**

HOUR-TO-HOUR CHECK-IN

Date: _____ Panic Location: _____

Intensity of attack (1–10): _____ Start Time: _____ AM / PM

Begin at the box closest to your start time and keep going for up to 12 hours. In each box, fill in your current symptoms, any ruminating leftover thoughts, and how you feel right now. Then, rate your current status (1-10). For a printable version, check out the Resource Index.

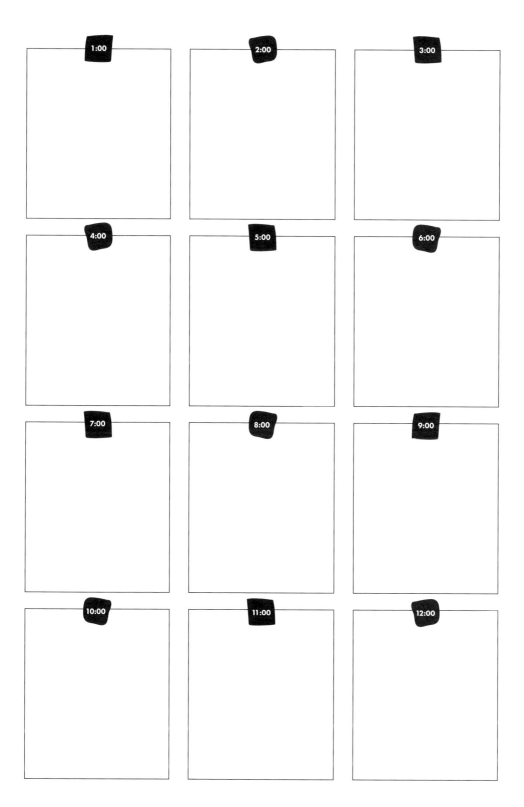

THE PANIC THERMOMETER

Color in the thermometer to show how you're feeling right now. Then, fill in the details below.

Time: _____

Situation:

_____

_____

_____

_____

Thoughts: _____

_____

_____

What ramped the thermometer to go higher?

_____

_____

Where/When/What were you doing last time you were relaxed and the thermometer was empty? How did your body feel? Can you get back to that place? Even if you need to fake it 'til you make it, how can you recreate that environment?

_____

_____

_____

_____

_____

_____

_____

_____

For a printable version of the thermometer and Panic Notes for Partners card, check out the Resource Index.

PANIC NOTES FOR PARTNERS

My Needs: _____

_____

What I'm Feeling: _____

_____

What You Can Do To Help Right Now: _____

_____

What WON'T Help: _____

_____

When I Feel Better, You Will Know Because: _____

_____

15 REALISTIC THINGS YOU CAN DO TO HELP ME THROUGH A PANIC ATTACK

I made this list when I was sitting in an airport in D.C. after I had just started dating my boyfriend, who has never experienced a panic attack before in his own life and, at this point in our fresh relationship, he had never seen *me* have a panic attack (even though he was aware of my panic disorder, which you can read more about in the Anxiety Tips For Partners chapter of this workbook!). Sitting at a restaurant bar, waiting for our flight, out of nowhere, I felt that all-too-familiar feeling that bubbled up inside me anytime I was going on a plane: that feeling of claustrophobia, lack of control, shortness of breath, the "oh fuck im gunna shit my pants and pass out in public" feeling. And I knew I wasn't going to be able to hide it from him. *Which made me panic more.* For a long time, I never knew how to explain how I was feeling during a panic attack—it just happened—it felt otherworldly—*and I fucking hated it.*

⚝ W. O. W. ⚝

Get that conversation out early with new lovers. If they have a problem with it, you don't want to be with them anyway! People are capable of learning!

At the time, I had been having success with journaling for a while, and I had my Moleskine journal on me. I watched him as he sat across from me at the bar, and he looked chill as a cucumber with his headphones on, playing some game on his phone. How could he be so calm while I felt like fireworks filled with poison were going off in my brain? If I took that moment to reach out to him verbally, I felt like I would explode into tears. So instead, I did what I found to be most soothing at that time: I whipped out my journal and started writing. I knew a panic attack was coming, and it was going to be the first one in front of him. Instead of thinking about *myself,* which felt overwhelming and scary to tap into, considering my oh-so-fragile-state, I thought about him and how he might react to me. I considered, "The LEAST I can do is give him some advice and guidance on what's coming and how to 'deal' with me." *Spoiler alert: He's never felt that my mental health diagnosis has been an inconvenience or something to "deal" with and has really appreciated how much advice I've given him to help me through it. He loves knowledge, so he soaks it up. He's also a Libra. So, I got lucky on this one. I guess my advice is to date Libras??*

My bubbling panic gave me the energy to write. I doodled...I wrote in different fonts...I tried to make the list look...fun?? I read it over and thought it would be good to send to my core group of panic attack supporters as well, so I snapped

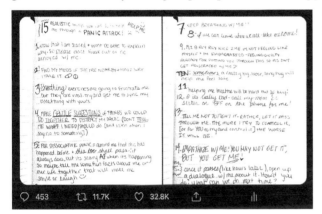

453   11.7K   32.8K

a pic of the pages on my iPhone. I had a thought that, since it was Mental Health Awareness Month at that time, I should post it to my Twitter. I'd started to publicly talk about my panic disorder in videos at BuzzFeed, so it seemed like just another tweet that made sense coming from me:

@KelseyDarragh May 11ᵗʰ, 2018: *I have panic and anxiety disorder. My boyfriend does not...but wants to understand it so he can help me. SO I made him this list! Feel free to share with your loved ones that need guidance!*

15 Realistic things you can do to help me through a PANIC ATTACK :(help me LOL

1. know that i am scared + won't be able to explain why so please don't freak out or be annoyed w/ me.

2. FIND MY MEDS IF THEY'RE NEARBY + MAKE SURE I TAKE IT

3. BREATHING exercises are going to frustrate me but they are vital. Try and get me to sync my breathing with yours.

4. make GENTLE SUGGESTIONS of things we could do TOGETHER to distract my panic (DON'T TELL ME WHAT I NEED/SHOULD DO [and listen when I say no to something])

5. FOR DISSOCIATIVE ANXIETY = *remind me that this has happened before + this too shall pass! It always does but its scary AF when its happening so maybe tell me some fun facts about myself or our life together that will make me smile or laugh :)*

6. *sips of water can be helpful but don't tell me i need to eat or drink b/c* **trust me** *i feel like i'm going to vomit :(*

7. KEEP BREATHING WITH ME!!!

8. *if we can leave where we are*—TAKE ME HOME!

9. *Plz be rly nice to me. I am not feeling like myself + i'm embarrassed + feeling guilty already for putting you through this so plz dn't get frustrated w/ me :|*

TEN. *sometimes a really big loose long hug will help me feel safe.*

11. *helping me breathe will be hard but so key!*

12. *if it's really bad call my mom or sister of BFF (Lacey) on the phone for me!*

13. TELL ME NOT TO FIGHT IT—RATHER, LET IT PASS THROUGH ME. THE MORE I TRY TO CONTROL IT { OR YOU TRY TO CONTROL IT } THE WORSE IT WILL BE.

14. EMPATHIZE WITH ME! YOU MAY NOT GET IT, BUT YOU GET ME!

15. *Once it passes (like, hours later), open up a dialogue w/ me about it. How'd you do? What can we do next time?*

♥ *Kelsey*

I wrote this tweet, attached the photo, and boarded the flying metal death bird with my boyfriend. I gave him the list because I let out some squeaks of panic, and he was SO intrigued by the material. I had written down shit that he would've never thought about offering as a hand of support. I was so relieved that he found it useful, and we walked through each step together. And, when I got off the floating titanium air shredder, my Twitter notifications were *blowing up*. This list had gone viral. There were hundreds of responses from other Twitter users, giving advice on what support works for them. They were tagging their therapists, their partners, and some news outlets. I had a few reach out to me, asking to interview me. It was CRAZY. I had NO IDEA this was going to be such an important topic that people were THIRSTY for answers about. It felt really great to have started a crucial conversation, but felt even better to see the way the community reacted to it. The list had spread across the world and was being translated into different languages! I even ended up on the front page of some British newspaper! I still get messages to this day about the list from people who just want to say thanks for posting something honest. In reality, I'm blushing behind my phone screen, because it was never meant to be a viral topic, but rather a selfish move of my own to avoid having a tough conversation with my partner face-to-face. But hey, now we have a physical list to look at when my panic pops up. We even made the list our phone backgrounds for a period of time when my stress was at its highest! I'm glad I took the chance on making the list, that I posted it, and that people had no fear about sharing their helpful tips, too. That's what I love about the mental-health community I've fallen into online: I thought finding allyship online was going to be a depressing suck-hole of strangers' weird thoughts and unnecessary emotional work, but, it turns out, it's not all that depressing or weird when you find literally millions of other people who experience that one thing that you thought was "crazy" and insanely personal to your experience. **Can you make your own personal list for your loved ones and friends that describes your specific and personal needs during a panic attack?**

_____

_____

_____

_____

_____

_____

_____

_____

_____

_____

_____

_____

_____

SO, WHEN DO PANIC ATTACKS BECOME A PANIC DISORDER?

THIS IS A VERY GOOD QUESTION

Some people will only have one, or very few, panic attacks in their lifetime. We cannot understand these people. Maybe we can't empathize with them, or perhaps are downright jealous of them. And I know YOU are not one of those people, because you're reading this sentence. I'm sorry.

But if you've had recurrent, unexpected panic attacks, and spent long periods in constant fear of another attack, you may have a **panic disorder** (always check with your doctor tho, of course). But fear not! Take me as an example of someone who's not only alive and surviving them, BUT THRIVING BECAUSE OF THEM! It took a LONG TIME, but I was eventually able to get to a place of acceptance and successful management of my panic disorder, which is exactly why I wanted to create this workbook—so that others diagnosed with panic disorder might get a little head start on recovery. :)

EASY NO-BRAINER WORD SEARCH PUZZLE
TO KEEP YOUR HANDS BUSY

```
N  Q  G  Y  L  T  M  A  E  R  T  S  Z  C  J
T  O  N  E  G  A  S  S  A  M  K  I  W  W  S
F  Y  I  E  L  V  V  R  H  C  L  R  F  E  U
O  F  L  T  Q  E  Y  E  O  I  U  I  I  U  N
S  F  S  T  A  Z  N  S  N  P  K  N  G  B  S
E  U  O  T  O  B  M  N  V  D  N  I  R  H  E
L  L  G  C  N  R  R  A  A  U  E  E  N  J  T
G  F  N  B  A  I  N  U  B  L  E  R  P  G  P
G  H  A  W  E  I  M  N  T  Z  F  E  K  E  U
I  C  Y  N  L  Z  V  J  E  S  A  V  R  B  P
G  O  R  L  E  B  C  U  P  C  A  K  E  S  P
Z  C  A  B  A  T  H  V  E  A  G  M  I  C  I
R  O  M  C  O  M  T  B  R  E  A  T  H  A  E
F  A  W  W  G  K  N  I  H  A  R  P  O  L  S
L  A  M  I  H  B  A  B  K  I  N  K  D  M  R
```

BATH	CUPCAKES	LIGHT	ROMCOM
BREATH	FLANNEL	MASSAGE	RYAN GOSLING
BREEZE	FLUFFY	MASTURBATION	SOFT
BUNNIES	GIGGLES	MINT	STREAM
CALM	HIKING	OPRAH	SUNSET
COCOA	KITTEN	PEACE	VANILLA
COZY	LAVENDER	PUPPIES	WARM SOCKS

A SOOTHING PAGE OF
SUDOKU TO BUSY THAT MIND!

INSTRUCTIONS:

Fill in the symbols (there are 9 total) exactly once in every row, column, and 3x3 region

SLOW TRACING

Need a physical distraction?
Trace these numbers while you breathe in and out.

Breathe in: 1, 2, 3, 4
Hold: 1, 2
Out: 1, 2, 3, 4, 5, 6

1 2 3 4
1 2
1 2 3 4 5 6

1 2 3 4
1 2
1 2 3 4 5 6

1 2 3 4
1 2
1 2 3 4 5 6

1 2 3 4
1 2
1 2 3 4 5 6

1 2 3 4
1 2
1 2 3 4 5 6

1 2 3 4
1 2
1 2 3 4 5 6

TAPPING

TO RELEASE EMOTIONAL ENERGY

This is one of those "Kelsey, this seems like a silly one" pages. But hey, you're in the PANIC section, so you're willing to try ANYTHING, RIGHT?! This is an EFT (emotional freedom technique) exercise that is quick to try and keeps your hands and brain busy. If you can, try doing this one in a private space where you can speak freely to yourself—if not, no worries! I've done this on a plane, in a lunchroom, and other public places. People will just think you're meditating, so if you can get over the idea that some people might wonder what you're doing smackin' your own face—LET'S BEGIN!

The explanation of EFT tapping sounds a little ~*weird*~ but can be an incredible resource when done correctly. The idea is to TAP, **with a bit of energy**, with your hands on certain *acupressure points* to try to release emotional energy.

Let's do a practice round! Tap, with some "umph" behind it, with four fingers (no thumb action), the fingertips of your right hand, onto the outside of your left hand. Practice those taps and get a good rhythm going.

RATE YOUR FEELINGS WHILE YOU TAP

While you practice tapping, start by rating your anxiety or panic on a scale of 1-10. Acknowledge the core feeling while you tap, and speak about the feeling out loud or in your head. It can be as basic as "I'm having a panic attack," or "I am anxious," or something more specific like, "It feels like my lungs aren't getting enough air," or "I am stressed from the interaction with Karen at work."

Rate the discomfort (1-10): _____

What's the recurring feeling?

_____

_____

_____

How do you feel about it?

_____

_____

That wasn't that hard, was it? See, I've always said I would try LITERALLY ANYTHING to get the feeling of panic at a manageable rate (even if it hurt my body or ego). So, if this didn't do ya any harm, let's dive into it!

- **You're going to do three rounds of tapping over various places on your body while speaking.**

- **For round one, we will be using "negative" speaking,** a.k.a. talking about the "problem," along with answering the questions you filled out above, either out loud or in your head. Don't take a pause to write down the answers, as we don't want to break the flow of tapping, but feel free to look down if you need a reminder of what the questions were.

- **In the second round, we will switch to a more positive dialogue** while you tap, giving yourself _answers and explanations_ of the fears and feelings that were mentioned in round one.

- **For the third round, we will speak positively, as if the issue is solved and we are free from the discomfort!** Remember, your mind has powerful influence over your body, even if, in this moment, it can feel like we're "faking it 'til we're making it." Tapping is a mixture of acupressure and talk therapy. You're literally tapping into these meridians, sending messages to release the fight-or-flight-or-freeze response.

ROUND 1

The first round of tapping is all about letting out each stress, saying it over and over (in your head or out loud). Using the same amount of force, tap onto these points on your body for the first round, again, speaking negatively about the issue, how you feel, and rating the discomfort. Spend about 10 seconds tapping each of these sections of your body:

1. both eyebrows
2. side of the eyes
3. under the eyes
4. side of the nose
5. chin
6. collarbone
7. under the arm (by bra strap)
8. top of the head

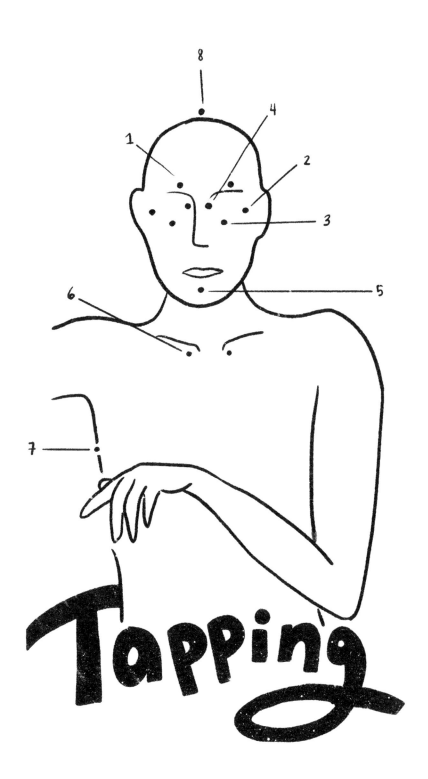

When you've finished these points, take a DEEP BREATH.

Rate how you are feeling now (1-10): _____

ROUND 2

In this second round, we are going to tap those same points in the same order, but instead of speaking your fears and feeling like you did in round one, we want to put a *positive spin* on the dialogue you are saying out loud or in your head. For example, replace the fearful dialogue with healing sentences, like:

- "I know this won't last."
- "I've been here before."
- "I give myself permission to vent to myself."
- "This too shall pass."
- "I'm giving myself permission to feel relief."
- "I know I am capable of being calm, and I welcome that shift."
- "I honor my situation and accept myself completely."

Tap the same places in the same order as you did in round one while choosing from the sentences above (or create your own!). Spend about 10 seconds tapping each section of your body.

When you've finished, don't forget to take a few nice DEEP BREATHS.

Rate your discomfort again (1-10): _____

ROUND 3

For this final round, we are going to speak to ourselves with complete love and adoration for body and mind. We are going to find compassion in our discomfort and speak as if we've resolved the conflict within ourselves with our emotions and physical feelings. Remember: Even if you don't believe it or feel it in this very moment, you've experienced peace at some point in your life, and you know it's possible to achieve. Help your brain tell your body to get there!

Try using phrases like:

- "I choose to relax now."
- "I am calmer now."

- "I give myself space to surrender."
- "I have found space."
- "I choose to find peace."
- Close your eyes. Take another deep breath in.

Rate yourself one final time (1-10): _____

How did that feel?! Was it silly as fuck? A total waste of time? Or maybe it was just "meh?" Did it HELP, perhaps? Even distracting yourself for a few moments? Maybe it took your panicky feelings away completely? SOUND OFF:

_____

_____

_____

_____

_____

_____

_____

_____

_____

_____

_____

_____

_____

_____

_____

THE BEST GAMES ON YOUR PHONE

I'm not really into video games, but I AM guilty of downloading a popular phone game and becoming obsessed, though I've never downloaded *Farmville* or *Animal Crossing* and I'm very proud of that (does one play *Animal Crossing* on a phone? Idk.). Even though I really only play games on my phone in times of high anxiety, apparently that still makes me a "gamer." Sidebar: I learned this info when I went to a wall-to-wall packed gamer panel where people were passionately chanting "PHONE GAMERS ARE STILL GAMERS! PHONE GAMERS ARE STILL GAMERS!" Who knew there was so much prejudice in the gamer community?

I highly recommend downloading these games BEFORE you get to an environment or place that might cause you anxiety or panic, just in case they don't have WiFi. In fact, just put this workbook down and download these games NOW, so you'll have them forever. I even made an "anxiety" folder with these games and the meditation apps listed below to have when I'm feeling ehhhhhhhSHAKEY.

BALLZ	**Minecraft**	**Mind Ease**
COLOR BUMP	**Alto's Adventure**	**Lava Lamp** (just what it sounds like: a lava lamp you can squish around)
Two Dots	**Monument Valley**	
Love Balls	**Scrabble**	
Falling Ballz	**Duolingo**	**Mind Numb**
Angry Birds		**SuperBetter**

WHILE WE'RE TALKING APPS! Let's focus on some meditation apps that have popped off in the charts in the last few years. Some are free, and some might be pricey, but I see it as an investment in my health. Most of the apps that cost money will also offer a free trial if you are in a pinch.

FREE MEDITATION APPS

Headspace	**WhiteNoise**	**Insight Timer**
Omvana (iOS)	**Equanimity**	**Happier**

buddhify	**Oak**	**Daily OM**
CALM	**Smiling Mind**	**Meditation for Fidgety Skeptics**
Stop, Breathe & Think	**Glo**	
Sattva	**Aura**	

Self-hypnosis YouTube videos are also free! Lately, I've been playing Spotify play-lists of frequency tones or binaural beats for HOURS while working. The sound is so beautiful and calming that, a few times, I've burst out crying for no reason. According to *Psychology Today*, "Some studies have found that binaural beats can affect cognitive function positively or negatively, depending on the specific frequency generated. For example, a study of long-term memory found that beta-frequency binaural beats improved memory, while theta-frequency binaural beats interfered with memory."[37] I prefer positive and uplifting beats, like "Love Tone" or "Miracle Tone."

I have to say that if, by the time you read this workbook, any of these apps have started charging fees for membership, know that this isn't uncommon with how big meditation apps are starting to boom. Find one you LOVE and consider it a wellness investment. If you can get a note from your doctor stating meditation is required to lower your anxiety, panic, or depression, you can even write the expense off! Personally, I use Meditation Studio by Muse. There are tons of courses and collections that are specifically themed for its users. For example, they have Sleep, Confidence, Pep Talks, Eating, Chronic Pain, and Fertility courses, just to name a few! My favorite teacher is Chodo Campbell; his voice sounds like if taffy melted into Leon Bridges's voice and someone wrapped it in a velvet blanket on a cool foggy morning in the mountains, and you're there, cozied in the blanket, holding a perfectly temperatured caramel macchiato that has no sugar in it but TASTES like dessert. WHEW!!!!!!

37 Breus, Michael J. "How Can Binaural Beats Help You Sleep Better?" *Psychology Today*, Sussex Publishers, 11 Oct. 2018, www.psychologytoday.com/us/blog/sleep-newzzz/201810/how-can-binaural-beats-help-you-sleep-better.

CONNECT-THE-DOTS TO REVEAL A RELAXING IMAGE

FLYING PANIC ATTACKS

AH, YES, MY ~*SPECIALTY*~

Once upon a time, I was having a panic attack upon takeoff. Takeoff, for me, is always the *worst,* because it solidifies in my mind that for the next XX hours, you have zero control over this speeding airtube! On this particular flight, I tried getting up AS WE WERE TAKING OFF to run to the bathroom to puke, or shit, or try to catch my breath—I don't know—and the flight attendant got on the intercom and said we need everyone to sit down immediately or we will land this plane, and I shouted back "YOU PROMISE??!!!"

Needless to say, I didn't make very many friends on that flight. But part of my job requires me to fly all across the world, to make videos and meet clients and make partnerships!

A very smart pilot once said, "When you're a baby, you have two fears instilled in you from birth—*fear of loud noises and fear of falling*—and planes give you both of those feelings." Essentially, being on a plane is tapping into an evolutionary fear. As much as these elongated-people-air-carriers suck ass, this is actually a good opportunity to practice sitting with your panic. Not only because you're forced to literally sit, but because your odds of making it to your destination are INCREDIBLY high—it's just about the hours between now and landing.

SOME KELSEY TIPS:

First, we need to assess the environment: Find your exits, survey the people sitting around you, know that most humans are good and will help if you really need assistance. This is also the moment you have to be a bit brave—letting the people around you know about your panic disorder or fear of flying will save you time when you ARE panicking, trying to explain what a panic attack is?? Yeah, no thanks. I'll usually smile at them when I sit down and catch the vibe if they're a talker or not (and TBH, sometimes I'm not a talker...but, that's pretty rare. I love to hear my own voice.). I'll take some deep breaths, calming my nervous system, and when they inevitably look over at my meditative practice, I hit them with the "I'm a very nervous flyer" and a smile. Maybe I'll even wave my Xanax* at them, if I get the right reaction. That way, if they see I'm getting up often, they'll be more empathetic; I've even had times where I've been sitting next to someone who can relate or offers up one of their Klonopin* (I believe I'm legally obligated here to say "don't take drugs from strangers," but, like, I don't even follow my own advice. So. Be smart. We're all adults here.). Once, on a transatlantic flight, I sat next to a dad who, after I introduced my own anxiety, shared with me that his daughter was suffering terribly from panic attacks back at home. He told me that he was convinced it was "all in her head" and that she was just a "stressed-out teenager." But her therapy and pharmacy bills were starting to stack up, and he worried that this was a "real" problem. EH OH EL. oOOoOOOoOO boy! I pulled up my bootstraps knowing I had some work to do. After boasting to him that I was that same "dramatic teenager," but 10 years later and diagnosed by multiple mental health professionals, he asked if he could pick my brain more about it so he could help her! YAY DAD! It felt amazing to have a real conversation, knowing in a few hours I'd probably never see this dude again, so I might as well just lay it all out there! We never spoke again or exchanged info, but I know for certain he walked off that plane with a completely different mindset about his daughter's disorder.

Talk to your doctor before taking drugs. PLZ

Second—board early! I had my therapist write me a note stating my medical condition and that I needed extra time to get settled. I've never had to use it, because airline workers are trained that they shouldn't ask about someone's medical condition when boarding, the same way you shouldn't ask someone why they have a therapy dog. It's just rude. But I'd have no problem whipping that baby out if I need to and educating some people on the old PANIC DISORDER if they REEEEEEEALLY wanted to get into it and have that discussion right there in the boarding line.

Third, remember: Humans are good. Almost everyone will be willing to help if you just ask. Need help getting your luggage up? Need directions? Water for your meds? Just ask.

Fourth tip: Sleep on the flight, if you can, if you're not ready to fly without fear of an attack. I HIGHLY RECOMMEND the Trtl Pillow for your neck. It's unlike any pillow you've tried before, and trust me, I've tried them all. All airplane pillows suck, except the Trtl Pillow. Additionally, Dream Water, or taking a small dose of Benadryl, which all airports sell in their little shops, is known to give even the biggest and strongest of people a nice drowsy glaze.

Tip 5: Download the app SOAR. It was invented by a former airplane pilot who helps people with flying anxiety. It has an IN-APP TURBULENCE READER that measures G-force in real time to prove that most flights never get close to the limit of danger, even if it might feel like it! *Remember, I'm not a doctor, so be sure to get proper medical advice before taking legal, over-the-counter medications, too!

Coming in hot at number 6: Keep YO HANDS BUSY! When you feel fidgety, and the seatback movie just ain't cutting it, get some small bursts of energy out with your hands.

- Braid your hair. Or your seatmate's hair. (Weird way to make a new friend, huh?)
- Bring a fidget cube or spinner. They really work, IMHO.
- Try to make your own weird fun cocktail or mocktail. Ask the flight attendant for three of the most random liquids you can find in the menu and create your own concoction!
- Make your own "Chopped" competition, like that Food Network show! Chop up your snacks and try to make edible bite-sized snacks, or mix your snacks together. Have a competition with your seatmate and ask the third person to be the judge of whose Chopped snack is better!

✹W.O.W.✹

FOR AGORAPHOBIA TRAVEL ANXIETY: *I like to watch cool travel/food and lifestyle YouTube videos of the city I'm going to; it will weirdly make you feel more familiar with the city. You'll be able to see the vibe and the amount of people that walk around depending on what time of day and part of the year it is. When I went to Thailand, I followed some of Anthony Bourdain's food map, and it felt super comforting to see the signs I'd recognized online, as if I had been there before, and felt more familiar with the establishment!*

Finally, tell yourself that STATISTICALLY you are not the only person on this flight who has flying anxiety, so take comfort in knowing this is a very common fear, and if you just keep an eye out, you might find a fellow white-knuckled friend you can chat with—and maybe share some tips or play tic-tac-toe together!

FLIGHT ATTENDANTS
ARE YOUR BFFS 4EVA

Out of all the flights I've taken in my life, I can tell you I've only run into one airline attendant who was a dick. She was probably having a rough day (bc flight attendants are hoo-mans too), and I tried not to take it personally, but basically, she yelled at me for using the first-class bathroom while the seatbelt sign was on. I told her I had started my period (A LIE) instead of telling her the truth: that I was feeling panicky. I got frustrated, she got frustrated, and she purposely skipped me when handing out cookies.

Most flight attendants are the nicest, most caring, and helpful people you'll run into on your travels. And, like your mom always says: *honesty is the best policy*. It makes no sense to try to cover up your panic, anxiety, or depression when you're stuck in a giant tube for many hours with a stranger that you're going to see once or twice every hour and have to make eye contact or light conversation with. I used to be the person who drank four glasses of wine, Valium'd up (DO NOT DO THIS), and boarded early without so much as a smile to the crew, put my sunglasses and headphones on, and prayed to GAWD I would sleep through the whole flight. I kept my anxieties balled-up inside my giant hoodie and closed myself off to the world, not realizing that airplanes come with a built-in support system: FLIGHT ATTENDANTS. Of course, their first job is to make sure we're safe, but I've never had a flight attendant dismiss my needs when it came to my mental health and flying. USE THEM!!!!!!!!!!!!!!!!!!!!! I wish I had more pages in this book to write all the AMAZING interactions I've had with flight attendants, especially when I've had to fly alone. Most of them know tons of facts about planes (and yes, statistics to prove how unlikely crashes and emergencies are) and will be happy to share them with you. I've had flight attendants break down the mechanics of turbulence like I was in flight school myself. And the best part about flight attendants is that they WANT to help. Once I'm honest with them about my fear of flying, 9.999/10, they will make sure to check on me frequently and even give me extra snacks and treats. The more support from humans I received, the less I needed support from medication (THANK GOD, ONCE AGAIN I CANNOT STRESS ENOUGH TO NOT MIX ALCOHOL AND DOWNERS. JUST PICK ONE). I felt as though I had a partner-in-crisis-crime. There have been a few times, however, when the panic overloaded the rational brain, and I found it hard to spit it out to a flight attendant just how tough flying really is for me, especially because I'm someone who smiles when I speak about trauma or during confrontation—I think I do this to put less stress on the person I'm speaking with, but just end up looking at them like a smiling-yet-terror-filled clown you see in your nightmares. When I haven't been able to speak up for myself, I would write them a note instead, usually on the spaces of a magazine or on the barf bag (sometimes, though, I've needed that for my PANIC PUKES), and either slipped it to them when they came by or when I've gotten up to use the restroom. If you can prep with one of these nifty notes, you can fill it out and give it to them while you're getting on the flight! I've even included a downloadable version (see the Resource Index) you can print and pass out to whomever you'd like!

 SERIOUSLY DO NOT TAKE DRUG ADVICE FROM ME IN THIS SECTION

Hi! My name is _____
and I'm sitting in seat #_____. This note is to let you and your crew know that I have an intense and sometimes debilitating fear of flying. If your duties allow (thanks for keeping us safe!), I could use some of your help by _____
_____.

Sometimes, I feel embarrassed by my fear, which is why writing these notes helps me get my thoughts out clearly and identify my needs. :) Thanks for being awesome! #DONTF*CKINGPANIC

MY FLYING ESSENTIALS BAG

I keep a small toiletry bag that's about the size of the 5th Harry Potter book in my carry-on at ALL TIMES. This bag never leaves the carry-on and sits under my seat or in the seatback pocket as I fly. Inside are what I consider to be ESSENTIALS for flying with anxiety. This does not include my medications, which I keep in my pocket while I fly. I consider this bag of goodies to be special add-ons, like when you get guac at Chipotle. Treat yourself and stay comfy. Flying doesn't have to be the most miserable experience of your travels. I try to keep all of the products to NO or minimum smell, because I know people are sensitive to things like that. But also, I'm taking care of myself, so if shit starts to smell a tiny bit like delicious mint and you're giving me the stink eye, I will kindly tell you to suck my dick, then pay for your in-flight cocktail. 'Cause I'm balanced like that. Here's what I keep in my Flying Essentials bag:

- ADVIL

- MINTS

- SILK EYE MASK

- O HUI FACE MOISTURIZER—I like to keep my face SLICK the entire flight, since I normally get dry as beef jerky when I fly. I will apply every two hours. I'm not kidding. Keep yourself hydrated and slick, and you'll be thanking me upon touchdown!

- GEL EYE MASKS—ironically, these usually come out pretty cold when I keep them under my seat, since airplanes tend to be FREEZING.

- LYSOL mini-disinfectant wipes for the tray table and arm rests. I don't need to get sick on this trip.

- EMERGEN-C, that powdered orange supplement that I usually use for hangovers also is great for those multiple cups of water they are always passing out on planes.

- YEAST INFECTION CREAM AND COOLING WIPES—sorry, not sorry.

- VISINE for dry eyeballs, especially if I'm watching a good flick.

- Three different kinds of CHAPSTICK

- NASAL SPRAY or SALINE SPRAY—that airplane air dry as heck tho.

- MOIST TOWELETTE

- TISSUES

- COMB
- MOSQUITO BITE CREAM, because nothing is worse than traveling back from an EXOTIC location scratching the whole way home.
- ESSENTIAL OILS: This one might be considered controversial, but I'll do a very diluted version of a roll-on essential oil or personal essential oil sniffer. I don't recommend bringing a bottle of oil on the plane, as your seatmates might be bothered by the smell, blah blah blah I feel like those people are the same people who get mad about flying next to a dog. STAY AWAY FROM DOTERRA & YOUNG LIVING brands as they are known to be multilevel marketing (MLM) schemes that don't pay their employees. My favorite brand of EO's is Baer Intentions (made by my good friend, and next door neighbor, Steph Baer.)

Thank you, and have a safe flight.

AVOIDANCE

Stepping outside of your comfort zone is a place where anxiety can pop up, but staying inside your comfort zone is a life not fully lived! And with that comes major anxiety, depression, and panic! Sure, you might argue that you're not an extrovert ("anxiety = introvert" is a harmful stereotype that diminishes extroverts' mental health struggles! I got this comment a LOT on a video I made about trying a Muse headband for anxiety, which measures EEG readings from your brain [you can find it on YT, "I tried this $250 headband for my anxiety"] and ALL the top comments were "she doesn't have anxiety...she's too outgoing," "how could you have anxiety and have that much energy?? I smell an attention whore"...etc. which you could imagine was NOT GREAT FOR MY MENTAL HEALTH AND CONFIDENCE LOLOLOL), but, there's a difference between not gaining any energy from being around other people and actively AVOIDING that as to not feel uncomfortable. Some people really do get more energy from social interaction (I think I did more as a teen than an adult; now, my alone time is VERY PRECIOUS and recharging for me), but for others—it can be draining. You might feel drained. But feeling drained after a long social event is NORMAL for anyone that's not an extrovert—it doesn't mean it's BAD. You feel drained after a long run, right? Doesn't mean you should stop running! The way to avoid the avoidance (lol) is with ACCEPTANCE & APPROACHING. Only when you *accept* that you might indeed have high anxiety about a certain place, subject, or conversation will you then truly be able to stop

Extraverts primarily obtain fulfillment from outside interactions and are often highly social.

Introverts are content in their own mental world and prefer to spend time alone or in small/intimate settings with others.

Ambiverts are fairly comfortable in groups and enjoy attention or crowds, yet actively seek and appreciate alone time, too.

AVOIDING the matter. Because, I hate to break it to ya, but anxiety that causes avoidance will only bring MORE anxiety in the long run. The longer and longer you AVOID doing something, the more the anxiety will build and build. AVOIDANCE PREVENTS LEARNING, and remember, my friend, we told each other we'd be down to LEARN MORE ABOUT OURSELVES TO BE LESS AFRAID OF OURSELVES when we started this workbook journey together, right?! When you accept, you can APPROACH. Approaching your fear is critical and sooooo fucking rewarding when you realize you've had the ability INSIDE YOU all along to do the thing!

How have you avoided emotional and/or psychological discomfort?

_____

_____

_____

_____

Remember to approach your avoidant behavior with COMPASSION! If a toddler were afraid of heights, you wouldn't just push him off the highest slide on the playground, right?! NO! I CAN HEAR C.P.S. COMIN' ROUND THE CORNER AS WE SPEAK! You'll want to use your self-compassion skills, along with mindfulness, when choosing to accept and approach your avoidant behavior. If you allow yourself to get caught up in your swirling intrusive thoughts, you might get caught between acceptance and approach, and negative-talk your way out of it!

What are some ways you could make yourself more uncomfortable?

_____

_____

_____

_____

Perhaps you're not physically avoiding environments or people, but rather trying to AVOID YOUR OWN EMOTIONS OR SYMPTOMS. This fear of new symptoms will trigger more anxiety. Your body can see the smallest symptom as a danger! Also, not to be *too* blunt here, but YOU are experiencing the symptoms. YOU feel them. **And you can't avoid yourself forever.** Remember, it will be beneficial to LEAN INTO that discomfort.

Ask yourself: Can I make ROOM for this sensation?

_____

_____

_____

_____

_____

What does discomfort REALLY feel like? From my head to my toes? Where does it start? Where does it end?

_____

_____

_____

_____

What are the behaviors that you do to avoid or control the panic attacks?

_____

_____

_____

_____

Ask yourself: Can I make room for this feeling without judging it? Can I just FEEL it without a thought attached?

_____

_____

_____

_____

THE PANIC POOS

Humans can defecate during times of extreme fear due to the fight-or-flight response. The bladder and bowels can "let go," a.k.a. THIS SHIT LITERALLY EVACUATES ITSELF. Now that we've got the medical jargon out of the way, I can say it: You might almost or most definitely shit your pants during or after a panic attack. Personally, I drop a huge gift off in the Comfort Room 10/10 times after a panic attack. AND THAT'S TOTALLY NORMAL. Your nervous system is not in sync with your gut during extreme moments of stress, and it has no choice but to fall out of line...and out of your body. There has been more than one time where I have almost landed a plane after takeoff because I got up out of my seat before reaching cruising altitude to absolutely create my own bowel landslide. I've had to do that awkward dance over the person sitting in the aisle seat before my body decides that... I don't know how else to put it?? It's like, everything liquefies? And the muscles in my ass are just like LOL BYYYYE SEE YA NEVER! The stomach in general is WILDLY connected to our emotions. Thank god scientists are starting to do more studies on gut health—but, none of these studies tell you what to do during that MOMENT when you're dealing with 15 different bodily symptoms.

- *How do you manage them all?*
- *How do you keep yourself from shitting your pants in public?*
- *How do you find a bathroom when you absolutely are nowhere near a bathroom when it happens?*

Kelsey's

TOP TIPS FOR NOT TOOTIN TOOTSIES in your trousers

1. Don't wait until it's too late. The toilet paper brand Charmin has a website where you can find public restrooms and actually rate them!

2. If someone is giving you shit (no pun intended) for needing a restroom, like at a gas station or store, use urgent language like "It's a medical emergency" (because it IS).

3. Stay hydrated, and don't be an idiot about what you eat before you go into an environment that makes you panic or panic about the panic. For instance, I once ate a 10-course exotic Thai meal from a fancy restaurant, filled with butters and fat, right before getting on the international flight home to the US. I literally had to LEAVE THE PASSPORT/CUSTOMS line (which notoriously takes hours to get through), abandoning my partner with my luggage and backpack. I then spent the rest of the flight MISERABLE, waiting for the next wave to hit. And y'all—I know I don't have to tell you, but there is NOTHING worse than having to take one of those stomach-stabbing shits in an airplane bathroom. Carry a collapsible water bottle with you when you know you'll be out of your comfort zone for hours at a time! Hydration is key after...idk how else to say this...SHITTING A LOT! Or travel in general.

4. Caffeine is a diuretic, which means not only can it give you the jitters if you can't handle the amount of caffeine, but it'll make you pee a lot. And with pee...and coffee... comes...poop. Just be mindful of *when* and *where* you're going to chug your latte. For so many of us, it's just a staple in our morning routine. But if you have a big meeting that day, maybe stick to water?

5. Remember. Everyone poops.

KELSEY'S TOP 5 PANIC ATTACKS

SPOILER ALERT: I SURVIVED THEM ALL

I'm about to expose myself so you can feel less embarrassed about yours!

#5

THE WORST HANGOVER ANXIETY ATTACK (AND THERE HAVE BEEN MANY)

In a last-ditch effort to save our relationship, I organized a surprise birthday trip for the boyfriend that broke my heart (you'll read more about this in the Depression section!), where all of his friends would meet us in San Diego for a giant Halloween-themed birthday bash. Well, we were on the verge of breaking up, so I DRAAAAANK. And, since it was also a Halloween party, I DRAAAAAAANK. And, I was generally just stressed and unhappy with my life, so I DRAAAAAAAAAANK! When I somehow woke up the next morning, I could barely make it through brunch without it feeling like the world was falling in on itself. Being in an unfamiliar city added to the confusion. We were supposed to go spend the day on a duck boat (I know, wtf is a duck boat anyway??), but one of my bathroom trips to puke turned into one of my bathroom trips to panic. I finally came out, embarrassed as fuck, and asked my boyfriend if we could drive back to LA. I told him I couldn't explain what was going on, but things weren't right, and I needed to go home. He obliged. I spent the rest of the two-hour drive (which felt like 10 when you're THAT hung over) counting my breaths. One. By. One. In. And. Out. FOR TWO HOURS. I WAS ON MANUAL, BABY.

I held his hand the entire drive and called my mom a few times on the ride home, to make sure I was still alive and not a figment of my own imagination. The next four to six days were filled with DAILY panic attacks, and I didn't leave my bed except to go pee. We broke up not long after.

#4
THE RAPTURE LMAOOOO

Once, during early childhood, before we'd known that I was suffering from panic disorder, I thought the Rapture had happened. The Rapture, for those who don't know, is supposed to be the day that God comes back to Earth and takes all of his followers with him back to heaven, like some exclusive club, and everyone left on Earth gets stuck there where it's, like, a purgatory? Or maybe we go to hell? I don't know. I gave up on the religion thing a while ago.

ANYWAY. It was a regular-ass day, and I was home with my family—OR SO I THOUGHT. I went out into the kitchen and it was eerily quiet...tooooo quiet. I began to get anxious. I checked my sister's room, and all her gadgets were on... but no sister. I ran to my parents' side of the house and couldn't find them. I SPRINTED TO THE GARAGE AND ALL THEIR CARS WERE THERE. "OH, FUCK," I remember thinking in my child brain, "THE FUCKING RAPTURE HAPPENED!!!" I basically FLUNG myself across these giant hedges that separate our house from our neighbors and BANGED ON THEIR DOOR. Only about five seconds went by before I assumed they'd evaporated up to the Pearly Gates and FLEW to the next neighbor's house...to...you guessed it, BANG ON THEIR DOOR IN A FIT OF PANIC. Another five seconds before my heart was pounding out of my own chest, and I decided that going back to my own home would be safest before the devil-demon-lizard came up to get the bad humans left on Earth (even though I was a super-religious kid and was "saved"). But. I didn't make it even 20 feet down the sidewalk before my panic was SO INTENSE that I fell to my knees. And peed. My. Pants. I PEED MY PANTS YOU GUYS!! OUT OF FUCKING PANIC!!! Jesssuuuusss Christ LITERALLY!

I somehow found the wit to take my soggy, cargo-shorted self into my house where, from the garage entrance, I could see into the pool and patio area...where my mom, dad, and sister were all standing, looking out into our back yard looking at a family of deer. Fucking. Deer!!!!! That's why I couldn't find them! Fuckin' BAMBI and her CREW!! I ran into my room, unable to face them, and jumped into the shower, shoving my wet pants into the dirty hamper underneath a bunch of already dirty clothes hoping to cover the smell of FUCKING URINE hhahahahah. Anyway, while I was in the shower, apparently the neighbor came and knocked on our door and asked if I was okay, since they saw me running away from their house frantically like a fucking crackhead in soaked shorts. When my dad asked me what I was doing, I told him I was playing ding-dong ditch.

#3
NYC

There's something about NYC that gives me anxiety, which makes me SO SAD, because my favorite TV show ever in the world still to this day is *GOSSIP GIRL*. I wanted to be Serena van der Woodsen more than ANYTHING. I loved that she was ALL CITY CHIC with a touch of California. I even moved to NYC after I gave up on going to a traditional college to follow my dreams of being an actor, film-maker, and Serena van der Woodsen clone. I bought the headbands and everything, y'all. But when I arrived in the beautiful concrete jungle…I learned very quickly that I DID NOT like riding the subway. It was too claustrophobic, and I had no control about how fast or slow it went, or when it would stop randomly for minutes on end. As convenient as it was, I quickly enacted avoidant behavior and stopped riding it altogether. Which got EXPENSIVE for a 19-year-old. I also could never get used to how TALL and TOWERING the buildings were. Every time I went outside, I felt like I was being hugged by the giant gray walls that seemed never-ending. And the elevators. OMG, the elevators—THEY'RE EVERYWHERE!!!

The two panic attacks I remember most in NYC involved a hangover and coffee. The first was when I was in NYC for work at BuzzFeed. I was sent there for two days to meet with the NYC office and help collaborate on some ideas. The night before my first day at the NYC office, my anxiety got the best of me, and I drank my balls off at some shitty dive bar in Turtle Bay to calm my claustrophobia. I woke up with a RAGING hangover and tried to make it to the BuzzFeed NY office. I paid for a $60 cab, so I didn't have to ride the subway, and arrived outside the building. There was scaffolding covering the sidewalks, which made it feel like I was in a giant box of metal sticks. I stepped out of the Uber, took ONE LOOK UP at the giant Soho building, and it looked like it WAS SWAYING. I swear to god, it could've been my vertigo or hangover or maybe the wind was really strong that day, but only two seconds on the sidewalk created that too-familiar rush of panic, and I turned on my heel just fast enough to catch my Uber before it drove away. I told him to take me back to my hotel IMMEDIATELY AND I CANCELED THE DAY AT BUZZFEED. All the meetings, all the brainstorms, I can't imagine how many people I let down that day or ruined their schedules, which made me feel even MORE guilty, and I spent the next 48 hours wrapped up in a duvet in the hotel with my eyes closed, counting down the moments until I could breathe the California air again. I told them I was sick. The second big panic attack caused by the NYC aesthetic was when I had just moved to Brooklyn Heights to go to school for acting. I was living in this apartment/dorm and was paired with a total stranger, who turned out to be a cool musical theater chick named Jess. Our first morning as roommates, we went to the corner cafe to hang and explore. She ordered a coffee. Now, listen, at that time, I was 19 years old AND HAD NEVER EVER DRANK OR EVEN TRIED COFFEE BEFORE. Her ordering her honey latte sounded tres chic, like something SERENA VAN DER WOODSEN would've done, so I ordered one, too! I wanted my new roomie to think I was a cool, grown adult who drank coffee like every other New Yorker. What. A. Mistake. Five minutes after walking out of the cafe and into the subway station. It happened. The sounds and winds of the fast-moving trains combined with this new HIGH of coffee caffeine I was unfamiliar with came whooshing in like the train itself. I grabbed my chest and closed my eyes. My roommate asked if I was okay. I could not even form a word to come out of my mouth. It was so UN-Serena van der Woodsen of me!!! I started sweating as the trains rushed by, while Jess stared at me, totally clueless on what to do. The train door opened and Jess was asked if I was getting on the train. My eyes were still closed, and all I remember was shouting, "I HAVE TO GO" and running up the stairway exit. I still remember Jess's face, concerned but wildly confused, looking out the train window as I ran up the stairs, needing to take a massive anxiety (and now coffee) poo. It was the worst first impression anyone could've made. I ran directly back to our dorm, pooped, and laid in my safe space under the twin bed covers in our small dorm. When she got home later that day after perusing the city ALONE, I told her that I had a stomachache and that I never wanted to bring up that moment again. Things weren't ever really the same with us. It was always a little weird after that. Now, 10 years later, I drink a trenta coffee every day and visit the city often, since my BFF, Lacey, still lives there. But I'd be lying to you if I said every time that skyline comes into view when the plane is landing, my stomach doesn't still do a few flips thinking about walking back into that concrete city.

#2
THE PANIC ATTACK WE DIDN'T EVEN REALIZE WAS A PANIC ATTACK

I was SO YOUNG, my parents didn't even THINK about mental-health concerns the night I came home from a soccer game, telling them I couldn't swallow correctly. I had childhood asthma, and my mom and dad were concerned that this new swallowing issue was somehow linked to that. I was probably around the age of six or seven, and recreational soccer had consumed all of my free time. But during one game, and I still don't know what the trigger was—maybe all the running around and exercise I did during the game—I sat on the bench and started noticing my breathing. Not in a good way. And not in an asthma-attack way, either. I thought about the blood pumping through my body and how it was magically doing it on its own. I felt my heart...hmm...I didn't like that. The flight response kicked in as I walked up and down the bench, asking my fellow teammates how their lungs and hearts felt. My coach thought I was having an asthma reaction, so he kept me out of the game, which, in hindsight, might have been a bad idea, because there I sat for 30 minutes on the bench, hyperventilating and over-breathing. I didn't say anything to my dad on the car on the way home; I just tried to drink my blue Gatorade and CHILL OUT. But when I got home, I found myself feeling like I couldn't SWALLOW. I ran into the kitchen, where my parents thought maybe I was choking on something or needed my inhaler. I remember a very specific moment of my dad sitting me up on the kitchen counter as my mom and dad's hands poked and prodded on my chest and face. I threw my hands out and said "STOP!!!!" I closed my eyes, gathered all my energy, and tried to swallow. *And I couldn't.* I started freaking out even more, so my parents threw me in the backseat of the car and rushed me to the children's urgent care, which was only a 10-minute drive away. As soon as I got there, the doctor tried to run some tests, but I kept my hands out, trying to create a distance and regain control of the situation. The doctor finally said to my parents, "We need to give her some Valium to chill her out so I can run my tests." (I'm sure she said it in a way more doctorly way.) They agreed, and I drank this liquid baby Valium and fell into a sleep haze moments later. I was OUT LIKE A LIGHT. They ran a bunch of tests and found...nothing. The doctors literally told my parents that I was being a "hysterical child." They chalked it up to a one-time thing, and for years, I lived in the gray area of never being diagnosed with a panic disorder. The *one* funny part about that night was that the Valium was SO STRONG, I couldn't walk out of the urgent care on my own two feet. SO, this very kind, huge, nurse dude scooped me up like a baby and carried me out to my mom's car. My mom said there was an absolute look of horror on the sea of parents' faces in the waiting room as this giant man carried the body of a limp and lifeless girl across the room. They probably thought I was dead. *laughing emoji and clenched teeth emoji*

#1
THE FIRST CONSCIOUS PANIC ATTACK

I was on a plane flight with my family, heading back to Florida, where I grew up. We had just had an amazing ski vacation in Canada, and I was looking forward to the long flight ahead to catch up on some Zs, since I'd spent the last week getting up super early to catch the first tracks on the mountain. However, our flight got canceled, and we were put on a later flight that had an overnight pit stop in Houston. Lucky us! My aunt lives in Houston, so we had a place to stay overnight. Just a nice little family reunion surprise pit stop, right??? NO. Wrong. VERY WRONG. I was sitting on the plane, next to my sister, mid-flight, watching a movie on a portable DVD player (which was something that existed back then!! hehe!! I'M OLD.), when, without any warning, my body went into my first conscious FULL-BLOWN PANIC ATTACK. I'm talking BLOOD-RUSHING, HEAD-FILLING, CHEST-TIGHTENING flight response. **This was the big one.**

It freaked me out so bad, I got out of my seat, climbed over my sister, which annoyed the shit out of her, and ran to the bulkhead, where my mom and dad were sitting. "I can't breathe. I can't breathe. Something's wrong, something's wrong." My mom took me to the back of the plane, where she was trying to handle my freak-out privately—remember, at this time, I still hadn't been diagnosed with a panic disorder, so my mom was still running down the list of "Is it something medical or mental health related?" She couldn't control me flailing around, and I started to get...LOUD. I was screaming in the back of the plane, "I GOTTA GET OUT OF HERE!" A group of flight attendants approached us, which caused me to feel more claustrophobic. The walls were closing in, and the air on the plane felt unbreathable and stale. The flight attendants kept asking if they needed to call a doctor, which my mom kept denying. I kept trying to walk around the group of people who had now gathered in the back of the plane, looking at me like a freak. I couldn't explain what was happening, and they all wanted to know how to help. Well, after 10 minutes of this back and forth, the head flight attendant said they were going to land the plane. "Oh fuck," I thought. "Oh fuck NO," my mom replied. At this point, we were already delayed due to this layover in Houston, and my mom knew we just needed to get home. Causing an emergency landing would not only delay us further, but THESE HUNDREDS OF PEOPLE WHO WERE NOW STARTING TO STARE AT THIS CHAOS HAPPENING IN THE BACK OF THE PLANE WITH VERY CONCERNED FACES would be furiously inconvenienced. My mom went into full "fuck this" mode and told the flight attendant, "Get me some vodka. For her." "How old is she?" the flight attendant asked. "GIVE ME THE VODKA," my mom replied. **I was 17 years old**.

It was probably the tone in my mom's voice, and the idea of doing an unnecessary emergency landing, that finally pushed the flight attendant over the edge. Another flight attendant grabbed a mini airplane bottle's worth of vodka and handed it to my mom. "Two more," my mom said. They obliged. My mom cracked open all three bottles of vodka, desperate, with no clue what else to do, and put it up to my mouth. Lest I remind you, I grew up in the public school system in TAMPA, FLORIDA; I had been drinking since I was 13 years old. I grabbed the bottles and threw them back with the speed and skill of an old alcoholic man sitting at a bar after signing divorce papers. The rest of the flight was a blur. *Apparently*, I sat with my mom in the bulkhead, cradled in her arms like a baby. A grown-ass 17-year-old. We didn't make an emergency landing and got to Houston. I started to sober up when we got to my aunt's house; at this point, it was past midnight, and as I lied in her guest bedroom, I stayed up the entire night with my hand on my chest, counting my breath. I'll never forget the feeling I had in my chest as I stared up into her ceiling, thinking, *"My life is going to be completely different now."*

And I was right. My life has been different since then. It was unmanageable for many years.

We arrived safely in Tampa after my mom had snuck me a few breakfast cocktails at the Houston airport to convince me to get back on an airplane. I didn't have a choice. My parents wouldn't even entertain the idea of *driving* back to Florida. I was so scared and unsure, but I felt safe with my mom. The next few days were filled with a similar feeling of panic. It was daily, and interrupting my quality of life, so I forced my mom to drive me to the ER. I know, she's VERY cool and understanding, and I'm SUPER lucky she didn't tell me to suck it up or walk it off. She agreed that if I was still feeling this "fucked up" days after the big panic attack was over, she wanted to make sure (along with me) that there wasn't anything wrong with my heart. The ER in the suburbs of Tampa, Florida, luckily, was not busy on a Tuesday night at 7 PM, and they took me in right away and ran a bunch of tests. Because of the results showing nothing out of the ordinary, I began to believe there was nothing medically pointing to what was causing my supposed heart palpitations. The doctors didn't dismiss me completely, though, and gave my mom the name of a psychiatrist. We were clueless on what else to do, so my mom made me an appointment, and I saw my first psychiatrist ever when I was 17 years old. From then on, I've been deeply and profoundly involved in the mental healthcare system and the activism along with it.

✵ W. O. W. ✵

Also don't feel bad if you've gone to the ER when you've experienced a panic attack. There are studies that show[1] people showing up to the ER for mental-health-related issues due to anxiety and stress are on the rise—and why WOULDN'T they be? Though we normalize the word "anxiety," people don't realize when it's becoming unhealthy in their own bodies. So, naturally, when you have your first panic attack OUT OF NOWHERE, you might think something is wrong with your heart or lungs, or wherever your main symptoms are. If you feel like your panic attack is severe enough to visit an emergency room, be sure to bring up mental-health concerns, and don't leave without resources.

1 Weiss, Ph. D., Audrey J, et al. "Trends in Emergency Department Visits Involving Mental and Substance Use Disorders." *Agency for Healthcare Research and Quality*, 6 Dec. 2016, www.hcup-us.ahrq.gov/reports/statbriefs/sb216-Mental-Substance-Use-Disorder-ED-Visit-Trends.jsp.

HEY! I'M GLAD I CAUGHT YOU HERE READING!

Do me a favor: Drop your shoulders, soften your tummy, loosen your eye muscles, and let your jaw hang open. Take a few, nice, deep breaths here. Check in with yourself. How are you feeling right now?

_____

_____

_____

_____

_____

_____

_____

_____

_____

_____

_____

_____

_____

_____

ACUPUNCTURE

PANICKING? POKE IT!

I'm not going to lie—when I first heard about acupuncture for treating anxiety, panic attacks, and depression, I thought, "This is bullshit. There's no way there's any science to this. Why would stickin' li'l needles in my body make me feel BETTER?! I HATE NEEDLES!" I was wrong. Very, very, wrong.

Acupuncturists are like, REALLY GOOD PEOPLE. THE BEST PEOPLE I'VE MET ALONG THIS CLUSTERFUCK OF AN EMOTIONAL MENTAL HEALTH JOURNEY. They spend their whole day making other people feel well. There's also TONS of friggin' science behind the benefits of acu treating anxiety, including changes in neurotransmitters involved in emotional regulation such as serotonin, modulation of the autonomic nervous system, and changes in immune function.

In my very personal opinion, if any doctor you meet is anti-acu, it's because they're deeply afraid of Eastern and alternative medicines after they've spent their whole lives studying modern medicine. They fear these types of treatments will have people spending their coins elsewhere and not at their offices. And it also feels a little racist.

A big myth about acupuncture is that it hurts. It does not hurt—and that's coming from a pussy ass li'l bitch who doesn't have much of a pain tolerance and still makes her boyfriend come to any appointments that require shots so he can hold her hand.

The needles are usually very thin and are made with rounded tips, so they don't cut the skin but instead stimulate the area they are applied to. The areas in which they are inserted depend on what's going on in yo' head and body. I've had needles in my ears, toes, nose—you name it!

So wtf does sticking needles in our bodies actually do for our mental wellbeing?

One of my very dear friends and all-around-incredible-badass-women, Emily Broderick, DACM (Doctor of Acupuncture and Chinese Medicine) says:

> "How I usually describe it is this: Our body has the sympathetic nervous system (aka fight or flight) and the parasympathetic nervous system (aka rest and digest or rest and repair, when we're chilling and perceive no threats). When you're having anxiety, you could say your body is stuck in the fight or flight sympathetic nervous system (SNS) response, even though the threat isn't necessarily real. We live in a hyper-stimulating, high-pressure world that amps us up. Acupuncture helps by helping to bring the body back into a parasympathetic state of self-healing (rest and repair) by stimulating the peripheral nervous system via acupuncture points on the skin and muscle."

She goes on to say,

> "One of the reasons I love acu is that when you're looking at how to treat someone, you always take into consideration their mental and emotional health because they are inextricably linked to physical health. For example, anxiety can be caused by a physiological problem, or a physiological problem can cause anxiety....but it's never a separate thing. If you want to treat a physical ailment, you have to look at all the mental/emotional stuff. It's all interconnected like an ecosystem that needs to be in balance."

Emily has not only treated me when I've been in emotional pain, but also when I had the worst chronic pain flare-up of my life with a neuropathic chronic pain condition called Trigeminal Neuralgia and Anesthesia Dolorosa. I hadn't slept for over 48 hours, and the pain was causing me to hallucinate. The emergency room sent me home with an icepack and told me that opioids can't help neuropathic pain (true), and I just had to "wait it out" after my then-boyfriend had driven me around to three other ER's looking for help. *FACEPALM* Eventually, my dad had to fly in from Florida because I couldn't blink without falling to my knees in pain. I didn't know what else to do. I had posted about it in an Instagram story, and that's when Emily reached out like the literal angel goddess of light that she is. She commented:

> *"So, if you get an acu treatment because your face hurts, the acupuncturist is also treating some emotional component of that just because that's how we're trained to diagnose and treat."*

Emily came to my apartment as a house-call, treated me with acu (after actually listening to me about how the past few days of my pain had manifested emotionally and physically), and then I drifted off to sleep with tens of needles in my face and body. Emily, a true healer and good person deserving of a front-of-the-line-spot in heaven, then sat on the couch with my 70-year-old dad and watched old movies with him while I FINALLY SLEPT FOR HOURS. *HEART EYES*

While acu didn't *cure* my pain forever, it made my life feel manageable again. My anxiety about getting out of bed vanished. I didn't spiral into a depressive hole of self-hate because my body always felt so against me. In fact, acu has helped me cherish, nourish, and be grateful for the mind and body that I do have…even if my mind and body get a bit hot, fiery, and flarey sometimes.

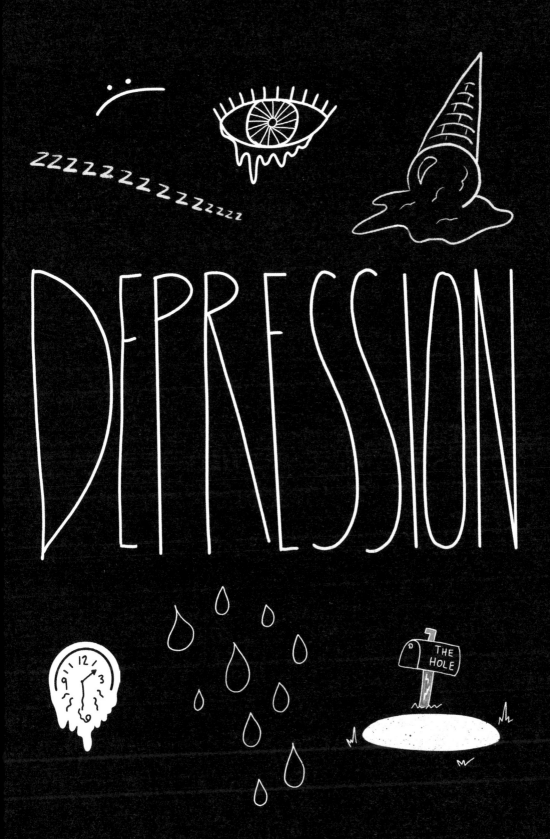

DEPRESSION

MY RELATIONSHIP WITH DEPRESSION BEGAN IN MY PRETEEN YEARS.

I very specifically remember being tired *all. the. time.* I would have to nap constantly by the age of 12 and 13 years old. To this day I have an unhealthy association that napping = I'm falling back into a depression. Seven hours in a public school felt like absolute torture, and each day felt like a new challenge to see how long I could stay awake. I'd consider it a win if I could make it to 5th period without having to put my head down in Mr. Leitzski's psychology class (a class I wish I would've paid more attention in, because maybe I would've LEARNED SOMETHING TO HELP MY BRAIN...alas, a nap prevails). On top of the constant fatigue, I quickly lost interest in my many after-school sports and activities, such as theater, flag football, and piano lessons. The exercise and socialization was slowly replaced by after-school naps and a general mood of fuckin' blehhhhhhhhhhhhhHHHH. I'd go home directly from school, not having the energy to even wait around for my crush at the bus stop, and get right into bed.

Eventually, my dad would have to force me out of slumber around 4 PM to whatever event was on the calendar that day, and, as the months went on, I dropped out of each hobby, slowly but surely. My parents had me tested for a bunch of thyroid diseases, which all came back negative. The word "depression" was never even *mentioned* by any doctors. In my mind, that word only belonged to sad adults in commercials: sad cartoon eggs, or grayscale B-roll of a mom who looked like she'd just buried her husband. Depression couldn't be happening to me! I was a YOUTH!!! What responsibilities did I have that made my life hard? I didn't have bills or a family to feed. Like most teens my age, I'd stay up late, watching TV shows I wasn't supposed to or chatting on AIM[38] with my BFFs—but not enough to be EXHAUSTED by life each day. I was a teenager, for fuck's sake! Shouldn't I be bouncing around social circles, giddy with crushes, and expanding my hobbies for college resumes? It wasn't like I didn't have *passions*—I always knew I wanted to be in entertainment—but I could only THINK about it. I couldn't bring myself to DO any of the steps required to put me in a position of excelling in the subject. I also wasn't ever tested for ADHD until I was well into adulthood; ADHD and mental health disorders like depression and anxiety are often linked. Furthermore, the symptoms of ADHD can look a lot like anxiety, too! It took scientists until 2009 to find definitive evidence that people with ADHD lack proteins necessary to build healthy rewards systems in the brains! That lack of motivation would've been helpful to identify as my brain coexisting with depression and not me being lazy.

When people living with depression say "I'm tired" they may also mean:

- I don't really feel attached to the idea of being alive
- I'm not super stoked about doing another day in this lifetime right now
- Please go buy me a Starbucks iced coffee for no other reason than you love me
- I'm tired of faking it
- I don't like being at war with my mood
- I feel like a burden
- I don't see the point of doing anything

As a teen, I was the queen of procrastination, and while I would always get my assignments done, I was barely scraping by. I also began to become really...I don't know how else to say this nicely about myself...CUNTY. I became a full-force cunt to everyone around me. My family chalked it up to hormones, but I knew this anger I felt inside was more than just horny, angry cell DNA bouncing off one another manically: I was tired, sad, and angry *all the fucking time*. I had lost interest in things I used to thrive at. Everyone and everything either made me sad, angry, or

38 For you even YOUTHIER YOUTHS: AIM was an instant messaging system before texting was free with your plan and FB Messenger didn't exist yet.

exhausted. Every conversation with a teacher or authority figure would conjure up a hate in me so deep that tears would well in my eyes every time I had to have a conversation lasting longer than a few sentences. God forbid I'd ever be YELLED AT by a soccer coach or teacher—that would result in a temper tantrum SO GREAT, it would be the talk of school for days. I once told my television productions teacher (whom I liked deeply as TV was one of my favorite subjects—again, shout out to Mr. Lennox!) to "take the tampon out of his ass, for fuck's sake," in front of a classroom of 30 students. WHY DID I SAY THAT?! He was my favorite teacher!!! He's the reason I stayed in film and got to where I am now!! Mr. Lennox reacted cool and calm and told me to stay after class. Ah, fuck. That white-hot rage was now bubbling as sour embarrassment inside my stomach.

The definition of **depression** has changed slightly over time. While many people think of depression as sadness, it should be highlighted that sadness is a REACTION to loss, disappointment, problems, or other difficult situations. DEPRESSION is a mental health mood disorder that distorts the way you understand yourself. It can also negatively affect the way you understand and relate to things around you. There are many names for this mood disorder, such as clinical depression, major depressive disorder, or major depression.

After class, Mr. Lennox asked that I apologize, which I did, and told me that he didn't recognize this behavior from me. Instead of reprimanding me, like he should have, he asked what was going on in my life. THAT'S a good teacher. At the time, however, I was so embarrassed, I brushed it off and didn't accept his help. I didn't think I needed help. Why couldn't I just feel GOOD for once? I remember being so frustrated at why I couldn't "snap out of" these frustrating feelings. I knew there was a lively, sweet girl who was empathetic and fun as fuck underneath, but all that came out of my mouth was cruel, dreary, and completely uninterested.

Even to this day, at 29 years old, I always feel exhausted. I've tried different diets, nighttime routines, getting more sleep, getting less sleep, doing sleep studies, medications, supplements, amphetamines, melatonin, etc., etc., etc. To no avail. My depression has always manifested as a pinch of irritability, fatigue, and a huge dollop of EHHHHHHHHH for life. I get angry that I'm not out and about LIVING LIFE TO THE FULLEST, as every T-shirt, Instagram story, and pop lyric reminds me that I'm supposed to be doing. I was always someone who would give 110% when she decided to do things. The problem was, I couldn't gather enough energy or fucks to give to DO ANYTHING. Even with routine, schedule, and accountability, whether it be school or work, I'd always find a way to get out of responsibility and lie in bed. I'm not proud to admit this—but in college, I faked many relatives' deaths to get out of going to class. I'd PHYSICALLY PHOTOSHOP pictures of random old people I'd find on Getty Images onto a pre-made funeral template that I'd find for free online and send it to a teacher as proof that I was "out of town for a funeral." The truth was, I was only a few blocks from campus, in bed, with the curtains pulled shut. I'd put more energy into making fake death fliers than any school activity I should've actually been doing. And the kicker was that, every time I did this, about an hour after canceling the class, I'd get an immense wave of GUILT that would wash over me. "I should've just GONE TO CLASS," I'd yell at myself. But why bother, if I'd spend the entire class wishing I was literally anywhere else? Depression feels uncomfortable, even in the most comfortable of spaces, like my bed. I painted my room dark-red and my sheets were black. I was fully living like a Victorian vampire.

While in my adult life, I've learned to take anger out *less* on people that are simply in my line of mental fire (though it definitely still happens from time to time), it's reversed and gone INWARD. Instead of the cunty, foul-mouthed teenager acting out to friends and family, I'm the cunty, foul-mouthed *adult* who has a viciously cruel internal monologue. The authority figure that I hated confrontation with as a teen was now inside my brain: the ADULT-NESS forever trying to crack the whip at being more "grown."

Depression has always *hit* me differently than panic and anxiety. With anxiety, I was always able to throw the feelings into a category with solutions, like self-care, medication, or meditation. Panic would ALWAYS pass. Always. But depression...this one feels a little trickier for me. Especially since so many people in my life have told me that I have nothing to be depressed about. They say I'm *insert compliment that I take as a negative*! How could I possibly be *depressed*? That's the rub with depression—it's not necessarily a feeling of sadness *per se, but rather a feeling of nothing*. Nothing excites me during a depressive episode. I'm perfectly content with the idea of staying in bed forever and letting someone else live my life for me. When I'm going through the worst bouts of it, I do my research and find that some people use ketamine injections for depression (and PTSD, among other things), but I'll tell myself that it doesn't ever feel like it's...THAT bad. "My depression isn't 'ketamine injection' bad," I'll always joke to myself and others. Ninety percent of the time, it feels like my depression only deserves an hour in a room with a therapist during talk therapy. But anyone who's experienced it knows that depression follows like a shadow that can dull your shine.

This section of the book can feel a little heavier for some, so I want to reiterate that *you can take your time with these pages.* It doesn't need to be done all at once, and make sure to check in with yourself and how your body is feeling as you use this section. And, another obvious but necessary TRIGGER WARNING that this chapter goes more in-depth about suicide, suicidal ideation, etc.

> *You have to be scared before you can be brave. That's how bravery works. Being brave means confronting what you're scared of, despite the overwhelming fear. That takes real strength, and you have it inside of you.*
>
> —Brené Brown

THE
BIG
FUCKIN' LITTLE
TO-DO-IF-YOU'RE-UP-FOR-IT
LIST

Like I've said many times in this workbook: HUMANS ARE MULTIFACETED. We can be depressed and *still get shit done*. In fact, that's how most of us live with it! So, remind yourself: You can take this day one step at a time. One breath at a time. Things will get done when they get done. So, let's give yourself a little boost for today. **Write down one thing you want to do today.** It can be anything (brush your teeth, make your bed, do the dishes, clean out that closet, answer the email, dance, sing).

Tell me what it is:

1. _____

Take pride in crossing off this thing when you've done it! X this bitch out with a BOLD RED PEN!! LITTLE WINS ARE STILL WINS!

What would you do today if you weren't feeling depressed?

_____

_____

_____

_____

_____

_____

1, 2, 3, 4, 5—
DON'T THINK, JUST DO IT!

I want to tell you about a very smart lady named Mel Robbins, who is an American television host, author, and motivational speaker who came up with the five-second rule. Mel believes that our minds are designed to not like to do things that are uncomfortable or difficult. Makes sense, right? The brain is there to protect us, not experience discomfort! However, if you want to live a life worth waking up for, you're going to have to take a risk, push yourself, and find the comfort in the uncomfortability. "Depression is designed to stop you," she says. "We all have a habit of hesitating. And, when you take that micro-moment to hesitate, it sends a signal to your brain that wakes you up going, 'Oh, whoa, wait, why are we hesitating here—this must be a risk!'" Mel continues on to say that she believes that all the problems can be boiled down to silence and hesitation. She says she realizes that, when it comes to doing what's at hand, she's NEVER going to wake up "feeling like it." That's what depression does. And that's she's ONE DECISION away from changing all of that: to waking up, to being a wife, to showing up as a mother, etc. But we check out because we're overwhelmed, or because we're afraid, or we hit that self-doubt. So, we hit the snooze button, and that's a *decision*. She talks about how she KNEW there was more to her life.

Sounds familiar, right?? She knew that there was more inside of her, but it felt too overwhelming; you KNOW what to do, but you can't do it, and you don't know why. I've never heard a more accurate description of depression before. It feels like you're missing the chapter in the manual of life that everyone else seemed to have. Instead, I get stuck in my head. Mel's five-second method helped me get past my stuck points—especially when it came to finding a light during a depressive episode. Mel considers this exercise a "skill" to learn: to hear that inner voice and lean into it quickly, before it takes hold of you. She says the second you hear your brain talking to you, to "get out of bed" or "take a walk" or "go show up as a friend," know that the answer is in you. **You CAN do it.** So, one day, when Mel heard that voice, she decided to get out of bed by counting down. **She said "5, 4, 3, 2, 1" and got out of bed.** Just like that. It was the first time she hadn't hit her snooze button. The next day, she did it again. 5, 4, 3, 2, 1—DO THE THING. It worked over and over for her.

She started to realize that she had a five-second window before her brain would step in and take over, recognize that hesitation, and sabotage any change she was about to make. And, those changes could change your entire life. Your counting out loud breaks these habits' loops. When you say number one, you've fully interrupted the brain's loop to ignite that gear of depression. She reminds people to remember that you ALWAYS have the five-second window. Do you have a hard time getting out of bed, like me? How about putting the phone down at night before bed? Deciding to speak up in that meeting? Confronting that asshole neighbor who leaves their dog shit on the shared patio? Try the five-second skill. Don't hesitate. Don't restrain.

What would you try the five-second skill for?

_____

_____

_____

_____

Try it and tell me how it felt.

_____

_____

_____

_____

COMPARISON IS THE THIEF OF JOY.

—someone smart.

Who are some people you've been comparing yourself to lately and why? What do you find yourself comparing?

_____

_____

_____

_____

_____

_____

_____

_____

_____

_____

_____

_____

_____

_____

DEPRESSION THAT FEELS CAUSED BY ANOTHER PERSON'S ACTIONS

Holding onto pain that someone else caused you is allowing them to still control you. Let yourself be free by accepting that you can't change what happened. Know that it's okay to still get sad about something you thought you've already healed from. It doesn't mean you've regressed. It means you're human. Accept an apology that you may never get. You cannot heal if you are pretending that you were never hurt. LET IT HURT *then* LET IT GO. Don't let your bad day, month, or even year trick you into thinking you have a bad *life*.

SET A S.M.A.R.T. GOAL

What is a S.M.A.R.T. goal, you may be asking me, as you assume it to be some nerdy acronym? Well, you're right, but that doesn't change the fact that IT'S HELPFUL! It's a goal you give yourself that is Specific, Measurable, Attainable, Relevant, and Time-based. SMART goals are a way to add structure to your goals. Your goals during depression can be as simple as getting out of bed, taking a shower, or going to the grocery store. When making a smart goal, ask yourself:

(S) What do you want to do? This should be something SPECIFIC. Use real numbers, and choose a realistic deadline. "Get out of bed" is simple, but too casual. Give me more details. HOW do you want to get out of bed? What kind of DAY do you want to have?

_____

_____

_____

_____

(M) How will you MEASURE your goal? How will you know when you've reached it? Is it trackable? Is it as simple as a yes-or-no answer? How will your answer accurately reflect success? Is it finishing a specific task? Sending that certain email?

_____

_____

_____

_____

(A) Is your goal ATTAINABLE? Clarify the actions you can take to make this goal successful. What's the action plan? Is it in your power to accomplish it?

_____

_____

_____

_____

(R) Are these goals RELEVANT to your overall life plan? Can you realistically achieve it? What hurdles might you face? Don't try to change the world overnight, or give yourself too many goals to accomplish at once. No one can do it all! Especially alone! Ask WHY you want to achieve it before you commit to it.

_____

_____

_____

_____

(T) When exactly do you want to accomplish it? You MUST have a deadline! A TIME-BASED limit gives you accountability!

_____

_____

_____

_____

If you get discouraged, what will be your mantra?

_____

_____

_____

_____

SMART goals can be applied to almost anything, and really help me face my depression. Even if I'm lying in bed, making a SMART list for the day on my phone under the covers!

MYOM

YOUR BRAIN CAN HEAR AND UNDERSTAND YOUR NEGATIVE SELF-TALK!

My little inner voice is a nasty cunt 90% of the time. But I'm working on it! As my mental health journey became more of a priority in my life, I've slowly started to see that inner voice become softer—knowing that, at its most basic form, all I'm trying to do in life, really, *is survive it.* And a fantastic way to soothe that nasty bitch is with MANTRAS! Mantras are like the sledgehammers to the concrete wall of self-hate that the vile inner voice had built up! The wall was built slowly over time, and I didn't notice how much my self-confidence had gone down at first: the impostor syndrome, the mood swings, all of the negative thoughts that no one could hear, all started to show outwardly. I fought back with MANTRAS! And, as basic or crunchy as they sounded, I started to look forward to hearing it—out loud—and referring to myself in first and third person. When I needed extra UMPH, I would say my name OUT LOUD with the mantra—like someone ELSE was saying it! Doubling its power!

MAKE YOUR OWN MANTRA

Fill In The Blank Fun Sentences Ad-Lib

May my life be _____.

This (insert choice language) _____ *shall pass.*

I allow myself to feel _____ *and* _____ *today.*

I can and will _____ *because I am a total badass.*

I am _____. *I am* _____. *I am* _____.

MANTRAS I LOVE, FROM FIERCE TO SOFT

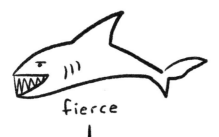

fierce

MY ANXIETY DOES NOT CONTROL ME, BITCH!!!

I am a boss-ass bitch who takes names and doesn't need help opening jars. Unless I do need help— then, I know how to ask for it.

There are no mistakes, only lessons to be learned. I did the best I could!!!!!

I AM STRONG. I let my armpit hair grow out and IDGAF who doesn't like it.

I will make this happen.

I am courageous and strong, like a lion from The Lion King—but, only the good lions, such as Nala and Simba. Sheesh, that movie got dark, huh?

I am attracting positive energy into my body.

I am strong and can persevere.

I am a good person who deserves good things to happen to them.

I am the master of my destiny. I am a powerful witch who can curse my enemies with the blink of an eye and a sprinkle of this magical pink powder I keep in my pocket.

I have the power to stop this.

I've survived this before; I will survive this again. Like Destiny's Child, I'm not gon' give up.

Today I'm going to search for as much fun as possible.

This is only temporary.

Feel the fear and do it anyway! SEEK THE UNKNOWN!

I take action with the right people at the right time.

I am worthy of everything good in life and deserve to be happy.

I am good enough.

I release the day!

soft

THE SOLO DATE

THE GREAT NEWS IS THAT NO ONE CARES ABOUT YOU

I know what you're thinking: Wow, what a sad-ass li'l bitch, all by her lonely-ass self, looking like a LOSER in the middle school cafeteria, like in *Mean Girls,* where they're like, "YOU CAN'T SIT WITH US," all by herself, eating something sad. I bet she's eating soup. That's such a sad dish. WELL, YOU'RE WRONG, DEPRESSED THINKING IN MY HEAD!!! I'M NOT A LOSER!! (But I do love soup. Even if it does look like liquid depression whenever you're eating it...like, no one looks HAPPY eating soup, right???) Look, I know, being in public by yourself might seem scary, but I almost fear being with too many people in public much much more—so many conversations to have, too many names to remember, YIKES. To be *alone* in public, it's all about managing the fear that everyone is looking at you like you're the "SHE DOESN'T EVEN GO HERE" girl in the aforementioned nod to the classic *Mean Girls* movie. BUT HEAR ME OUT.

I can promise you. No one is thinking about you.

AND THAT'S GREAT NEWS!!!!!!!

We spend so much time worried about what others are thinking, especially in moments of solitude. "Did I say something stupid? Are there pepper flakes in my teeth? Did I remind them of their ex and that's why they put icc in my water, even though

I VERY EXPLICITLY SAID 'NO ICE, PLEASE' and made eye contact while saying so???" Welp, there's a very high chance that they are thinking NONE of these things. IN FACT! They're probably thinking about *themselves!* WHICH IS GREAT NEWS! *Because you're also thinking about yourself!* SEE! We're all just a bunch of sensitive and selfish beans with crippling anxiety and depression. On average, people spend 60% of conversations TALKING ABOUT OR CONVEYING INFORMATION ABOUT THEMSELVES.[39] WOooooOOOOW. AND 99.99999999% of waiters are truly there just to do their jobs of being the middleman from the chef to your mouth. So, no need to stress about them (but please, treat them like humans because...well...they...ARE humans. Look them in the eye and try to absorb their energy so you're not yelling "HI SO GLAD TO BE HEEEEEEERE" the way I do sometimes when I'm overly nervous about an interaction with a waiter. Why do I desperately need waiters to think I'm so thrilled to be there?! I fear waiters are going to go back to my therapist and tell them how I REALLY was acting that day. The way I order my burger conveys much more about how I'm feeling than pressed pants and fresh makeup!!!!!!!!!! [this is not true— catastrophic intrusive thought]). So there's a chance that if they ARE asking questions about you, such as "What can I get you?" Or "How you doin' today" they really just want to get you your food. And all those people sitting at other tables? THEY COULDN'T CARE LESS WHY YOU ARE OUT ALONE! We're usually using projection to push our own thoughts about ourselves onto others thinking that about us.[40] The sooner you can cut this invisible cord, the more fun you're going to have on a date with yourself!

Psychological projection is a defense mechanism in which the human ego defends itself against unconscious impulses or qualities (both positive and negative) by denying their existence in themselves while attributing them to others.[39]

Most solo dates, I'll pretty much wear my PJs out in public (shout out to onesie jumpers that you can totally freeball in and not even have to wear a bra or underwear!), but, other times, I'll take the time to get ready, as if I'm actually going out on a SEXUAL date! OOO LALA! Makeup can be pretty transformative, along with what we wear, how we smell, or the smile we wear out. (Okay, I know that sounded totes cheese, but try it next time you're out! Just smile to yourself while ya walk! Whistle a tune!) I'll even schedule the date on my calendar and not take any cancellations from myself unless I'm having an absolutely shit day and, in that case, will take myself on a date to my bed, where I can NETFLIX AND CHILL AND MASTURBATE!

39 Ward, Adrian F. "The Neuroscience of Everybody's Favorite Topic." *Scientific American*, 16 July 2013, www.scientificamerican.com/article/the-neuroscience-of-everybody-favorite-topic-themselves/.
40 "Psychological Projection." Wikipedia, Wikimedia Foundation, 29 Sept. 2020, en.wikipedia.org/wiki/Psychological_projection.

KELSEY'S TIPS FOR SOLO DATES

- **Movies are my favorites.** It's dark enough where truly no one is going to notice you're alone. 11 AM matinee is the best time to go because it's all old people and they're cute.

- **Sit at the bar.** Those barstools are made for people on their own. And, if you're feeling awkward, the bartender (if not super busy) might just keep you conversational company. I've scored many an extra topper of tequila by being alone at the bar and being kind to the bartender (even in sweatpants and no makeup!).

- **Bring headphones.** No one will bother you...but, like, take them off when the waiter approaches, you feel me?

- **If you're heading to a restaurant, approach the hostess with confidence.** I'll usually say, "ONE for lunch, please!" and if they repeat something like "Just you??" I'll smile with a "YEP! TAKIN' MYSELF OUT!" If you're not sad about it, they won't be either!

- **Not trying to break the bank?** How about a book in the park with a blankie! YES, PLEASE!

- **FEELIN' CRAZY?** Theme parks are the BEST solo dates. You get to ride the single-rider lines, and I'll bring headphones to catch up on podcasts, and get my steps in all day! The only time you'll have to talk to anyone is when you need help putting more sunscreen on.

IT'S OKAY TO BE
ALONE & DEPRESSED

(FUCK FOMO)

Most nights I spend at home with my cats, a vibrator, and my phone inches from my face...and I'm *totally cool* with that. It wasn't always that way, however. Growing up, I was not okay with being alone too often. I never got invited to things. During my later teen years, when social media really started taking off, I developed a bad case of FOMO (fear of missing out). I wanted so badly to be invited to all the parties that I saw the prettier, cooler, and more popular people attending on Facebook. I wanted to be involved in the Twitter threads between girls I thought were funnier than me. I wanted to be tagged in the Instagrams that cute guys were posting from their getaways that weekend.

I've always been a very independent person who liked doing things on her own. But that doesn't mean I didn't get sad, and even cry, thinking that I was missing out on a better life, filled with more friends and things to keep me busy. Of course, I wasn't taking into account that I moved away from all my friends straight out of high school and switched colleges three times in three different states. I lived alone and freelanced a lot before I found my first full-time job at the age of 25 at BuzzFeed. I never really had that solid group of friends you knew from birth who did everything together, like you see in movies and TV shows. I didn't meet my best friend, Lacey, until I was almost 21. Even still, she moved away a few years later for work and love (but we're still bffs & soul mates despite it!).

I would try hanging out with different groups of random people that I never really clicked with, just so I could have something to post over the weekend or have a party to attend. I would mentally exhaust myself trying to fit in, or physically exhaust myself trying to put together a hangout that I'd invite random people to. In reality, *I just wanted to be liked.* (And remember: that's HUMAN and OKAY! Who doesn't want to be liked?)

I've only learned in the last couple of years that I really enjoy and *prefer* my own company...and that's really okay! I get to do what I want, when I want, and how I want to do it. I've gained more time to throw myself into my work, which I really thrive on, and have even met some new friends in the process of minding my own goddamned business. I've also learned a few things that have helped me feel less lonely:

1. **Don't compare what you are doing right now to what someone else is doing on social media right now.** You are exactly where you are supposed to be.

2. **Start going out during the day.** I used to focus solely on my night plans: which party, which bar, which club to go to. And, if nothing happened for me that night, the weekend was considered a bust. Instead, I spend my days putting myself in public places, which means I'm surrounded by lots of people without having to hang out with them. I like farmers' markets, biking on the beach, and trying Groupon classes.

3. **Know that there will be millions of birthday parties, dinners, and opening nights in your lifetime.** You don't have to be invited to every single thing going on every weekend. SERIOUSLY. THERE WILL BE SO MANY MORE OPPORTUNITIES.

4. **Try new things.** Just 'cause you didn't like going to an amusement park alone as a kid doesn't mean it's not fun as fuck as an adult (I REPEAT: *single-rider lines*, baby!!!).

5. **Know that it is completely normal if you like being alone.** Go where you feel appreciated and if that means going somewhere to be by yourself, go be alone, babycakes!! And it's also completely normal to still feel sad when you see other people doing things you're not doing, even when you choose to be alone.

Sure, I still go out! And, hell ya, I post about it! But trust me when I say that just because you're not invited to things doesn't mean you're not smart, interesting, outgoing, fun to be around, and sexy as hell!

And, when it comes to experiencing a bad wave of depression, society tells us that we NEED to go out to "cure" it. GO HANG OUT WITH FRIENDS! MAKE A MEAL YOU ENJOY! Blah blah blah. Sometimes, what your depressive episode needs is just your damn self. The worst feeling is forcing yourself to go out when you know you're feeling blue and not enjoying being out. Wishing you were anywhere but there. I say, get comfy. Do what you want. If it feels forced, it's probably not right for right now.

SOMETHING FURTHER TO TRY WHEN GOING THROUGH A DEPRESSIVE EPISODE:

See if you can go an entire day without taking ANYTHING PERSONALLY. No matter what it is, tell yourself that a person's behaviors, words, or actions have everything to do with THEM and THEIR issues, and that someone else's behaviors, words, or actions don't actually **have anything to do with you**! It's pretty freeing! Remember, we can't change what's out of our control—**we can only control how we react to it!** And the way we can try reacting for an entire day is to tell ourselves that it has nothing to do with us. :) There's no reason to topple the expectations and responses of other people onto ourselves when we're already focusing on maintaining our *own* bodily responses and expectations!

"DON'T BE SAD, GO GET A TATTOO" —A TIKTOK PROVERB

Kelsey's tattoo's, all which she got during sore mental health spots in her life, include:

1. **An Italian quote** on both sides of her hips that loosely translate into saying "life is beautiful" and "live with love" and she got both when she was 17 and definitely wanted to kill herself. She did not want to live, laugh, love or think life was beautiful at all.

2. **A Beatle's quote on the inside of her lip** (yep, you read that right) that says "LET IT BE". She still thinks liking the Beatles makes her "vintage" and cool.

3. **ANOTHER Beatles quote on her rib cage** that says "you may say that I'm a dreamer..." She actually likes this one despite John Lennon being in an absolutely toxic relationship with Yoko Ono when he wrote it.

4. **A Woodstock symbol on her inner left foot** she got when she was 18 because she was born on August 16th—the same date of the Woodstock music festival's mid-point during the summer of love in 1969. Her dad attended the festival, and they both share a love for the music that was played there.

5. **The letter M on her inner right foot** because the letter is a significant recurrence in her life. The woman who raised her is named Marie. The tattoo artist who did it said it was ugly.

6. **A GIANT-ASS LION HEAD** on her rib cage that she got completely on a

whim during an episode of her BuzzFeed podcast AdultShıt with her cohost who was getting her first tattoo. Kelsey reeeeeeally identifies with being a Leo.

7. **A triangle on her left elbow** which is a matching tattoo with her best friend, Lacey. It represents water and fire (depending on how her arm is bent) which are the zodiac elements she shares with Lacey. They got them while drunk on Hollywood Blvd. at three in the morning and barely remember it. Kelsey's tattoo artist pressed way too hard into her skin, so now Kelsey's looks like a blurred smudge of dirt on her arm.

8. **On her left tricep she has her birth chart** tattooed which she got on her 29th birthday in Barcelona with her sister after an amazing chart-reading session with @andrada_astrology (this one is probably the only one she got sober & in a *decent* mental health space!)

MASTURBATION AND DEPRESSION

OKAY, MY FAVORITE CHAPTER!

I masturbate a lot! When I'm happy, bored, hungry...but *especially* when I'm depressed. Despite the taboo, shameful, religious shit that's attached to givin' yourself a rub, our society is finally starting to see masturbation how it should be seen: as an act of SELF-LOVE. Dare I even say it: SELF-CARE!

Self-care is a funny term that gets flung around a lot these days...on Instagram, it looks like a bubble bath and your favorite green-tea mask...but, self-care also includes the hard stuff (no pun intended), like cutting off a toxic friendship, forfeiting a day's pay for a mental-health day, and...jerkin' it when you just don't feel up for it. Naturally, your libido might feel decreased when you're in a state of depression, which is all the more reason to tap into that self-love aspect of the act and tell yourself that you're doing your brain a damn favor. There are SO MANY benefits to masturbating! It has both physical and mental benefits. These include:

- greater sexual desire
- feelings of pleasure and satisfaction
- improved mood
- greater relaxation
- relieving stress and anxiety
- easing stress-related tension
- releasing sexual tension

- better sleep

- a greater understanding of your body

- a better connection to your sexual preferences

FUN FACT:

"Some research suggests that regular ejaculation may lower the risk of prostate cancer, though doctors aren't exactly sure why. A 2016 study found the risk of prostate cancer decreased by about 20 percent in men who ejaculated at least 21 times a month. A 2003 study also discovered a similar link between frequent ejaculation and lower prostate cancer risk."[41]

Masturbating ALSO releases those feel-good chemicals in your brain, dopamine and oxytocin! Which are just the right substances you need to replace those feelings of anxiety and depression. Masturbating also forces a sense of mindfulness, to be present in your body instead of too much in your head. Also, it's empowering as hell. One REALLY GOOD orgasm can explode those fireworks of happy brain powers, showing you the badass self-love goddess/god/powerful being that you really are! And just like sex, there doesn't *need* to be a climactic, firework exploding, confetti-popping orgasm at the end. It's a good reminder, too, that your body can just feel *good*, even if you haven't felt like yourself for a while.

41 "Can Masturbation Cause or Treat Depression?" *Healthline*, 18 May 2018, www.healthline.com/health/masturbation-and-depression.

THE FIVE GIVENS OF LIFE THAT WE CAN ACCEPT TO REDUCE SUFFERING

(ACCORDING TO SOME DUDE NAMED DAVID RICHO)

I remember being on my own for the first time when I went off to college and thought, "WOW. ADULTHOOD!" I was 17, living in an off-campus apartment paid for by my parents, smoking weed to my heart's content every day. THIS IS NOT ADULTHOOD. ADULTHOOD IS FILLED WITH STRUGGLE AND DUST AND BILLS AND CRYING. I wish I would have known about these "givens" sooner. These five "givens" are presented as rules to accept as you enter adulthood. It's not meant to feel bleak or dreary but...realistic. And the sooner we all accept this, I believe, the less struggle, dust, bills, and crying will come.

1. **EVERYTHING CHANGES AND ENDS.** The sooner you can teach yourself to yield to changes instead of resisting them, the less you will find yourself disappointed by life.

2. **THINGS DON'T ALWAYS GO ACCORDING TO PLAN.** I KNOW I KNOW—this is a big one because we're learning how to let go of control! But if life went exactly according to plan—it would be boring as shit.

3. **LIFE IS NOT ALWAYS FAIR.** Evil will prevail. Bad things will happen to good people who don't deserve it. It's okay to have imbalance so that it forces you to recognize and shape your morals—to make you GIVE A SHIT about something outside yourself!

4. **SUFFERING IS A PART OF LIFE.** EHHHHhhhhHHH I hate this one. But the truth is, without suffering, we wouldn't know how strong we are. And trust me, *you are stronger than you think you are.*

5. **PEOPLE ARE NOT ALWAYS LOVING AND LOYAL.** You are going to get fucked over. You are going to get your heart broken. IT'S JUST FACTS. But remember, the best way to flex on those shitty people is to love yourself more than you had wished they loved you.

REMEMBER:

INSTAGRAM IS A HIGHLIGHT REEL...

Fill in this post with a <u>real</u>, nofilter post with your handle and hastags that show the <u>real you</u>.

Don't compare their outsides to your insides.

DEPRESSION & CREATIVITY

THIS CHAPTER IS SOMETHING I HAVE TO READ OVER WEEKLY.

I host a podcast, make weekly Internet videos, and star in a comedy television show and am now an AUTHOR! I can't be "ON" all the time. Trust me—I've tried. Red Bull, L-theanine, cocaine, coffee...IT ALL GETS EXHAUSTED EVENTUALLY. I beat myself up when I don't think I'm being funny enough, creative enough, etc., etc. I strive to make each episode of the podcast better, funnier, and more successful than the last. I find it easy to throw away all the successes and impact I'd created before, just based on numbers. I had to unlearn that thinking. Downloads don't mean shit compared to someone sending me a DM, thanking me for being open enough about a certain topic that they were able to take something away from that made their life easier.

THE DEPRESSED ARTIST IS <u>SO</u> NOT
A NECESSARY LOOK TO BE SUCCESSFUL ANYMORE.

You are enough. As you are right now.

Say it! Stick it to your mirror! Write it on your hand, like Taylor Swift! Remember, in times of depression: You are MORE than what you make. You are more than your career. Your productivity does not determine your value. It's OKAY to do nothing sometimes. You gotta recharge those batteries, baby—and, once they're full, you'll get back up and get after it. Not EVERYTHING you do has to result in a successful end product. You can just make things for yourself, too! For instance, I got super into gardening during the pandemic of 2020. I didn't make it so people would walk by and compliment me on my hard work. In fact, the garden wasn't even visible to the naked eye; it was hidden on the side of our building. I made it because I realized the longer I was in the garden, the less I was on my phone. I fell into a rhythm in the garden. It pleased my OCD tendencies to lay sod; watering the bushes was a repetitive movement that soothed my ADHD symptoms, it gave my heart something to care about when I planted a new flower. This was art. I was creating it! Just not the kind I was used to creating. And, guess what? Some of the flowers died (and like, ALL of the herbs...and a fiddle fig), but...I reminded myself that, "Kelsey, you have to know that not everything you make will be important or impactful or significant, or even good. Hell, it might actually be bad. But it is not the product we make that matters at all, *it's what we do with the result.*" So, I threw out the dead weeds and planted way easier plants (succulents & spearmint)!

Do we celebrate ourselves enough? If you bought this workbook, then probably not! But you are working on it, and that's the most important thing. You're doing something with the results of depression. LOOK AT YOU! THAT'S WHAT MATTERS! Try to be in the stands of your own game of life. Cheer yourself on. Your game is YOU v. YOU. Play your hardest, give yourself the best coaching, take water breaks, and, when you're done, leave it all on the field.

What creative endeavor do you not give yourself enough credit for?

_____

_____

_____

_____

What's something creative you can do for ONLY YOURSELF TO ENJOY?

_____

_____

_____

_____

GO DO IT!!! ORDER THE SUPPLIES ONLINE! GO TO MICHAELS AND GET IT!! I'll be waiting to NOT see what you made, since this is something only for you :) No tagging, no posting, no TikToking. Just create whatever your heart is calling you to make right now.

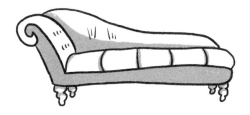

THERAPISTS

Therapy is the greatest gift you can give yourself. I am a firm believer that EVERYONE should go to therapy. IDC who you are: Oprah, Joe-Schmo, or a therapist yourself (therapists DO have therapists quite often!). Having a therapist is like having a cheat code for LIFE! I've seen close to 30 therapists in my 30 years of life, all for varying reasons/roadblocks/rough parts of life. Knowing therapy is a privilege, I made sure to do my research and find a therapist who specializes in my "issues." Therapists are like doctors (some are doctors) in that they study and have experiences in certain specialties of mental health. Finding the right therapist can take TIME. It's kinda like dating...Don't get discouraged if the first meeting is an awkward flop as you make weird eye contact from across the room, stepping on each other's sentences. My best advice is that if you don't vibe with the person ON THE FIRST APPOINTMENT, don't waste your time and money. The same way I hope you would feel confident leaving a first date (bc we're not wasting our time with people who don't immediately recognize our fabulous-ness!!), you should feel that similar confidence after meeting a therapist for the first time. And hey, not everyone you see is someone that you are going to click with, and it's OKAY TO BREAK UP WITH A THERAPIST! In fact, they get broken up with every day! I used to lie to my therapists and tell them I could no longer afford treatment, or that my insurance had changed, rather than being straight up with them.

I've had a therapist fall asleep on me, a therapist who was way younger than me, a therapist who was such a dick and his advice was too straightforward, a sex therapist, a chronic-pain therapist, and, most recently, a couples therapist! A good therapist will make sure you feel that you have the right resources to find someone that you connect with, a better match, if you don't think you are clicking—and you'll feel it. You'll have to trust your gut and ask yourself if you really feel comfortable with this person knowing everything about you, and if their listening skills match your communication style. Some therapists will tell you that they are just a bouncing board, a third-party opinion to your life, and some therapists will straight-up tell you what to do. I've even had a therapist help me write out a script for a difficult conversation I needed to have with a boss! It's okay to take a BREAK from therapy, and it's okay to hate it at first. It's okay to go twice a week or even twice a year. The best part about therapy is there really is no one way to do it. Some insurance plans have apps where you type in your insurance plan and it will list the therapists in your area that are covered under your plan. Additionally, *Psychology Today* is a great resource for research on finding the right match for you. However, note that if you are using your insurance to cover therapy appointments, your insurance company will have insight into your diagnosis and treatment. This *could* cause your insurance premiums to rise in the future because of a "pre-existing condition." GARHHHHHHHHH I'm sorry, I can't explain ALL the fuckery with insurance and mental health in this one workbook. It causes me great stress. Isn't that ironic?? But know that if you don't have insurance, there are affordable online video chats, and even FREE volunteer-based websites (7 Cups of Tea!). There's even a chance that you will *outgrow* your therapist! And that's to be expected if you're in a transitional period of you life. So don't feel bad if you have multiple therapists over your lifetime. In fact, I ENCOURAGE IT!

Lastly, you guys, there's no reason you should be paying money to LIE to your therapist or NOT TELL THEM THE WHOLE TRUTH. You're just cheating yourself, then! Find someone you feel comfortable telling the truth, the whole truth, and nothing but the truth to!

Have you ever tried therapy?

What does your ideal relationship with a therapist look like?

What are you are most worried about sharing with a therapist?

_____

_____

What are you afraid that they will feel, or how do you fear they will react to you sharing your feelings?

_____

_____

_____

_____

How much are you willing to budget for therapy per month?

_____

TYPES OF THERAPISTS &
WHAT ALL THOSE LETTERS MEAN

Type of Education:

MD: Doctor of Medicine

MA: Masters of Arts

MEd: Masters of Education (in Counseling)

MS: Masters of Science (in Counseling)

MSSW: Masters of Science in Social Work

MMFT/MFT: Master of Marriage and Family Therapist

PhD: Doctor of Philosophy

Type of License:

LCSW: Licensed Clinical Social Worker

LCDC: Licensed Chemical Dependency Counselor

LPC: Licensed professional Counselor

BC-TMH: Board certified Tele-Mental Health Provider

CADC: Certified Alcohol and Drug Counselor

CSAT: Certified Sexual Addiction Therapist

AND THERE ARE TONS MORE! A quick Google search and light stalking will help you determine what kind of therapist will suit your needs!

!!! TRIGGER WARNING !!!

JUST STAY

When things are at their absolute worst, and shit is just all sorts of fucked-up, know that there is strength in numbers—that there is at least one other person that feels at their rock bottom, too. **You are not alone.** When you can't get out of bed or even call for help, know that you don't have to do ANYTHING. **Just stay. That's all you have to do. Stay.**

And, if today, all you could do was stay, then I am proud of you.

Sign a contract to yourself to stay:

_____

_____

_____

_____

_____

_____

_____

_____

_____

_____

X _____

Sign It Here

SUICIDE
& SUICIDAL IDEATION

There was a depressive state that I was in after a breakup when I wanted to kill myself. I didn't want to DIE, necessarily; I just wanted to close my eyes and not feel anything, specifically the heartbreak, any longer. That's pretty common with suicidal ideation, or suicidal thoughts; it's not *you* that you want to end, it's a *feeling* inside of you that you want gone. I get angry, thinking back on the girl who tried to take her own life that night. How selfish it was to go that far into my state of spiral that I would leave so many people I love behind. People that love me. But I wasn't thinking about anyone else. I was in tunnel vision of self-loathing.

I had this breakup I was dealing with. I had just lost an acting role that might have propelled my name into stardom. I was fostering kittens at that time, and one of them passed due to a "fading kitten syndrome" disease (didn't know that was a thing!). I was hungover all. the. time. I wasn't treating my body right, and I just wanted to stop feeling this intense sense of LOSS and GRIEF.

I had suicidal ideation of taking my own life many times before this heartbreak. Suicidal Ideation just means "thinking about" or "planning." It's not the actual, physical act. I'm not sure that what I did would be considered a "real" attempt—whatever that means—by societal standards. I just wanted to see what it felt like if I hung a belt from my shower curtain and put my head through it. That's all. I was crying, numb, and stood on the edge of my tub. I remember my bathroom becoming blurry because of the tears in my eyes, and I liked that I couldn't see anymore. I didn't want to see the life I had in front of me anymore. My bathroom was this awful, off-yellow color that was so distasteful, I felt like I could smell it at times. I let my head hang in the belt, slowly at first, but then tilting my toes over the edge, just slightly, so the belt tightened. I inched back and forth, just getting used to the feeling, when my shower rod came crashing down. Was it a sign? Eh, probably not. I was trying to hang my body weight from a belt and plastic shower tension rod. I don't think I would've really done it...but, I honestly can't say with 100% certainty that I wouldn't have, either. I hit the floor and cried a lot more. I grabbed my cell phone and called the suicide hotline. I was too embarrassed, fucked-up, and ashamed to phone a friend. I felt as though I had already "used up" my phone-a-friend calls during the breakup, and that no one wanted to deal with another middle-of-the-night heartbreak call from me.

The phone only rang a few times. The woman on the other end asked if I had attempted to kill myself. I told her that I didn't, even though I wasn't really sure. She said she could send an ambulance to me. I begged her not to. Instead, she sat on the phone with me. All night. Just listening. And talking. Long enough to get me out of the thickness of the feelings of crisis. She was totally nonjudgmental and empathetic. I can remember exactly what her voice sounded like. She sounded older... maybe in her 50s. I could picture what she looked like. I wondered why she worked there. I wondered if she was a volunteer. Or was she a trained professional? Had someone in her life died by suicide? Does she devote her time to helping people like me so a loved one of mine didn't end up working as a suicide hotline volunteer, too? I finally fell asleep. I don't remember what she said, or even her name. Just the sound and the tone she used with me. Like a friend. Not a doctor or authority figure. I just remember waking up, incredibly hung over, with a phone pressed to my cheek that was as hot as a potato. I threw the phone across my bed and rolled back over to sleep. I was so ashamed and embarrassed. I felt so gross about what I'd done. I was SO disgusted with myself that the thoughts started to creep back up. I didn't like this sour feeling in my stomach that I'd live on knowing that I'd contemplated suicide. I found the grief coming back as a wave. I didn't want to get out of bed...but, maybe I could hang my shower curtain back up. Yes, maybe I'll get up to pee...and see how it holds. Then, lying there in my bed, feeling like a shell of negative space, wasting my life, I felt a buzz in my sheets. It was a text from my sister, and I believe this text saved my life.

"Hey kelsey mom told me about all the shitty stuff happening in your life right now. I'm sorry :(whatever you do—don't go into a tizzy and drink ur ass off and get depressed. This is all a part of life I promise! Do you know how long I looked for a job when I wasn't teaching anymore and I didn't want to be a receptionist anymore? A LONG TIME! I finally got a job at OT after 2 months of looking. God is watching over you and he's giggling because you have no idea the amazing things he has in store for you. Maybe if you would've gotten that part on that show you would've died in a tragic accident from the big light falling on your head or maybe somebody would be carrying a huge sharp object and trip and fall and impale your liver...you never know what the universe has in store for you. Don't get your hopes up. Keep trying. Don't let this bring you down. I'm here for you whenever you want to...i know you don't feel like talking right now. Let me know how you are and if you're okay. Hugs"

—My Sister 2:48 P.M. OCT 8TH 2014

284

So, just for that day, I decided to stay. And then, I stayed another day, and another, and then I smiled again, and then I stayed another day, and, finally, I went for a walk, and stayed some more to meet friends for dinner...and time passed. And I stayed. And I shudder to think about what would have happened if I chose not to stay. How I would've missed out on getting my dream job only three months later...then getting to travel the world because of it? I would've missed the trip to Europe to celebrate my mom's 60th birthday eating dinner in the Eiffel Tower, and I would've never gone to therapy, or peed my pants the time my sister and I went to Barcelona and drove a Vespa on the highway by accident. I never would've seen my dad kick cancer's ass, and how I never would've started a podcast and grew a fan-base and touch people's lives and help others through states of depression. I never would've gotten a job on a different TV show and wrote a fucking BOOK ABOUT ALL OF IT. If I hadn't stayed, I would've never gotten to feel what it feels like to have time stop when you meet the love of your life.

That feeling I felt that night that I put my darkest thoughts into action, the lowest I'd ever felt, was replaced easily by thousands of other good and true and real feelings of happiness that came *only because I chose to stay.*

You have survived everything you thought would kill you before. This time is no different. You've got this. Stay.

If you are on this page and you find yourself still struggling, please reach out to the National Suicide Prevention Hotline: 1-800-273-8255.

W.O.W.

A reminder: Emotions and urges have a natural arc of intensity. They typically last 15-25 minutes and can feel the most intense from minutes 7-10. During this time, the feelings will feel like they are going to last forever. We can't see an end and of course would do anything to stop feeling this way. Try setting a timer and notice how the intensity of emotions changes over this time period. Breathe, distract yourself, call a friend...stay.

THE AFTERSHOCK

Even after the initial wave of intense emotion, the ground might feel a little shaky, or the intensity might pop up again.

Keep taking time for yourself until you're YOU again (even if that takes longer than expected).

What are some self-care activities you can do that make YOU feel like YOU?
Get specific and detailed. What are the kinds of activities or people or shows that make you happy? Why? What are your favorite thoughts that pop up about these things?

_____

_____

_____

_____

_____

_____

_____

_____

_____

_____

_____

_____

Only YOU can heal yourself, no matter who caused the pain. You have to heal for you.

We're all going to die. We don't get much say over how or when, but we do get to decide how we're gonna live. So do it. Decide. *Is this the life you want to live? Is this the person you want to love? Is this the best you can be? Can you be stronger? Kinder? More Compassionate? Decide. Breathe in. Breathe out and decide.*

—Richard Webber, Former Chief of Surgery, Mercy West Hospital—'Seal Our Fate' *Grey's Anatomy* (Season 10, Episode 1)

10/10/10 EXERCISE

This exercise is intended to root up some ~good feels~ in recognizing your desires for life, what makes you tick and what beautiful shit you've already built for yourself

DESIRES—write 10 things you desire most in life. It can be physical, mental, or a mixture of both. Don't feel bad about writing down material items or "pie in the sky desires".

1 _____

2 _____

3 _____

4 _____

5 _____

6 _____

7 _____

8 _____

9 _____

10 _____

THINGS THAT MAKE YOU HAPPY RIGHT NOW—what in your life, right now, makes you happy?

1 _____

2 _____

3 _____

4 _____

5 _____

6 _____

7 _____

8 _____

9 _____

10 _____

GRATITUDE—write down 10 things you are most grateful for in this lifetime.

1 _____

2 _____

3 _____

4 _____

5 _____

6 _____

7 _____

8 _____

9 _____

10 _____

LIFE IS TOUGH,
BUT SO ARE YOU

DEPRESSION SLEEP

(TRYING TO) GET OUT OF BED!!!!!!!

I love sleeping. So much so that it scares me. I'd take sleep on a sweet date to Olive Garden, give it all the breadsticks it wants, move into a single-family home, get an orange cat, and marry it, if I could (no shade to my current partner, who wants all these things). In a depressive streak, I can enjoy living in my dreams more than in my daily life. I can't be the only one that feels that way, right? I don't mean it in a ~*suicide-y*~ way; life can be going swell—but, I swear, NOTHING can feel as swell as my comfortable bed, icy sheets, warm, cuddly comforter, 10+ hours of sleep, and the blissful ignorance of a sweet dream. Sometimes, I'd get so much sleep, I'd need a nap from all the sleeping I was doing. According to a quick Internet search, the average person spends 26 years of their lives sleeping.

LOLOLOLOLOLOLOOOOOLLLLLLOOOmotherufckingLOLOLOOLOL......
el......oh....el

......whew....oh..

.....

.

:(

Now I'm sad.

A: because I know my average will probably be *much greater* than that because of my depression and love of sleep.

And, B: because I fear that I am missing out on so much of my life because I'm always in my fucking bed. I don't know why I became this way. My parents are not like me. Both of my parents can run off of four to five hours of sleep. And they prefer it. And they are super-healthy and successful and happy. And it annoys me to no end. You mean to tell me they can pass on their genetically long legs and ability to grow leg hair at the speed of light, but they can't pass on the gene that makes me sleep "only because we biologically have to," as my mom said once?

When depression fatigue hits, my body and brain usually give me two options:

1. **I guilt-trip myself into WAKE-NESS** and spend every WAKE-NESS moment hating my life and circumstances, self-hating, and having negative thoughts until I can get back in bed.

OR

2. **I stay in bed and succumb to my depression sleep.** And feel guilty about THAT.

SO, if you're going to go with option #1, here are my tips to make it the least miserable depression sleep-less day.

- **Give yourself a whole-ass hour to wake up.** Give yourself an hour to do whatever you want. For example, if you need to be out of bed by 8:30 AM, set your alarm for 7:30. You don't HAVE to wake up, but if you can, open your eyes. Stare at the ceiling, read your phone, finish that episode you fell asleep to last night, meditate, masturbate, WHATEVER. Just don't go back to sleep.

- **Chug some water.** There's something refreshing about washing away that nasty-ass night breath that makes the day feel new. I keep a dedicated SLEEPING WATER BOTTLE next to my bed that can hold a few days' worth of water in it (QuiFit on Amazon) so I don't have to think about it every night before going to sleep. If that fails to wake you up, well, eventually you'll have to get up to pee—and that's one way of doing it.

- **Set a positive intention for the day.** Sounds cheesy, but your brain gets a to-do list.

- **Stimulate that vagus nerve, baby!** Splash some really cold water on your face—or, do the version of this that I had going for a while, which was using a spray bottle (usually reserved to scare my cats away from jumping on the kitchen counter) to spritz my own face in the morning! Listen! We gotta do what we gotta do, honey.

- **Try Mel Robbins's 5, 4, 3, 2, 1 exercise** that we reviewed in the beginning of this chapter! I gave it its own chapter for a reason!!!

- **Clocky!** If you're someone who wakes up and reaches straight for the phone because your alarm is on it, which results in you laying in bed way longer than you should (you're not alone here, Chrissy Teigen also admits to doing this every morning), try this INSANE INVENTION called CLOCKY...

They clearly tried to give this thing a cute name so that they could try to Baby Yoda their way into my room, but DON'T BE FOOLED! This powerful device BLARES your alarm and fully leaps and rolls off your nightstand, and THEN RUNS AWAY FROM YOU lmao. I'm sorry—I don't mean to laugh, but THIS IS SO FUNNY—because I can just imagine my depressed ass trying to BURST out of bed, chasing some Harry Potter magical machine that's running away from me like FUCK YOU AND YOUR DEPRESSION CATCH ME IF YOU CAN, BITCH!!! Hahahaahah. After doing some light EXERCISE and calming my heart rate, I'm sure I'd like to just crawl right back in bed, but hey, maybe drastic times call for drastic measures. *crying laughing emoji*

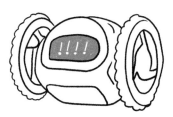

CLOCKY hahahahahahahaha fuckkkkk.

IF YOU'RE MORE OF A OPTION #2-ER, HERE IS THE BEST WAY TO MAKE THE MOST OUT OF YOUR DEPRESSIVE SLEEP:

- **Give yourself permission to do it.** Once you've done it, do it. But be honest to your cancellations that you're taking a mental-health day, if you can afford that.

- **Get a bed you like.** Make your safe space comfy! Almost all mattress prices are negotiable. It's like buying a car; the salespeople are capable of bargaining. (*$400 Green Tea mattress is the cheapest and yet the BEST mattress ever. I love this mattress so much I even wrote an article about it in The Strategist![42]*)

42 Darragh, Kelsey. "Thank You to My Twitter Followers for Telling Me to Get This $258 Mattress." *The Strategist*, New York, 9 Mar. 2020, nymag.com/strategist/article/zinus-memory-foam-mattress-review-2020.html.

- **HAVE YOU SEEN these bed desks???** They made fun of us for depression, but look at this future science space desk shit now! Turns out we were ahead of the curve!

- **Work on your phone.** Dabble in Notes and turn off your social media in your settings.

- **Take breaks to get up.** Do five jumping jacks. Go pee, run your wrists under some cold water, paint your nails, pluck your eyebrows, and sit up in bed using a few pillows as opposed to laying down. Get your blood pumping, or else you're going to get bedsores.

- **KEEP YOUR BEDSIDE TABLE CLEAN!!** It's the closest thing to you on those days you can't get out of bed. If a cluttered mess of water bottles, tissues, and empty gummy-bear bags is the first thing you see when you open your eyes, it can put an even heavier weight on your brain. If it's going to be your desk for a few days, treat it like a corporate desk. My suggestion is to buy an ultra-thin trash can to keep next to or under your bed. They sell them on Amazon for less than $10.

- **Naps?** LOVE & HATE 'EM! How to not feel guilty about 'em? Not sure yet. BUT! When I do nap, I have this little trick for waking up. First, ALWAYS SET AN ALARM. ALWAYS. Could be 30 minutes later...could be three hours later! Before I nap, I'll grab three small cups of water. Then, I nap. Hard. Fucking ooOOOoOO, I could nap all day. Then, when the alarm sounds, I'm allowed to hit snooze as many times as I want, EXCEPT, I have to chug one of the waters before I go back to napping. So, by the time I've snoozed three times, I've had three cups of water. I HAVE TO PEE. And, therefore, I must arise from my slumber!

GROW THROUGH

WHAT YOU

GO THROUGH

WAKING UP REALLY
IS THE HARDEST PART.

As you read in this DEPRESSION intro section, YA GIRL HAS HAD ISSUES WITH BEING TIRED HER WHOLE LIFE (yes, I've had my thyroid checked, stop asking plz, thanks AUNT CAROL and EVERY DEPRESSION FACEBOOK GROUP I'VE JOINED).

Waking up really is the hardest part. It can take a herculean effort to simply take that first step out of bed (my comfort zone) and into my day. And that's coming from someone who likes their life! Yet...why does this one simple act...take such mighty strength?

My boyfriend was helping me through a particularly tough morning when he started singing this very silly song that went like this:

> *PUT ONE FOOT IN FRONT OF THE OTHER!*
>
> *AND SOON YOU'LL BE WALKIN' ACROSS THE FLOOR!*
>
> *PUT ONE FOOT IN FRONT OF THE OTHER!*
>
> *AND SOON YOU'LL BE WALKIN' OUT THE DOOR!*

I had never heard this li'l jingle, but apparently, Jared told me, it comes from the animated Christmas classic, *Santa Claus Is Coming to Town*. The animations are hilarious and creepy. And in this snow-covered land, this li'l...clay elf? ...boy? Tells this old...Christmas Wizard...? Pope-lookin' guy that "changing from bad to good is as easy as taking your first step!" Then, he *bursts* into song, while a penguin in a scarf looks on like his hype-man, and, eventually, the whole forest of animals is singing the song. I don't recommend watching this movie on 'shrooms.

The point is—these lyrics hit HARD for some reason. It felt impossible to get out of bed, thinking of my Google calendar filled to the brim, driving across a traffic-packed LA—I was thinking of my day on such a large scale. But the truth was, all I had to do to get up and out of bed was...PUT. ONE. FOOT. IN. FRONT. OF. THE. OTHER. And if I could only take one step, that was good enough for me. Then, I took another step. And another. And before I knew it, *this motherfucker really was walkin' across the floor*. I got to the bathroom...put on my clothes...brushed my teeth. And I took each task by taking one literal step at time. And my silly-ass boyfriend was singing the song behind me the whole time. Eventually, when I did get out the door, I found myself humming the tune throughout the day.

Remember that the greatest adventure that lies ahead of you starts with a single step.

Can you find a way to look at your day tomorrow morning a little differently? Can you open your eyes and say, "All I have to do right now is put one foot in front of the other?" What would be the first thing you step toward?

_____

_____

_____

_____

Then, when your next task pops up—repeat! **Tell me how your day felt different:**

_____

_____

_____

_____

> *EACH MORNING, WE ARE BORN AGAIN. WHAT WE DO TODAY IS WHAT MATTERS MOST.*
>
> *—BUDDHA*

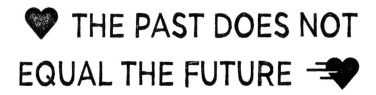

❤ THE PAST DOES NOT
EQUAL THE FUTURE ➤❤

DEPRESSED MORNING JOURNAL

Woke up just feeling like "ABSOLUTELY NOT" to the day? Same. Let's take a simple five minutes to journal and see if we can't turn this shit around, right?

Spend ONE MINUTE doing each journal entry:

MINUTE 1: Calm yourself and exercise those eyes. Open and close them nice and tight, like you're giving your face a good ol' stretch. Do the same with your jaw and mouth. Notice anything that feels tight? So many of us grind our teeth while we sleep, or have stress dreams...let's leave all that shit on the mattress. What did you feel in your face while doing this?

_____

_____

_____

MINUTE 2: Write out your goals for the day. No matter how big or small, tell me what your ideal day would look like today. After you make your list, read each goal OUT LOUD. YELL IT IF YOU CAN!

_____

_____

_____

_____

_____

_____

_____

_____

MINUTE 3: VISUALIZE yourself completing each goal on your list. Don't close your eyes! (Or else you gonna fall back asleep...I know you too well.) What outfit are you wearing? What's your energy like after you complete a task? Are there other people in your visualization? Who are they?

_____

_____

_____

_____

MINUTE 4: Gratitude time. Need some ideas? Ex.: Write one thing you are proud of yourself for. Write one sentence about someone in your life that you think is dope. Write down the last time you remember having a good day. What was good about it?

_____

_____

_____

_____

MINUTE 5: THIS IS IT! STAND UP!!! YOU'RE GOING TO DO 25 JUMPING JACKS! And then run in place for the remaining time. TELL ME HOW YA FEEL NOW?!?

_____

_____

_____

_____

OKAY NOW GO DO THE DAY BITCH!! I LOVE YOU!!! I'M PROUD OF YOU!!!!!

OKAY, WELL, MAYBE... THE FALLIN' ASLEEP IS HARD AS F*CK, TOO

Falling asleep can be just as hard to do, if not harder, for people with depression. Of course, we see those ads for antidepressants that show people in bed all day, "sleepin' their lives away," which, like, don't get me wrong, can be HELLA true...but, what happens when you get TOO MUCH SLEEP? Or you nap in the middle of the day? Or, perhaps like me, you get a rushing wave of anxiety creativity at 11 PM and, before you know it, you've made a Pinterest page for an Etsy business that you'll never actually start that sells magnetic dog clothes because you're furious at the current model for dog wear design and you don't even HAVE a dog and then it's 4 AM. And even though your eyes are red as fuck, you're exhausted, and ready for bed...the sleep just doesn't wanna come.

There are many ways why falling asleep can be the most difficult part about depression, but there are a few tips and tricks to use beyond the regular bullshit of "not eating past 8 PM," blah blah, "only use your bed for sleep and sex," blah blah, that just DOESN'T APPLY TO US DEPRESSED HOOMANS! (But ofc, try to apply those simple stupid rules when you can!)

- **Get some blue light glasses.** I'm not going to try to convince you to "stay off your phone past 9 PM," because I am also a young, phone-obsessed being who, at least once a week, falls asleep with their phone in their hand. So, instead—get them blue light glasses! So, at least when you ARE binge-watching a TV show while simultaneously Snapchatting on your phone while also reading your fav new crime novel on your iPad...you'll be blocking out some of that digital light that tricks the brain into thinking "Light? Must be time to get up!"

- **Lavender ANYTHING.** Bath bomb, Epsom salts, pillow spray, essential oils, WHATEVER—lavender is known to have calming-spa-ass properties that help you feel nice and cozy. I have the pillow spray and I soak my pillowcase every night of the week and sleep like an ANGEL. I even started GROWING lavender in my li'l garden, 'cause I wanted to make my own syrup for decaffeinated tea at night!

- **Melatonin can be your friend.** But stick to a VERY LOW DOSE of it because WHAT THEY DON'T TELL YOU ON THE BOX is that if you take TOO MUCH melatonin, you can actually start to feel MORE AWAKE. You will even feel more groggy the next morning if you try to up your tolerance. Also, duh, consult your doc before taking anything blah blah you guys know that by now, right?

- **Really, stop the fucking coffee past 2 PM.** I'm guilty as hell of this one, but find a way to curb your cravings for stimulation past 2 PM.

- **MASTURBATE TO SLEEP.** Y'all already know this one is my fav! There is no better feeling than the sleepies after a good O. Sometimes, the masturbating will put me to sleep before I finish! A success if you ask me! If I wake up in the middle of the night with a numb hand and overstretched PJ drawstrings, I know I was more tired than I thought.

- **Keep something next to your bed to store thoughts in:** a journal, sticky notes, a fucking voice recorder, for all I care. Use it before you go to bed to get all those ruminating feelings and ideas out. Or, if you wake up at exactly 3:17 AM every night, like I do, with a brilliant thought, have something in arm's reach so you can get that thought OUT and onto some paper for you to revisit in the AM.

- **If you have a partner, consider a separate sleeping arrangement.** I am a very light sleeper. I like to have 700 pillows when I sleep. I want to be a starfish and stretch all limbs into a final resting position. As you can imagine, this is not ideal for my partner, who is 6'4" and can confirm I will take your soul if you wake me up in the middle of the night (BECAUSE I HAVE SO MUCH TROUBLE SLEEPING, OKAY?! IT'S NOT MY FAULT!). The best goddamn thing I ever did for our relationship was build my "princess bed," as we call it. We took an extra loft space that was a weird-shaped room and fit a queen mattress perfectly in the corner. I bought a foam topper that was LAVENDER-scented and put up a bunch of Christmas lights and surrounded the room with books, and it feels like the coziest little reading nook that could house THE Princess Meghan Markle. (This is my extended invite to you, girl, if you ever wanna come over and try it, you are so welcome to!) The mattress is so fucking soft, I couldn't feel a pea even if you stuck a Costco-sized bag of frozen dinner peas underneath me! Hence the name: princess room. And when either one of us needs extra special attention in regard to resting, as a princess would, they get to sleep in the princess bed! It hasn't affected our intimacy, and the room is an open loft, so we can still see and talk to each other before falling asleep. It's very cute. Feels like we're in giant adult bunk beds. I think every night, before I fall asleep, "What fucking idiot decided couples need to sleep together? Fuck that guy."

- **Try listening to white noise.** I know. This might sound counterintuitive. "Kelsey, why would I want NOISE if I'm falling asleep?" And I hear you. I thought white noise sounded like TV static for a lot of my life, until I got an Alexa. I ask my li'l homie Alexa every night to play RAIN SLEEP SOUNDS, and it works like a freaking charm, because as soon as I close my eyes, my brain can run free while it imagines various scenarios of me in the rain, doing all sorts of fun shit. It's like counting sheep, but you are the sheep, and you are running, or trotting, I guess, in the rain.

- **ASMR also counts.** I thought I was one of the unlucky ones who didn't get a tiny skin orgasm whenever I listened to ASMR, until I discovered HEAD SCRATCHING ASMR, which is some stranger who scratches a manne-quin's head into a tiny and powerful microphone, and when it plays through my speakers it sounds like I'M GETTING THE HEAD MASSAGE, y'all. The Internet is a wonderfully weird and beautiful place.

BODY LOVE CHALLENGE

Write a love letter to a part of your body you hate.
In what ways has it served you? Been there for you? Can you get a little steamy? A little sexy? Or is it heartfelt? Appreciative?

DEAR *(Insert body part here)* _____

_____

_____

_____

_____

_____

_____

_____

_____

_____

_____

_____

_____

_____

_____

_____

_____

_____

Signed,

_____

What's something weird you love about your body?

_____

_____

_____

_____

What does your internal monologue sound like when you're feeling really confident? Well, scream it loud and proud into your brains! Write it here as many times as it will fit on the page. Feel each fuckin' word.

_____

_____

_____

_____

_____

_____

_____

_____

_____

_____

_____

_____

_____

_____

_____

I love routine > until I'm bored, then I love excitement > until I'm overwhelmed, then I love routine > until I'm bored, then I love excitement > until I'm overwhelmed, then I love routine > until I'm bored, then I love excitement > until I'm overwhelmed, then I love routine > until I'm bored, then I love excitement > until I'm overwhelmed, then I love routine > until I'm bored, then I love excitement > until I'm overwhelmed, then I love routine > until I'm bored, then I love excitement > until I'm overwhelmed, then I love routine > until I'm bored, then I love excitement > until I'm overwhelmed, then I love routine > until I'm bored, then I love excitement > until I'm overwhelmed, then I love routine > until I'm bored, then I love excitement > until I'm overwhelmed, then I love routine > until I'm bored, then I love excitement > until I'm overwhelmed, then I love routine > until I'm bored, then I love excitement > until I'm overwhelmed, then I love routine > until I'm bored, then I love excitement > until I'm overwhelmed, then I love routine > until I'm bored, then I love excitement > until I'm overwhelmed, then I love routine > until I'm bored, then I love excitement > until I'm overwhelmed, then I love routine > until I'm bored, then I love excitement > until I'm overwhelmed, then I love routine > until I'm bored, then I love excitement > until I'm overwhelmed, then I love routine > until I'm bored, then I love excitement > until I'm overwhelmed, then I love routine > until I'm bored, then I love excitement > until I'm overwhelmed, then I love routine > until I'm bored, then I love excitement > until I'm overwhelmed, then I love routine > until I'm bored, then I love excitement > until I'm overwhelmed, then I love routine > until I'm bored, then I love excitement > until I'm overwhelmed, then I love routine > until I'm bored, then I love excitement > until I'm overwhelmed, then I love routine > until I'm bored, then I love excitement > until I'm overwhelmed, then I love routine > until I'm bored, then I love excitement > until I'm overwhelmed, then I love routine > until I'm bored, then I love excitement > until I'm overwhelmed, then I love routine > until I'm bored, then I love excitement > until I'm overwhelmed, then I love routine > until I'm bored, then I love excitement > until I'm overwhelmed, then I love routine > until I'm bored, then I love excitement > until I'm overwhelmed, then I love routine > until I'm bored, then I love excitement > until I'm overwhelmed, then I love routine > until I'm bored, then I love excitement > until I'm overwhelmed, then I love routine > until I'm bored, then I love excitement > until I'm overwhelmed, then I love routine > until I'm bored, then I love excitement > until I'm overwhelmed, then I love routine > until I'm bored, then I love excitement > until I'm overwhelmed, then I love routine > until I'm bored, then I love excitement > until I'm overwhelmed, then I love routine > until I'm bored, then I love excitement > until I'm overwhelmed, then I love routine > until I'm bored, then I love excitement > until I'm overwhelmed, then I love routine > until I'm bored, then I love excitement > until I'm overwhelmed, then I love routine > until I'm bored, then I love excitement > until I'm overwhelmed, then I love routine > until I'm bored, then I love excitement > until I'm overwhelmed, then I love routine > until I'm bored, then I love excitement > until I'm overwhelmed, then I love routine > until I'm bored, then I love excitement > until I'm overwhelmed, then I love routine > until I'm bored, then I love excitement > until I'm overwhelmed, then I love routine > until I'm bored, then I love excitement > until I'm overwhelmed, then I love routine > until I'm bored, then I love excitement > until I'm overwhelmed, then I love routine > until I'm bored, then I love excitement > until I'm overwhelmed, then I love routine > until I'm bored, then I love excitement > until I'm overwhelmed, then

MEETING LITTLE KELSEY

AND YOUR FIRST CONVO MEETING "LITTLE" YOU.

All right—another one that perhaps a grown adult will roll their eyes at. But before you scoff at me asking you to play pretend—know that this exercise made me cry harder than anything I've cried about in therapy sessions. GET YOUR TISSUES OUT!

It was a particularly hard therapy session, beating myself up out loud, when the doctor did something he'd never done before: *He interrupted me.*

He said, "I need to stop you. I want to ask you something. What do you think Little Kelsey would think of the way you're talking about her right now?"

"Huh?" my face said back to him, still confused that this sweet, quiet man had INTERRUPTED ME FOR THE FIRST TIME IN THE TWO YEARS I'D BEEN SEEING HIM.

"I want you to think about yourself as a little girl. Younger than a teenager, but older than a toddler, who can understand the basics of relationships and emotion... maybe around the age of six or seven...Little Kelsey. Little Kelsey didn't know what anxiety, depression, or self-deprecation meant, did she? She took emotions and conversations at face value. I want you to think of her right now. How would she comfort Big Kelsey?"

"Is Big Kelsey...uh...me? Right now?" I asked.

"Yep," he said, curtly.

"Okay, well, when I think of myself as a kid..."

"No, no," this motherfucker interrupted me again, "don't think of yourself in your memory...I want you *to imagine Little Kelsey as her own person sitting next to you right now.* What's she look like? What's she wearing? And how would she feel if you talked to her this way?"

I looked at the empty space on the velvet green couch next to me and began to see Little Kelsey form. She was wearing this white, flowery T-shirt she wore so many times as a kid, that her mom secretly had to throw away because Little Kelsey would wear it days on end without letting her mom wash it. I saw her in these way-too-big navy cargo shorts that she ran around the neighborhood wearing because she LOVED playing outside...catching lizards...climbing trees. She wore these white lace-ankle socks and blue Velcro shoes...She had a half-up/half-down messy ponytail that came out like a fountain at the top of her head. And she had a permanently stained mouth from all the red Popsicles she used to eat. And she was looking at me with these big doe eyes and a faint smile. She was so innocent and vulnerable.

And

I

lost

my

fucking

shit.

I started crying...like, CRYING CRYING. Where you can't catch your breath and there's liquid falling out of your mouth and nose crying.

And then the strangest thing happened. I saw in my own mind, that small beautiful Little Kelsey reach over and hugged me, Big Kelsey, in that moment, and told me it was going to be okay.

And then I lost my shit all over again.

When I finally stopped crying long enough to make intelligent sentences, my smug-ass but wonderful therapist looked on at me, beaming. He knew he'd unlocked some magical shit, and I had to give it to him...*he fucking did.*

I think we get so wrapped-up in adulthood so quickly. We spend all of our teen years wishing we were older, and then when you're older, you just want to be more respected or successful, or whatever the next stage in life is supposed to be. Rarely do we go back and think of ourselves as "little," as having a relationship to ourselves now. Our "big" selves. Not just looking back on memories, but imagining what our little selves would *say* to our big selves. How would they think of each other? How do they speak to one another? They would be proud of us, no doubt. No matter what position we are currently in or feel like we are in, Little Us would be so happy that we'd made it this far. That we'd done so many things in our lives that Big Us surely forgets about or sweeps under the rug.

It's also important to accept what Little You has gone through. How have they been influenced? How do they understand love? How do they feel about critical parental figures? Do they have the freedom to explore passions and play at this age? Know that how Little You was impacted as a child will most definitely impact Big You.

In moments of pain or depression, it's easy to be cruel to ourselves...but, I've used this tool of Little Kelsey to imagine her sitting next to me in times of toughness. She would probably cuddle me when necessary and pull on my leg to go outside when needed. We're whip-smart together. We're curious and kind. I try to speak to myself the way I would speak to her. And, to think of it the other way around, I'd imagine all the things she'd want to know about all the fascinating shit I've done in my life...even down to the little moments of what it was like to kiss my crush for the first time, or was high school as fun as the movies, or if I still played piano as well as I did as a kid. I'd love for you to meet little you...and see what amazing and positive conversations can come from having them around.

So tell me,

Where is little you going to appear right now?

_____

_____

What is little you wearing?

_____

_____

_____

What is little you super-into right now in their life?

_____

_____

_____

What does little you's smile look like?

_____

_____

_____

_____

What does little you's laugh sound like (and what are they most likely to laugh at right now)?

_____

_____

_____

_____

What would little you be so proud of you about?

_____

_____

_____

_____

What would little you tell big you if they knew you were sad?

_____

_____

_____

_____

What would you say to little you, that is different than how you would talk to big you, if little you were sad?

_____

_____

_____

_____

Can you give little you permission to come visit from time to time when you need them?

_____

_____

_____

_____

Could they bring something comforting next time? Maybe a favorite blanket, or a pet, or maybe your favorite snack? What would they bring?

_____

_____

_____

_____

How do you say bye to Little You?

_____

_____

_____

_____

Now that Little You is back off to little-land, how did that feel?

_____

_____

_____

What would you accomplish if you KNEW you could not fail? That it was guaranteed to work? All your depression, anxiety and panic disappeared. Tell me how you'd do it and why:

_____

_____

_____

_____

_____

_____

_____

What do you need to hear right now? Tell yourself here:

_____

_____

_____

_____

_____

_____

_____

THE FIVE "INSTEADS"

IF YOU'RE TRYING TO BREAK A HABIT.

LET'S TAKE A WALK DOWN MEMORY LANE, SHALL WE? Nothing like reliving trauma, eh?! When I went through the worst breakup of my life, I felt as though I had truly lost everything. I hadn't realized it at the time, but my whole identity revolved around the person I was with. It wasn't their fault; I just hadn't built a life of my own yet, whereas he was an older dude with an established career and grew up in LA with many close friends. I was a 20-something young adult, trying to figure out my life and identity. He was a good pillar of stability! However, where I went to eat, what we did on weekends, birthday parties, and all sorts of activities had been absorbed into going out with his crew of friends. I had a few of my own friends, sure, but as most couples do, we found it easier to hang out in a group where everyone got along and never felt like a "wheel." So, it shouldn't have been a surprise to me that when the relationship ended, I lost a lot more than a best friend; I lost my entire social life, too (or, at least, the social life I had gotten accustomed to)! I knew his friends would take his side, and even the girls I had made friends with through him had to keep their distance until it was appropriate to reach out (and eventually they all did, and we are still gal pals till this day! SHOUTOUT TO #COOTERCLUB).

But in those post-breakup depressive days, **I had to make extra sure each day to remind myself that my depression was coming from heartbreak,** NOT the core of my soul or my depression diagnosis. Yes, I had been feeling depressed for a very long time toward the end of our relationship, and had been diagnosed and was on medication for major depressive disorder, but THIS EXTRA WEIGHT... this physical heaviness I could feel on my heart had to be SEPARATED FROM MY DEPRESSION. The scariest part of depression is when SOMETHING DEPRESSING HAPPENS TO SOMEONE WITH DEPRESSION! The unknown was what this high-stress situation would do to me and my body. I had to actively separate them in my head. I could not allow these feelings to stack on top of each other. I had to be able to treat the heartbreak properly and my depression disorder separately. For heartbreak, I needed to allow myself the space to cry, eat spoonfuls of frosting in bed, binge *Teen Mom,* and soothe myself. I told myself I would not allow this extra self-preservation to fall under the category of "slipping" in a depressive wave. I would not burden myself. I would not feel bad for feeling bad...and that took a LOT of daily reminders to achieve. I wrote mantras on my bathroom mirror, in my car, on my hand...as my iPhone screen saver. Any chance I could, I had to be my own best friend, helping her through a breakup.

When it came time to wipe myself off of the floor after a few days of hibernation, I knew I needed fresh air. But I had NO IDEA where to go or whom to call. When I thought of my favorite restaurants, I thought of him. When I wanted to go sit at the dog park and watch other people's dogs, I worried he might also be there, since that was a weird thing we did together to pass the time and look at dogs. I couldn't think of a weekend activity or even a hiking spot where I didn't think of HIM. Like the smog of Los Angeles was actually his spirit, and the air was cloudy and polluted with our relationship.

But just like I had to take back the power of my own life, I had to take back my environment, too. And that meant exploring new places I'd never been, doing things with my sadness that would force me into venturing out into the big city alone to make my FIVE INSTEADS. The Five Insteads can apply to situations more than breakup plans; they can be helpful when breaking avoidant behaviors, social anxiety, and even pushing your own boundaries, when you're feeling saucy. This exercise might require you to look back at some old memories or behaviors that bring up negative emotions, but it'll only be temporary, as we are actively using this exercise to replace the negative emotions and places associated with that environment.

I went back into my journal in 2014 to look at my Five Insteads. I wrote down the places/environments that most reminded me of our relationship. Everything from: our favorite restaurant (SUGARFISH, a bomb-ass LA sushi spot), to the place we visited most on the weekends (Will Rogers beach park for Sunday beach volleyball with friends), to very specific things I might feel when thinking of the relationship that threw me into a depression (when I saw a sweater with holes in the thumbs). Instead of getting sad, I would take a 10-minute walk INSTEAD of wallowing.

Find your own "insteads" that will be your go-tos when a certain emotion triggers you into a negative space. So, *instead* of doing/seeing/feeling the thing, you have an INSTEAD plan!

EX: Instead of eating at SUGARFISH, I will try to local go to the local Ethiopian restaurant that I've never had before! *Bonus points to myself if I take myself out on a solo date!*

Ex: When I hear the Adele song that reminds me of him and my sadness, INSTEAD OF LISTENING TO IT, I WILL take out my new watercolors and paint a li'l art for a friend! *Bonus points to myself if I take a walk to the post office and mail it to said friend!*

Heres a template to get you started:

a) Instead of_____,

I will do _____ to

replace the feeling and the thought.

b) I will _____

instead of _____.

c) Instead of feeling_____,

I will _____.

Make a list of five things you'd like to break a habit or relationship with and use this template to make your five "insteads." Put that paper somewhere that's easily seen and accessible.

JOURNALING

Journaling is something I thought I'd never had time for. It sounded stupid. I thought it was a waste of space on my nightstand, something I'd get excited about for two or three days, and then it would sit there, collecting dust, like so many other self-help workbooks I'd tried to complete. It was something recommended by so many therapists, and even that wasn't enough to get me to do it. But I got desperate. In the deepest parts of my brain, I was willing to try ANYTHING to get myself out of the black hole. I had to FORCE myself to write in a journal. I picked a red, leather-bound Gryffindor journal from Harry Potter World. At least THAT part of journaling made me happy.

What would your perfect journal look like?

_____

_____

_____

_____

It started with a simple, five-minute ranting. None of it made sense, and it was totally brain vomit. I even wrote "I HATE THIS JOURNAL" many times. My handwriting was bad and changed often, depending on my mood.

What's your BEST handwriting? Write me a sentence here so I can see. Write me a sentence about something that made you happy today:

_____

_____

_____

_____

How about your worst handwriting? Tell me about something that made you laugh recently:

_____

_____

_____

_____

I mostly wrote in it at night, while sitting in my bed, right before I'd go to sleep. While it started as a chore, I began to find relief in brain-vomiting right before going to sleep. I even bought a little book light that clipped to the top of the journal, so I could write with the lights off. Many nights, I fell asleep with the journal on my chest.

What would be the ideal time for you to write in a journal, and why?

_____

_____

_____

_____

I used the journal to write out texts or conversations to people that I didn't have the balls to send to in real life that day. Maybe I write a fake nasty text to an ex, or "send" an email to a boss who did me dirty that day. Anything goes in your journal! There are no rules!

Want to get anything off your chest to someone in your life? Write it here:

_____

_____

_____

_____

_____

_____

_____

_____

_____

Looking back on my first journal (there are many now, hidden in various spots in my room), I had decorated the interior with little doodles. There's a doodle of the Hollywood skyline, the Statue of Liberty (???), music notes, a bunch of film equipment, and my name and address LOL, ya know, just in case anyone finds it in my room, where it never ever leaves its one spot in my dresser. **What would you doodle on the inside of your journal?**

As the months went by, filling the journal felt really good. Seeing the pages dwindle down, getting close to the "end," felt like I was getting to the end of a really depressing time in my life. And it was CRAZY to go back and read some of the early entries. I didn't recognize this person. To see the growth I had made was astonishing. In a weird way, I'm super proud of these journals and plan on keeping them forever, and maybe sharing with my kids one day, if they are going through a tough time (if I ever decide to have kids, and they're old enough to understand why I was frustrated with the girl who made out with me in the bathroom at the club when we were drunk but ignored me at work). The way I wrote to myself shows tangible growth that I can touch and read. It's reassuring and a cool little time capsule of my life.

Where would you love to see growth in regard to the way you speak to yourself? Tell me what one year from now would look like for you, emotionally and physically:

_____

_____

_____

_____

Hey, guess what? You just did a journal entry without even realizing it! Isn't that cool? Think you can take this off the page and into your own moleskine?

I DID NOT COME THIS FAR TO ONLY COME THIS FAR

WHAT IS IMPOSTOR SYNDROME?

Impostor syndrome (also known as impostor phenomenon, impostorism, fraud syndrome, or the impostor experience) is a psychological pattern in which one doubts one's accomplishments and has a persistent, internalized fear of being exposed as a "fraud[43]."

How rude of myself to feel this way, right?! It's basically my brain LYING to itself that I'm not good enough!!

Often, impostor syndrome comes in the form of chronic self-doubt and intellectual inferiority. I feel impostor syndrome with the big, obvious category of CAREER (which a LOT of women are plagued with) and sometimes the lesser, low-stakes shit like dating. EVEN THOUGH...*clears throat preparing to rant a long list of accomplishments*...

I have millions of video views to prove my success as a creator, a loyal audience following who share my talents wherever they can, two people got TATTOOS of quotes I've said before, AND I EVEN PUBLISHED MY OWN DAMN WORKBOOK!!! I'm a great employee, I wake up early and go to bed only after I've finished the day's work. I lead creative brainstorms of entire teams of people. I'm great at public speaking. I'm a HAM for the camera. I LOVE my job and...yet...I still feel like I have ABSOLUTELY NO IDEA WHAT I'M DOING. OFTEN. Each time I meet a new person in the industry, I wonder how much more experience they have, and how they might look down upon my work as a "YouTuber." The fix? Self-confidence,

43 Langford, Joe, and Pauline Rose Clance. "The Imposter Phenomenon: Recent Research Findings Regarding Dynamics, Personality and Family Patterns and Their Implications for Treatment." *Psychotherapy: Theory, Research, Practice, Training*, vol. 30, no. 3, 1993, pp. 495–501., doi:10.1037/0033-3204 30.3.495.

right? Knowing that I have knowledge about the internet and content that a lot of brands and studios wish they knew. Yet, in the ACTUAL MOMENT of having a big meeting or pitch with these "higher ups," I never seem to remember all my accomplishments.

AND EVEN WITH A LESSER STAKES TOPIC, LIKE DATING...*takes a sip of water and sings "LA LA LA LA," making sure my voice is in tune*...

I'm a loud and proud bisexual with a bomb ass pussy and GREAT personality, who can make a motherfucker laugh just by looking at them the right way, who has been on more successful dates than not, DEFINITELY knows how to flirt with a girl and bump elbows like it was an accident but then compliment her on her necklace and maintain cute eye contact when securing their phone number 9.9/10 times... but, sometimes, I can feel judged by the queer community. Often bisexuals aren't fully accepted into the gay club, because we aren't seen as "fully" anything, but rather "half & half" or indecisive about our sexuality. So, whenever I enter a queer space, I enter with my guard up while internally screaming, "I KNOW WHO I AM. I AM QUEER. I BELONG HERE...but, please, like me more?"

But I want to tell you the good new about experiencing impostor syndrome the next time you notice it come up: You're only feeling inadequate BECAUSE you have the successes and confidence already. *You already know those feelings and how great they are,* so you know how shitty it feels to *not* have it! And that's a feeling based in fear, not reality.

Remember, confidence is a skill[44], and some days you'll be better at it than others. But when you know you got it deep down inside you somewhere, and your soul is just being a little tricky asshole that day—you can FAKE IT TILL YOU MAKE IT, BABY! Us depressed people are the QUEENS & KINGS & NON-BINARY ROYAL FOLK OF FAKING IT! Are you kidding?! The amount of FAKING it that it takes to attend that event, go to the birthday party, go on that date...we all should get Academy freakin' Awards!!!

Sure, it's a low-quality solution, but, sometimes, we just need to get through the "performance" of life. Goddess of Vulnerability Brené Brown warns us, however, that if you're "faking it till you're making it through ALL of life, and you're not able to get the response you want, potentially, people are subconsciously responding the the fake you—it's time to look under the hood of the car!"

Which is where *vulnerability* comes in with impostor syndrome. Sometimes, it's

---

44 More about Confidence in the Anxiety section!

okay to just be honest about how you're feeling. If you're nervous—tell them! If you feel uncomfortable—get comfy! Chances are, the other people you are dealing with in the current situation will see you as more human. Remind yourself in these scenarios that YOU ARE ENOUGH. Say it. And then say it again. Don't diminish your actual traits because of comparison to how "qualified" or "how much gayer" they are. There's that same feeling of fear you're taking on, that the other person might find out that you're a "fraud." And what does "fraud" even mean in your current situation? Don't we agree that no human being is perfect, and everyone is on this same Earth, learning and growing? Do you really have the same definition of "fraud" as everyone else? OR, could it potentially be that we're all worried that we might not be what the other person is expecting us to be? That's just a projection, isn't it? Can you prove that's rooted in fact? Probably not, right (unless you're catfishing someone—don't do that)? So, it's helpful to remind ourselves that we can't change other people's feelings about us; we can only control what <u>we</u> do and how <u>we</u> react. They are going to think whatever they want, so you might as well be yourself!

Letting go of the idea of who we think we're "supposed to be" can be liberating when you can recognize and celebrate who you really are.

Are you feeling some impostor shit syndrome in some facet of your life? Tell me about it:

_____

_____

_____

_____

_____

_____

_____

Are you comfortable with the idea of being successful? Why or why not?

_____

_____

_____

_____

_____

_____

_____

_____

_____

_____

Does impostor syndrome feel more comfortable to you than presenting your true self to the world? As if it's a motivating factor to keep finding the better and better version of yourself?

_____

_____

_____

_____

What qualifies you for this position, meeting, or space that you feel inadequate to exist in? Brag a li'l!

_____

_____

_____

_____

_____

_____

_____

For a moment, let's think about a typical childhood experience growing up in America. Parents often think their babies are the best and cutest baby on the planet, with constant Insta-stories and themed birthday parties. What did those kids do to deserve so much lavish attention?! THEY'RE JUST SITTING THERE, DROOLING, AFTER ALL, RIGHT?! Oh, wow! Your baby put the right block in the hole...? A genius! Your kid got the answer right to 1+1...? The teacher delivers a gold star sticker! Your toddler shit in a porcelain bowl instead of a plastic one...? MONUMENTAL! POST ABOUT IT ON FACEBOOK!

But there's something to this: Chances are, your guardians (hopefully) often PRAISED you whenever you did something growing up—maybe a little to the point of detriment. But of course, why wouldn't they? You're a STAR in their eyes! Then... at a certain age, we might not even realize it, but the authority figures in our lives (often our parents) STOP giving that amount of praise, and all those actions just become *expected*. If parents kept praising adults at the rate in which we praise li'l bbs, then it'd be considered coddling or arrogance. We stop getting it from our parents, so we look for it in other places...maybe a bad boyfriend, or a toxic friend? And it's the same cycle over and over again. At some point, we need to learn how to shift that need for praise and validation from others into getting validation and praise from ourselves. Are we proud of the person we've become? Do we like the work we put out into the world?

Would you want to be your own friend or coworker? In what ways can you be better at praising yourself and your own accomplishments?

_____

_____

_____

_____

When I'm feeling dat IMPOSTORY SHIT, I remember my favorite tweet:

"Because, at the end of the day, when you don't feel smart enough, remember: Apple (the smartest, chicest, most modern brand in the world??) decided to make the mouse charger like this: "

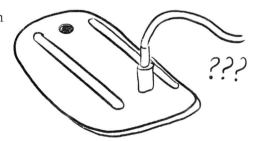

THIS IS A LIST OF SONGS YOU LISTEN TO AT YOUR VERY MOST DEPRESSED TO CHEER YOU UP!

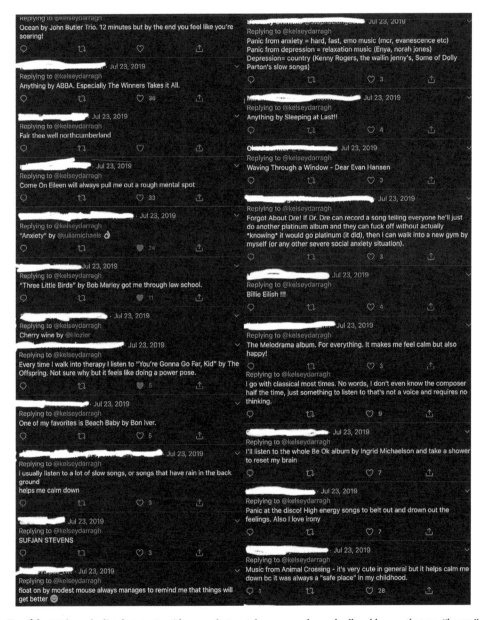

Try this: *Make a playlist that starts with songs that match your mood...gradually add songs that are "happy" and upbeat that make you wanna dance. Try listening to the playlist and see if it helps elevate your mood!*

NO APOLOGIES NECESSARY

ALTERNATIVE LANGUAGE EXERCISE

Remember how you're an amazing gorgeous warrior battling a mental illness? You have nothing to apologize for. Try this: Instead of saying "sorry" all the time for your emotions or actions, try saying "THANK YOU."

INSTEAD OF THIS:		SAY THIS:
Sorry, I'm being a bitch.	→	Thank you for being supportive.
Sorry, I'm a mess.	→	Thanks for your patience!
I'm scared. I'm sorry.	→	You're the best for understanding how scary this situation can be for me.

Remember: Everyone else's opinions about you or your mental health are neither your business nor your problem. It's THEIR opinion, so it's THEIR problem! Not yours! So, get that load of thought off your shoulders, and let them carry their own thoughts and feelings. You just keep being a fabulous warrior.

SELF-CARE BINGO

Brushed my teeth!	I spoke my affirmations out loud five times to myself!	I watched my fav movie without any interruptions!	I made a happy music playlist.	I took myself out on a date.
Took my pet for a walk outside!	I took a well-deserved nap!	I took care of a plant! (Dusting a fake one counts, too.)	I resisted self-harm! Whether it's physical or mental!	Masturbated :)
Meditated!	I danced around the house.	FREE ✺ SPACE	I got outside for a hike/walk/jog/skate/bike ride.	I did something creative that I enjoy.
Made a Pinterest board of some inspo for my next DIY!	I tried knitting!	I took a moment to recognize my feelings!	I made someone aware of my true feelings and boundaries!	Tried scent therapy (lavender, chamomile, cinnamon, citrus, eucalyptus)!
I set an intention for my day.	I screamed into a pillow!!!!!	I made a list!	I tried a puzzle!	I got off my phone and read something on paper (article, book, magazine)!

GET UP! AND DO 25 JUMPING JACKS RIGHT NOW! THEN, YOU CAN GO BACK TO WHAT YOU WERE DOING! BUT JUST REAL QUICK! DO IT!!!!!

GET THAT BLOOD FLOWING!

**Too little serotonin for too long is no bueno.
Here are some simple and quick ways to raise your serotonin:**

1. **Food.** You can't directly get serotonin from food, but you can get tryptophan, an amino acid that's converted to serotonin in your brain.

2. **Bright light.** Go sit outside or by a window for just a couple mins!

3. **Supplements.** Things like Vitamin D.

> **Serotonin**
> *is a chemical that has a wide variety of functions in the human body. It is sometimes called the "happy chemical," because it contributes to well-being and happiness.*

4. **Massage.** Big fan of the self-shiatsu massaging devices from Amazon! They squeeze you harder than any human hands I've found!

5. **Mood induction.** Long explanation short for this one: Watch a series of happy images online, or pics on your phone that you know will make you smile!

6. **Neurofeedback therapy!**

7. **Masturbate or have sex!**

HACK YOUR HAPPINESS

DOPAMINE:
the "reward" chemical

Try completing a task that's been on your to-do list for too long.

Eat your favorite snack.

Stretch for 10 minutes!

ENDORPHINS:
the "pain killer"

watch some funny youtube compilations.

Sniff those essential oils!

Netflix your favorite comedy.

Go for a fast-paced walk.

OXYTOCIN: the LOVE hormone. Ooh la la

KISS SOMEONE YOU LIKE!

Play with a pet!

Hug a friend.

Compliment yourself.

YOU PROBABLY
NEED A SHOWER

We don't like to talk about the lack of hygiene some of us go through when struggling with depression because it's such a personal topic...but, as this is the book with NO FILTER, BABY, I'M HERE TO TELL YA! I've seen it first-hand how your pitties and undercarriage can STANK during the hormonal/chemical shakeup of a depressive episode. If you're going through it right now, remember that you are BATTLING A MENTAL ILLNESS. YOU'RE IN THE BATTLEFIELD, BABE! Things are going to get messy, muddy, rolling around in the grass and dirt. You are a soldier. Waging a battle today! And, even on the battlefield, the soldiers were given a shower every now and then, or would wash off when possible. **You deserve cleanliness**. So, take this time and go ahead and take a shower or bath. This book will be waiting for you ready when you come back.

But before you go!! Consider this:

I made over my shower during the pandemic of 2020 (hi, corona, COVID-19—you suck) because I found myself working from home, falling slowly but surely into a small li'l depresh moment, and...not showering. So, I decided, instead of doing work (like finishing this workbook, teehee), the best use of my time would be giving my bano a li'l DIY makeover! First, I bought a waterproof suction-cup Bluetooth speaker ($9 on Amazon) that automatically connects to your phone when you turn it on for a seamless transition from when I ~*crawl*~ from the bed into the bathroom.

Next, I brought my eucalyptus essential oils into the shower, and just two drops are enough to fill the entire shower with a spa-like smell that'll melt any tough bitch into a watery rainforest dewdrop. The bottle now lives on my shower window shelf. If you don't have essential oils, you can use an orange to create a beautiful smell. Bring that bright boy right into the shower and PEEL IT IN THE SHOWER—just let the peel fall to the drain. All that acidic oil will create a really fun scent that just feels CLEAN—right?! Aren't all cleaning products scented like acidic fruits after all?!

REALLY feelin' myself a Martha Stewart at this point, I made a mini rainforest in my shower! AND BOY DID IT CHANGE THE GAME. You can do it, too!

You'll need a shower curtain rod, small shower plants (recommend succulents, eternity plants, orchids, snake plant, bamboo, and my favorite, motherfuckin' FERNS. Ferns just drip down the shower tiles in a way that makes it almost sexual. UGH I LOVE FERNS. HIGHLY RECOMMEND), and macrame or hanging plant pots (you can find tons of macrame patterns online for free to make at home with nothing but STRING! YAY, we love a DIY moment!).

1. Hang shower rod.

2. Place air plants or succulents into a small pot with a hanger or your handmade macrame.

3. Hang high so you're not covered in vines and let those babies flourish!

4. Name your new plant friends. Kelsey's plants are: Mason, Penelope, Reign, North, Chi, Psalm, True, Stormi, and Dream.

These plants require very minimal maintenance. Whenever I'm in the shower, I give them a spritz with the shower head, which is plenty to keep them alive, and, yes, I eventually named them all and gave them all personalities of the Kardashian grandchildren. There's something about doing the minimum effort to keep something alive when I can barely take care of myself that gives me a fulfilling task while also getting clean in the shower! A TWO-FOR-ONE!

In those super-stinky depray-pray (depression) days, I try to imagine a shower cleansing me of those negative feelings and thoughts. It might sound stupid now, but just visualizing those thoughts going down the drain can be powerful imagery for your brain, and REMEMBER HOW POWERFUL AND INFLUENTIAL your thoughts can be! Good, bad, right, or wrong!

OKAY, now go get in that shower, you li'l stinky cute garlic onion! <3 I'll wait.

...How was it? Tell me if this shower felt different than others?

_____

_____

_____

_____

_____

_____

_____

_____

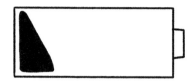

DAILY HABITS THAT DRAIN OUR ENERGY

- **Overchecking social media**
- **Skipping meals** (don't let that blood sugar drop or spike, honey—it can imitate feelings of panic and depression)
- **Gossiping or bullying others** (that ain't gonna make u feel better about yourself, boo)
- **Caring about what others' opinions of us are** (the sooner you accept that not everyone in life is going to like you, the easier this one gets. Except for Beyonce—EVERYONE LIKES BEYONCE)
- **Taking things personally**
- **Oversleeping** (even if it feels better in the moment, there's no better anxiety spike than missing your first appointment! Or, even if your day is empty, you don't want to throw off your internal clock [for the children, this is something you start to feel like shit about around the age of 28])
- **Letting petty shit bug you** (choice theory: allows one to take responsibility for one's own life and, at the same time, withdraw from attempting to try to control outside factors)

INSTAGRAM HASHTAGS THAT WILL MAKE YOU HAPPY INSTANTLY

I've never claimed any page in this entire workbook will "cure" you, or even work for, fuck's sake (have you tried BREATHING???). This page is the exception. These Instagram hashtags to follow WILL IN FACT CURE YOUR DEPRESSION!* Even if momentarily.

EVERYONE'S feeds could use more love and happiness on them. What we mindlessly scroll through for hours a day can have more effect on our sadness than our well-being. Fill your feed with as much brightness and color as possible.

These hashtags also work for TikTok too, and whatever cute Gen Z app has taken over the Internet by the time you're reading this workbook.

#superhappy	#nationalparks
#brusselsgriffon	#charcuterie
#germanshepherdpuppies	#blackheadextraction
#kittens	#earthfriendly
#babiesbeingfunny	#earthporn
#peoplestandingweird	#randomkindness
#satisfying	#latteart
#shibainupuppy	#powerwashingporn
#ocdfix	#vanlife
#foodporn	
#miniatures	

HOW TO CHANGE CHORES INTO ACTS OF SELF-CARE

CLUTTER IS THE CULPRIT OF STRESS

Housekeeping and cleanliness are funny things—some of the most successful people and artists I know keep their house a MESS. It doesn't seem to affect their creativity, and, as a Marie Kondo meme would say, some people "Love a mess!"

I.   Do. Not.   Love.   A.   Mess.

Even writing that unevenly spaced sentence gave me ANXIETY.

I.Do.Not.Love.A.Mess.

Ah, much better.

This chapter is for the people whose arm hairs tingle when they read that mis-spaced sentence! If you thrive in a chaotic home environment, by all means, feel free to skip this page! But if you're like me and tend to lean on the OCD or OCPD side of organization as self-soothing, then this is for you. I know that if my space is messy, I tend to take on the guilt that my LIFE is a mess, and it's always sitting in the back of my mind as another task I need to cross off my to-do list—therefore, I'm never able to function creatively at 100% when my workspace and comfort zone (my bedroom) is a mess. It doesn't feel like I can retreat to a place that isn't inviting. And, as much as my brain jerks off to the idea of a crisp, freshly made bed and perfectly stacked books and a dust-free staircase—I don't particularly like the act of DOING THE CHORE itself. For some with disposable income, a cleaning person or housekeeper/nanny is the way to go. Usually, the price is worth the gained free time. If you do your own housekeeping, like me, I have some tips and tricks to make the "chores" feel less like a mountain of work and more like an opportunity to take a break from life and give yourself the cleanliness you DESERVE to function!

- **If you work from home** or spend a lot of time at home, my first recommendation is to keep an eye on the pileup from the get-go. If you can avoid letting work pile up, the less it will feel like an overwhelming task. My household bought very cheap but cute-looking woven baskets from Target and Marshalls to keep in all the rooms of our house. So, even if we are quickly dropping in a blanket, or some extra cords, and even laundry that didn't make it to the bedroom, we know that we at least have these buckets to contain the mess. Then, when you decide it's chore time (which is *all the time*—see: tip 2), you know to start with organizing your cute and stylish basket.

- **I try not to have the idea of "cleaning day" happening all at once.** If you believe that, let's say, SUNDAY is always your day to clean, it can get... well, messy—no pun intended. Rather, spreading out small tasks throughout the week will keep your space and, therefore, your mind clear in the meantime helps avoid a pile-up situation. I have a rule in my head that if it will take less than five minutes for me to do, THEN I JUST DO IT! If it's a bigger or longer task, like laundry or mopping/vacuuming, I save that for a day when I know I can block out the chunk of time.

- **DON'T BE AFRAID TO ASK FOR HELP!** I live in a three-story townhouse with two other people (hi, Bryan and boyfriend). I tend to take on the load of the work simply because it makes me feel in control of the the space's ~*vibe*~, and, as mentioned above, soothes my OCD tendencies. HOOOOWEEEVVVVERRRRRR—in couple's therapy, I found myself complaining about my boyfriend not doing as much of the work as I did, how that catered to the patriarchy, even though I was willingly taking on the work myself. I never told him I needed help. And *that was on me*. Not him. It's hard to monitor your needs as someone living with a mental health condition, but usually the fear of how the other person will react or do the task is much more high-stakes in my brain than IRL.

- **Doing laundry or static movement cleaning**—use this time to listen to a podcast or catch up on a reality TV show! Science has been debunked that we can multitask successfully (yes, even that "fact" that women can do it better than men, sadly), so let your brain take a rest by watching something you don't have to think *too* hard about to enjoy. The characters in reality TV will give you LIFE (and more pop culture knowledge on where all those memes originate from). It's not time for that thrilling murder mystery vignette. Try *90 Day Fiance, Teen Mom, Below Deck, Jerry Springer*, etc., etc.

- **Marie Kondo up in this bitch.** Check out the book *Tidying Up*.
- **Cooking can go from stressful and hectic to fun and social** if you cook over a Zoom meeting with a friend (or multiple friends, if you have those, you lucky duck!). Schedule an online conference meeting with this free app, or use FaceTime with all your pals, and pick a meal you can make multiples of, so you don't have to cook too soon again :).

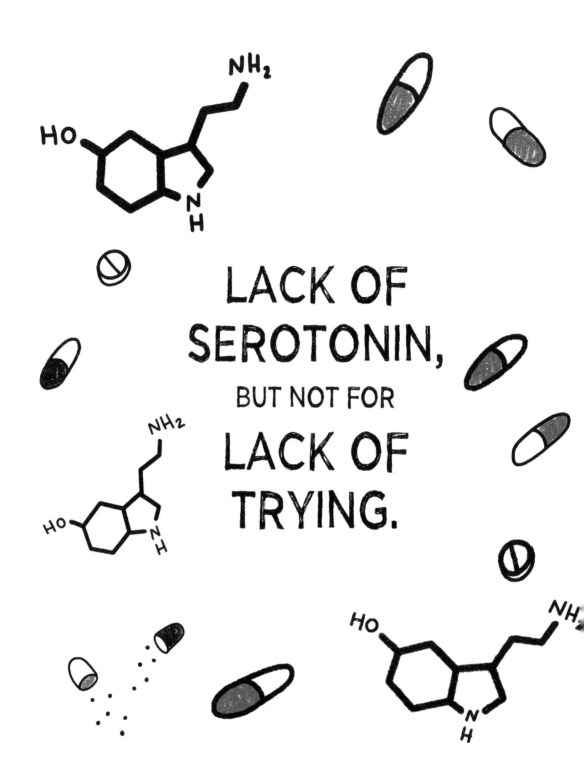

LACK OF
SEROTONIN,
BUT NOT FOR
LACK OF
TRYING.

DEPRESSION EATING

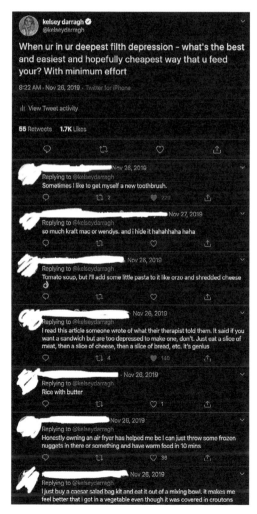

HERE'S ANOTHER LIST!!! THAT YOU GUYS! YEAH! FUCKIN' YOU!!! (unless you're new here...then, hiiiiiii, welcome. I like u) MADE!! ABOUT WHAT TO EAT/ORDER WHEN YOU ARE FEELING AT YOUR LOWEST!!!

All kinds of ramen (fancy or cheap)

Tyson's frozen chicken strips (micowaved)

Peanut butter via PBJ or straight from the jar.

UberEats

Cereal

Anything w cheese or jelly

Sharp white chedder with pretzel crackers and a Granny Smith apple

Mac + Cheese

Tuna packets or cheese sticks

Chef Boyardee Mini Ravioli

Ensure

Instant Oatmeal

Soup

Salty, buttery popcorn

Turkey sandwich with chips

Baked beans

Doritos

Instant mashed potatoes loaded with salt and butter

Pastroni

Burger

Champagne and donuts

Nachos

Pizza

Hamburger Helper

TRAIT VS. STATE

The saddest and most depressed I've ever been was after a breakup (which, y'all know pretty intimately now, huh? It feels so silly to think back on, considering how much better my life got later!!). Months before he broke up with me, I was having regular panic attacks, I was switching my meds every other month, and this mental and the emotional back-and-forth was too much for him to empathize with. To this day, my biggest fear is being called "too much," or perhaps "extra," as the kids are calling it now. On the day of the breakup, life didn't feel real. I felt like I was reading a script, as words came out of my mouth to make it feel amicable. When, in reality, I wanted to SCREAM. Cry. Shit. Even puke a li'l, at the same time. I felt like I had lost so much of my life. My friends, my routine—how do you go from doing EVERYTHING with one person to the very next day—just...not?

I was terrified that I'd NEVER stop hurting. It's hard to understand how you could love someone else so much and the other person has the FULL RIGHT to not want to be with you. It's like that movie, *500 Days of Summer*—people hated Summer for all the cruel things she did to Tom when, in reality, Tom was the asshole. He was trying to *make* someone love him that didn't feel the same way back. It's just RUDE! And that's what I was going through. I didn't know this level of hurt could exist, and I was SURE that this would last forever. Of course, many years later, I'm not only fine, but I look back at that period of my time like, "Whoa wtf what that shit all about?" I couldn't believe I had been in a hole that deep. So dark. So lonely. It was scary as fuck. After much therapy, and even a li'l stint at an inpatient therapy clinic, I learned that that period of time in my life was a STATE. Not a TRAIT.

This is a crucial lesson to recall for people who deal with depression. Let me explain further...

LET'S SAY A DISASTER IS HAPPENING IN YOUR LIFE. OH FUCK. I'M SO SORRY FOR YOUR TROUBLES YOU ARE GOING THROUGH. However, your body, mind, and feelings are in a STATE. You are in a STATE; this is not who you usually are and how you usually act and respond in life. You are in a state of crisis, or a state of depression. It is happening TO you. You must separate this crisis or depression state away from what your true personality and soul are when you are at your best. It is not a fixed TRAIT of yours to respond or feel this way. During this disaster/trauma, you acknowledge and treat the STATE the proper way trauma should be treated, and note that life won't feel normal for a while. SEPARATE THIS DISASTER from your core of who you really are. Note that the following things are NORMAL to EXPERIENCE during trauma or disaster:

- **Relationships to food and eating will be challenged.**
- **A surge of compulsive or addictive behaviors will surface.**
- **You might get sicker easier.**
- **You will feel exhausted, even after long periods of sleep.** Perhaps fatigued, unmotivated, and lethargic, or "lazy."
- **You might start to think of money, food, and shelter in a more panicked or confused way.** Do I have enough? Do I need more? Do others that I love have enough resources?
- **New and old trauma can resurface, causing the feelings to feel like they are stacked on top of one another!** STACKS ON STATES.
- **You might get angry, irritable, frustrated, sad, confused, etc.**
- **Crying spells or anger bursts.**

After this breakup, I let the state CONSUME ME. I thought it was who I WAS now. How would I ever get out of this depressive hole? I didn't know at the time that I could learn how to nurture my breakup with the time, love and, self-compassion it deserved.

Although this STATE took over my ability to function, I survived it. And I thank the universe every day. I learned a lot about self-reliance in that time. Of course, since I've seen what my rock bottom looks like, I fear going back to that place. I know it exists, and that it's a STATE I am capable of falling into. When I'm feeling down or sad, my mind immediately goes back to this moment of my life—and I worry that my life might end back up in this deep, dark, shitty, suicidal, hung over, and tired place. But I'm different now. I have a better relationship with myself. I have the tools. I take care of myself. And, I can tell the difference between being in a STATE and my fixed TRAITS. I have to constantly remember that I'm not going to spiral, and that those weren't and aren't my normal circumstances.

So, how do we get out of that state? Besides having a support system, therapy, and/or an outlet for our true emotional state to flow freely... *time* is the answer.

Time!!!!!

Can you remember a time where you thought your pain attack would never end, and THEN IT DID? Same with heartbreak. It's a quote that's as old as time, but truly, really got me through it: TIME HEALS ALL WOUNDS.

TIME.

TIME.

TIME.

And, when you live with depression, the idea of the clock being the gatekeeper of happiness can feel like a sick joke. Daydreaming takes on a new meaning with depression. It's like living in slow motion—but, I told myself I would get to the other side. I had to recognize that my healing might not look like what I saw in the movies. Maybe I needed more time than I'd originally thought. **It's okay to still be alive and not be okay for a really long time.** It's okay to not be okay. Without that deep state of depression, I would've never learned how strong I really am. The pain I suffered *then* has given me the power and strength that I have *now* to take on any dark time, head on.

PAPER PLANE EXERCISE

1. **Get a piece of paper out and write whatever the hell you're feeling right now.** It can be a stream of consciousness, a very specific problem, or even a retelling of a conversation you had that left you feeling a type of way.

2. **Then, follow the instructions on the next page to make an easy but badass paper airplane using the sheet of paper you just wrote on.**

3. **Find your nearest highest place and take your plane with you.** Meditate or be mindful of the thing you wrote down for a few minutes. Say thanks for being around, but that you don't need it anymore! THEN THROW THIS BITCH OFF THE ROOF!* TAKE OFF, BABY!!!!!!

4. **Say goodbye to toxic things, persons, habits, negative self-thoughts, etc., etc.**

But then go pick it up and be environmentally friendly. Maybe just throw it into a garbage can to begin with.

THERE IS NOTHING SO BAD IN THIS WORLD THAT CAN HAPPEN TO YOU THAT IS STRONGER OR MORE POWERFUL THAN GOOD. SOMETHING GOOD WILL ALWAYS COME ALONG (especially alongside something bad). To me, this means that good will NEVER abandon you. It might be subtle. But it's there. Always.

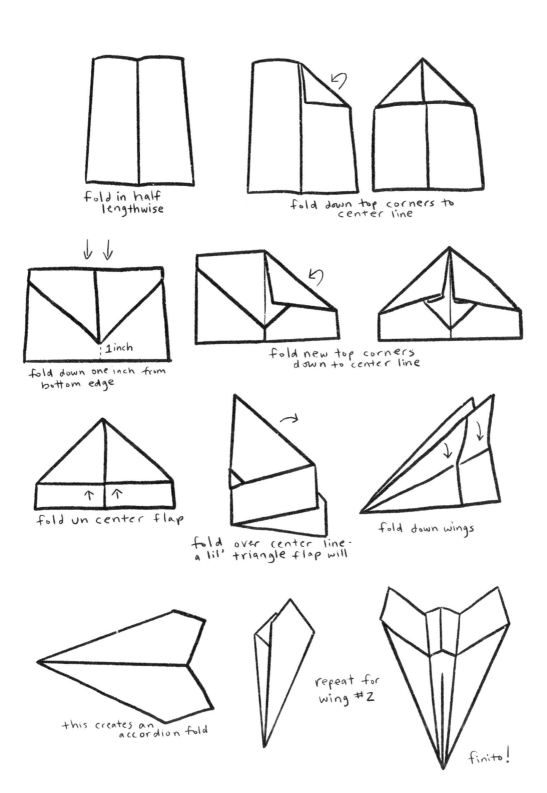

fold in half
lengthwise

fold down top corners to
center line

fold down one inch from
bottom edge

1 inch

fold new top corners
down to center line

fold un center flap

fold over center line-
a lil' triangle flap will

fold down wings

this creates an
accordion fold

repeat for
wing #2

finito!

REINFORCE THE GOOD

Let's take a good look at the good in your life. It's all around us but might be difficult to see when you're squinting through a cloud of depression. So, let's get outside of ourselves. Try to take the worry and sadness off yourself and focus on others for this exercise.

Tell me something that you love about your favorite people (pets are people, too):

Your BFF: What do you love about them? What's your funniest memory with them or of them? How did you guys meet?

_____

_____

_____

Family or chosen "family" member:

_____

_____

_____

How about a challenge? **Tell me something you like about an EX oooOOOooOOOOoo:**

_____

_____

_____

A complete stranger passing by:

_____

_____

_____

A furry friend:

_____

_____

_____

Hey—can you text, call, or show a person/pet some love right now? Use what you just wrote as a jumping-off point. That song "I Just Called to Say I Love You" totally makes sense now.

don't

trip

over

what

is

behind

you

Like Elsa said, "Let that shit go, dawg." That's verbatim what she said. Remember, anxiety is rooted in overthinking about the past or future. The past is the past. Be better right _now by thinking about the right now._

PAYING IT FORWARD

Ever cry your eyes out watching "Ellen's 12 Days of Giveaways?" Or how about those viral YouTube clips of strangers risking their lives to save someone else's dog caught in the river riptide? What about that TikTok of a bone-marrow donor meeting their recipient?! OH GOD IS SOMEONE CUTTING LARGE ONIONS WHILE PLAYING FRANK OCEAN IN HERE?!

Sure, ya pessimist, there might be some companies or people that are doing it for the PR, but there are many MORE out there who do it for altruism. Altruism is defined by the belief in or practice of disinterested and selfless concern for the well-being of others. The Dalai Lama says that his main daily practice is altruism and that it's good for physical health. He's 84 and not only one of the most important people on the planet, he's one of the HAPPIEST. So, like, we should listen to him, yeah?? There's an actual science to why selflessness makes you feel good, especially if you expect nothing in return (including praise from friends, family, or social media). One 2014 study, published in the journal *Social Cognitive and Affective Neuroscience*, says, "engaging in compassionate actions activates the areas of the brain associated with the reward system including the dopaminergic ventral tegmental area and the ventral striatum (LMAO WTF DOES THIS MEAN). The positive feelings created by compassionate actions then reinforce altruistic behaviors."[45] If you need more inspiration, one of my favorite YT channels to watch to get some smiles and good energy flowing is from MR. BEAST, who is known to have given away millions of dollars to strangers who deserve it.

When's the last time you practiced altruism?

_____

How did it make you feel?

_____

45 Klimecki, Olga M., et al. "Differential Pattern of Functional Brain Plasticity after Compassion and Empathy Training." *Social Cognitive and Affective Neuroscience*, vol. 9, no. 6, 2013, pp. 873–879., doi:10.1093/scan/nst060.

If you could do it again, what would you do differently?

_____

_____

_____

Reduce stress and anxiety; it makes someone ELSE feel good in return.

EASY WAYS TO PRACTICE ALTRUISM:

- **Browse GoFundMe and donate $5 to a stranger's cause with a note of support.**
- **Pay for the person's coffee behind you at Starbucks.**
- **Marie Kondo the shit out of your closet and donate those extra things.**
- **Invite someone to sit with you at lunch that you haven't really interacted with before.**

LETS PLAY A GAME

You've won ONE MILLION DOLLARS!!! WOW, congrats.

Except oop—there's a stipulation in the contest rules that says you can't spend ANY OF THE MONEY ON YOURSELF (ugh, we never read the fine print, do we?). You have to dole out your million in service of others. How would you use the million? Feel free to split it up as much as you want.

AMOUNT: _____ TO WHOM: _____

FOR WHAT: _____

WHY: _____

While writing this workbook, I started spending a lot of time at an animal shelter. It's not one of those beautiful Beverly Hills boutiques with shiny floors and clean, poofy dogs. It's quite the opposite. It stinks and has bird shit on the walls. It's doing the best it can with the resources it's given. I wasn't sure why, late in my 20s, I became obsessed with the idea of volunteering at this shitty shelter. Perhaps I was trying to escape from my own life and feelings with this distraction? Since I had left my full-time job the year before, I was having a rough time filling my time with meaningful work. I got pretty depressed and blase about all the days that show up on my GCal with no events. I thought to myself, "Maybe it's true. Misery *does* love company!" These skinny, shaken, dirty animals seem to be doing just as bad as I was feeling (okay, and LOOKING. Sometimes, I wouldn't shower for four days on average over the sad summer of 2019). But something I noticed being at the shelter over time: All of the volunteers were some of the happiest, most caring, and helpful people I've met in Los Angeles (which is saying something, since almost everyone here is smoking weed and doing an all-plant-based diet with 364 days of sunshine). I interviewed a volunteer about why he spends so many days a week there, working *for free*. "Some people think they'll get too attached working here, or it's too sad when you see a foster dog returned for the fourth time that year...but, the good moments FAR outweigh the sad. Seeing the tiniest improvement and success from an animal brings more joy to me than I've felt with any human." I LOL'd at this, because I used to have a hard time celebrating other people's successes. But with animals, it felt so natural. "And it didn't have to be an adoption, which was obviously the dream. No, it could be as simple as seeing a sick cat finally get rid of his kitty kennel cough, or a nervous dog finally lick my fingers—they were baby steps that felt like LEAPS!"

I started to find myself wanting to visit the shelter, a 45-minute drive away with shitty parking, any free chance I got. And then, it hit me: Seeing progress in these animals felt easier to see than seeing progress in myself. I was learning how to celebrate small wins through these shelter animals. I'd spend all week sleeping in too late, unable to finish a script, or canceling lunch, but then become ELATED when a kitten could switch from wet to dry foods. I was treating those animals the way I should be treating myself. I started to try to accept my own small wins and celebrate them just as hard. I got out of bed that day—HURRAY!!! I was able to eat dry food instead of wet—FUCK YEAH! The best part was, I expected nothing in return from these animals except...*to keep on living*. And I started to feel the same for myself. That's the rub with paying it forward; you can't expect to get anything in return, and you shouldn't...but you'll come to see how quickly the karma comes back inward. Not to mention, petting kittens is a really good stress-reducer.

After a few months of volunteering and fostering a cat, I thought I'd try my hand at fostering a dog. I self-identify HARD as a cat person, but this shelter carries over 200 dogs at once, and I found myself starting to wander the alleys of the dog section over and over. One day in November[46], I took my friend Zach to the shelter to drop off some blankets. We roamed over to the dog area, and then I saw him. Barry. My boy. My sweet, sweet, perfect boy. I already believed in love at first sight and soul mates and all that shit, but this moment actually felt like time froze...I fell in love with Barry, a 29-pound bulldog mix with a stumpy tail and pirate eye that wouldn't open. He was labeled a "medical case" with entropion (a condition where eyelashes grow the wrong way on a dog's eyes, causing pain and blindness), and no one would adopt him because they knew they'd have to pay for medical care. I took him home.

My Barry bear,

I have no idea where you'll be by the time this book comes out. Maybe I caved and convinced Bryan and Jared to let me keep you in this tiny zoo of a townhouse. Or, maybe I let you get adopted by that nice hairdresser who loves to hike and posts lots of thirst traps. But right now, you are curled up next to me in the living room, with your big boxy head rested on a pillow. Speaking of, we found out you're NOT a boxer at all! You are part Chow and part English Bulldog, with a sprinkle of Staffy! I just changed out your bandanna that hangs around your collar from blue to black checkers. You pooped once outside and once inside on Bryan's bathroom rug today. And you are absolutely perfect. I remember the moment I decided to foster you. I ended up at the shelter and saw you in the 5th cage on the right. You were sitting on your butt, shaking, with one eye closed. They told me you were a medical case because your eye was all fucked-up and wonky, and that's why no one would adopt you. You were two years old and a stray at the shelter for three months, with no microchip, and hadn't been neutered, but I'm convinced you must've been a savant dog because you knew how to sit like a good boy. Your huge head and tiny body, at only 29 pounds, looked miserable. You had just been fixed, so your peen was all fucked-up and stitched together. I don't know if it was the Valium or my altruism, but I took one look at that ball-less, square-headed, one-eyed body of yours and knew it would fit perfectly in my arms. And it did. I carry you around like a baby all the time. Your personality is so goofy. My cats hate you, but they are doing their best. You can't understand why all dogs don't want to be your best friend, and you can keep up with all the big dogs, even though you're a little big dog. You've taught me so much about what it means to prioritize myself. You

---

46 Before I finish this chapter I should mention the morning I met Barry, I had a 6:30 AM MRI scan. I am very claustrophobic, so I had some Valium before the appointment as a preventative measure since I had canceled the prior two appointments due to panic attacks in the MRI machine. So...was I high on my anxiety meds when I met Barry, time froze, and I fell in love with a dog? Maybe. But that's NOT THE POINT HERE!

helped me learn how to love getting up in the morning. Like, I NEVER thought I'd be a morning person. Ever. At 7:30 AM, your little tail wakes up before you do. It's almost like your tail knows I'm coming down the stairs before you do. Our walks allowed me time for ourselves. To bond, or to just walk alongside each other in silence. You gave me purpose at the lower points in my life. In the moments of inexplainable depression, where it didn't feel like I deserved to be depressed but just WAS, I just took one look at your dumb little face, and that frustration was replaced with unmatched joy. You snore. You burp like a human. And your farts could clear a large room. You're so gentle with me, and you trust me. You look to me to do EVERYTHING. I didn't think I could ever handle that responsibility when there are some days I don't even think I can take care of myself. But you never gave up on me. You are my shadow and my Jiminy Cricket. You were miserable when I met you, and so was I. And then we were happy together. A lot. Like, all of the time. You have the most kissable forehead I've ever seen in my goddamn life. You never bark—like, ever. Maybe four times since we got you. Also, I love the way you smell. You don't have doggie breath, and you don't shed. You smell like wood, with a tiny hint of fresh Doritos. You get your eyeball stitches out tomorrow since we finally got you the surgery. You needed to see the world with two whole eyeballs!! I don't like to think about the day you may leave me, but I try to remind myself that if you get adopted, then I have room in my heart for another foster and the chance to feel all of that...that magical, natural antidepressant bonding...all over again. And I know that THAT'S the best gift I could give you. A good home and to save more good bois just like you. There are so many doggos that need help. Thank you for letting me be your first human. I love you. I love you. I love you.

Here is a pic of Barry, hugging me while I was on the toilet.

Which he did.
Every. Single. Day.

POWER STANCE

For four years, I worked at one of the most competitive, fast-moving Internet digital companies in the world: BUZZFEED. It took me about six months to feel like I actually deserved my jobs, promotions, and recognition. The environment is so chaotic and exhilarating, it's easy to get lost in the shuffle. If you don't know how to speak up and have confidence in your ideas, you'll never stand out. Point of view is everything, so you'd better have strong self-reliance if you want to keep up at a company where the news and trends change literally every hour.

On particularly tense days, something fun we all used to do in the middle of the day, totally unprompted, was a group POWER STANCE. It would often happen in a moment of inappropriately long silence for the bustling company. Perhaps the whole floor had their headphones on, deep in the edits. Or, maybe, the company Slack had just reported some not-so-great news, and we were feeling dampened as a team. But POWER STANCES were someone's way of saying, "HEY, WE'RE IN THIS INSANITY TOGETHER. LET'S TAKE UP SOME SPACE FOR A MOMENT."

The goal of a power stance was to regain control of your space. To fill it up with whatever emotion you'd like to and *fuckin' own it,* baby. And the great thing about a power stance is that it's incredibly easy to do. All you do is stand up, stretch your arms and legs as far and wide as they'll go, and try to create a giant X with your body. Feeeeeel the stretch, and release the negativity inside. Feel free to roar and make noises. Once you've emptied your body of the badness, start breathing in the good. Make yourself even wider. Pour in positive thoughts. Nothing too good is off-limits. Perhaps it's as simple as crushing the rest of your day, or nailing a meeting, or finishing that long edit sequence. Take up as much positive space as possible. Kick your chair out of the way, for all I care!!! Try to keep this stance and positivity flowing for at least 60 seconds. When you sit back down, you should have a renewed surge of energy running through your veins. Try it. It's fun.

Try a power stance next time you're feeling cramped physically, emotionally, or mentally. **How did it make you feel?**

_____

_____

_____

_____

_____

Did you feel silly? Was there goodness in that silliness?

_____

_____

_____

If you had to ask a friend or coworker to do it with you, who would you ask and why?

_____

_____

_____

THE PURGE: A CHALLENGE

CUE THAT CRAZY PURGE MOVIE ALARM BELL

It's time...It's happening...the SOCIAL MEDIA PURGE!!!! I challenge you to unfollow accounts (at least five on each social media account) that don't make you feel good or have you questioning your appearance or the validity and importance of your life. This can apply to anything: food accounts, hot Insta-influencers, fashion brands that aren't size-inclusive, media sites that focus on celebrity drama (ahem, *Daily Mail*), or even that dickhead from 7th grade who told you that you were "too flat to wear a bra" and never did a day's work in his life and somehow ended up running for office while still posting shirtless soccer selfies from practice every weekend and has a pool AND A JACUZZI before the age of 30. Just giving an example here, of course.

What are you initial thoughts about this challenge?

_____

_____

_____

What about that account you're going to unfollow makes you feel unsatisfied with your own life?

_____

_____

_____

Why, if at all, are you resistant to unfollowing them?

_____

_____

_____

Do you feel like you'd be missing out on things?

_____

_____

_____

How much space in your life and brain does this person/place/thing/company hold in your life?

_____

_____

_____

What OTHER accounts, Pinterest pics, comedians, SJWs, ideas, daydreams, brainstorms, and happiness could you fill that negative space up with on social media?

_____

_____

_____

YOU ARE ALWAYS CHANGING

AND GROWING

Your brain is constantly making brainwaves and activity—that means you always have an opportunity to change and reroute thoughts. It's about breaking thought patterns. This can happen at any time; any moment. It's never too late to start. Remember when you were a kid, and you were afraid of monsters under the bed, and then, one day, you never thought about it again? Or maybe, in your early tweens, when you never thought you'd get over the heartbreak of a crush, but you DID?

Below, let's list some fears and worries you've overcome in your lifetime, just to remind you how much your mind, thoughts, and feelings have grown and changed. Let's think back to times in your life where your brain has changed its own way of thinking. What were some childhood fears, worries, or nightmares that you now know are no longer rational and have overcome:

Kelsey's example: I had this insanely irrational fear that a SHARK was going to end up in my backyard pool when I was a kid. Now, I don't have that fear. Because I've developed logical thinking skills. LOLz.

CHILDHOOD WORRIES AND FEARS:

_____

_____

_____

_____

_____

_____

_____

TEEN WORRIES AND FEARS:

_____

_____

_____

_____

_____

_____

_____

_____

ADULTHOOD WORRIES AND FEARS:

_____

_____

_____

_____

_____

_____

_____

_____

♥ REFLECTION ♥

How were you able to overcome these negative thoughts and fears? Was it the wisdom of age? Was it facing the fear head-on?

_____

_____

_____

_____

_____

_____

_____

How about after using this workbook? Have things changed at all? Slightly, or in significant ways?

_____

_____

_____

_____

_____

_____

_____

What did you find most useful as a tool for managing your mental health?

_____

_____

_____

_____

_____

_____

_____

Name any of the people you shared some of your new ways of managing with:

_____

_____

_____

_____

_____

_____

_____

What are you excited about for the future?

_____

_____

_____

_____

_____

_____

_____

OKAY! THAT'S IT!

HOLY FUCK!
THAT'S THE END OF THIS WORKBOOK! THE FINAL PAGES!

But here's the thing, my dear friend (at this point, we're dear friends...right?) You're probably not cured. And, if you've done the work, you know that being "cured" of anxiety, panic, or depression doesn't exist. You are different now, after reading these pages. You have new insight and, hopefully, more tools in your tool belt.

Go back and fill out or try any pages you didn't use previously—remember, you are always changing...so, what may not have worked before might just be that exercise you need to get back in the right headspace. I wanted to create this book to help people the way I wish someone had helped me during the scariest parts of my life. I would please encourage you to give this book to the next person who could use it. It might be just the thing they need to keep going.

RESOURCE INDEX

DOWNLOAD PRINTABLE EXERCISES FROM THIS BOOK

thoughtcatalog.box.com/v/free-from-panic

GENERAL HELP

The Tribe therapy wellness community

7 cups of tea

BetterHelp.com

National Suicide Prevention Lifeline

1-800-273-TALK (8255)

Crisis Text Line

Text HOME to 741-741

TrevorLifeline, TrevorChat, and TrevorText (LGBTQ+ crisis support)

1-866-488-7386

Text "Trevor" to 1-202-304-1200

Trans Lifeline

US: (877) 565-8860

NAMI—National Alliance On Mental Illness

Depression and Bipolar Support Alliance

International OCD Foundation

National Eating Disorders Association

Emotions Anonymous

PTSD help—Gift From Within

The TLC Group—for Body-Focused Repetitive Behaviors

MORE READING

Truly *anything* written by Brene Brown

*F*ck Feelings : One Shrink's Practical Advice for Managing All Life's Impossible Problems* by Michael Bennett MD and Sarah Bennett

Attached by Amir Levine (note: the pronouns are a little outdated from 2010)

*Hardcore Self Help: F**k Anxiety* and *Hardcore Self Help: F**k Depression* by Robert Duff, PHD

The Hilarious World of Depression by John Moe

Maybe You Should Talk to Someone: A Therapist, HER Therapist, and Our Lives Revealed by Lori Gottlieb

Are u ok?: A Guide to Caring for Your Mental Health by Kati Morton LMFT

How to Be Happy (Or at Least Less Sad) by Lee Crutchley

Shame: Free Yourself, Find Joy, and Build True Self-Esteem by Joseph Burgo

The Five-Second Rule: Transform your Life, Work, and Confidence with Everyday Courage by Mel Robbins

The Four Agreements by Miguel Ruiz

The More or Less Definitive Guide to Self-Care by Anna Borges

Essentialism: The Disciplined Pursuit of Less by George McKeown

Hyperbole and a Half by Allie Brosch

How to NOT Travel the World by Lauren Juliff

GROUPS

Blessings Manifesting Facebook group

Alcoholics Anonymous

Narcotics Anonymous

ACKNOWLEDGMENTS

This workbook idea was something that amalgamated from a fuck-ton of pain. I never thought I could use that pain for good, to relate and connect to other people in the world, until Bianca Sparacino from Thought Catalog told me it could. B—you already know I'm a huge fan. Thank you for believing in me.

To KJ—who has read this probably more times than me—you fucking rock. I cannot say enough about your ability to design and transform the garbage in my brain into a fucking book. That's crazy. You are a superwoman. Thank you to everyone at TC, including the editors & Noelle. Sorry for all my spelling errors.

Thanks to my team at UTA & Select MGMT, Ale Catanese, Laura and Karson, and anyone in a position of making entertainment decisions who actually gave me a chance and believed in my powers.

To the Ree's family for showing me what true strength looks like.

Brooke, I don't deserve you. Sanjana, you're a true friend and creative partner.

To all my #HappyPlace friends and employees from BuzzFeed, for encouraging my art and supporting my journey of "coming out" publicly with my mental health disorders.

#CooterClub, I love you crazy, strong bitches. ZNT & Curly, my sobriety fairy godmothers.

To my exes, fuck you, look at me now. I wrote a workbook about myself!!! I'M GREAT!!! AND I KNOW IT!!!

To all the therapists, psychologists, psychiatrists, pharmacists, ER nurses, and strangers from 24/7 hotlines: You've saved my life. Many times. Thank you.

Thank you, flight attendants.

To Marie—for shaping me. My heart.

To my Confidantes & followers: I only exist because you do. I owe you all everything. *Fucking everything.* Thank you for sharing your stories and vulnerabilities with me. I trust you. I love you.

To my dad, Mike, who may not understand my panic & anxiety but has always been a pillar of strength and support in my life, who has dropped everything to fly to

LA on multiple occasions when I've needed it most. I was never alone because of you. You've made me believe I can do ANYTHING I set my mind to. I love being a Darragh. I thank you for everything.

To Lacey & Mikey—*my fucking ride or dies.* You've given me these experiences and are the reason I've survived it and why I'm still here. I can't believe both of you will still be seen in public with me.

Megwah, my big sistow, any day spent with you is my favorite fucking day. No matter how far apart we are in distance, I feel closer to you every day. I can't wait to continue growing up with you.

Jared—My love. My face. My grotto. You are the greatest surprise and adventure that life could've possibly given me. We've created our own fairy tale, and I thank you for proving that stable, healthy, and true love exists. Thank you for letting me be a firework. Your soul is my home forever.

And finally, to my mom, Kristy, Mammy Jammy MaMa D: Because of you, this book is possible. I made this for you, of you, and by you. I was able to write it because I was not consumed by my own mind or deepest anxieties because you gave me the strength to get through it. Because of you, I look at the world with fire in my eyes instead of fear. You taught me how to make my own toolkit, and that I can only rely on myself in this world, but asking for help is part of that resilience. I am a strong woman because a strong woman made me. I could not ask for a better mentor and best friend. If I could turn out to be an ounce of how fabulous you are, then this life will have been worth living.

P.S.

Barry update: Barry did eventually get adopted after four months with me, to an incredible couple who, I couldn't believe it, love Barry just as much as me. We kept in touch with his parents, and here we are a few months later dog sitting, reunited. Please foster. It saves lives.

KELSEY DARRAGH is a comedian, filmmaker, and mental health advocate living in Los Angeles. With over 250MM views of her anxiety videos, she's quickly become the "big sister" of mental health on the internet. Formerly of BuzzFeed internet fame, Kelsey moved on to E!'s flagship LGBT show, "Dating No Filter," and hosts her own chart-topping podcast, "Confidently Insecure."

WWW.KELSEYDARRAGH.COM
TWITTER.COM/KELSEYDARRAGH
FACEBOOK.COM/KELSEY.DARRAGH
INSTAGRAM.COM/KELSEYDARRAGH